Reforming the Public Sector

Brookings-SSPA Series on Public Administration

Published in conjunction with the Scuola Superiore della Pubblica Amministrazione, Rome, this series is devoted to the study of international issues of public administration and public management.

Federiga Bindi, *Italy and the European Union* (2011)

Federiga Bindi and Irina Angelescu, editors, *Frontiers of Europe: A Transatlantic Problem?* (2011)

Giovanni Tria and Giovanni Valotti, editors, *Reforming the Public Sector: How to Achieve Better Transparency, Service, and Leadership* (2012)

Reforming the Public Sector

How to Achieve Better Transparency, Service, and Leadership

GIOVANNI TRIA
GIOVANNI VALOTTI
Editors

SCUOLA SUPERIORE DELLA PUBBLICA AMMINISTRAZIONE (SSPA)
Rome

BROOKINGS INSTITUTION PRESS
Washington, D.C.

ABOUT BROOKINGS

The Brookings Institution is a private nonprofit organization devoted to research, education, and publication on important issues of domestic and foreign policy. Its principal purpose is to bring the highest quality independent research and analysis to bear on current and emerging policy problems. Interpretations or conclusions in Brookings publications should be understood to be solely those of the authors.

Library of Congress Cataloging-in-Publication data
Reforming the public sector : how to achieve better transparency, service, and leadership / Giovanni Tria, Giovanni Valotti, editors.
p. cm. — (Brookings-SSPA series on public administration)
Includes bibliographical references and index.
ISBN 978-0-8157-2288-5 (pbk. : alk. paper)
1. Public administration. 2. Organizational change. 3. Organizational effectiveness.
I. Tria,Giovanni, 1948– II. Valotti, G. (Giovanni)
JF1525.O73R44 2012
352.3'67—dc23 2012011886

9 8 7 6 5 4 3 2 1

Printed on acid-free paper

Typeset in Minion

Composition by R. Lynn Rivenbark
Macon, Georgia

Printed by R. R. Donnelley
Harrisonburg, Virginia

Contents

GIOVANNI TRIA AND GIOVANNI VALOTTI

Introduction: Challenges of Public Sector Reform

Public management reform has become a priority on the political agenda of governments in major industrialized countries since the 1980s.[1] Nowadays, the reform of public administration can be considered a stable and autonomous public policy and the object of a distinct stream of studies.[2] According to Hood and Peters, "the formalization and normalization of the field" of public management studies is the third and last stage of maturation of this discipline.[3]

The purpose of this volume is to contribute to this growing body of literature, highlighting the main issues in the ongoing reform processes, and to help develop suggestions for public decisionmakers involved in public sector reforms by offering a comprehensive picture of the main challenges that governments face today.

Previous studies have focused their attention on the main factors and determinants that underlie the impetus for change in the public sector.[4]

1. The environment in which governments operate has become increasingly unstable, calling for flexibility and adaptation skills on the part of bureaucrats and administrators in the public sector. The "stable and slow changing environment" that suited traditional public bureaucracies has been subjected to huge transformations.[5] These turbulent changes have influenced bureaucracies in different ways, such that they now appear to be characterized by the increasing need for information about the environment. They need to gather such information and respond on the basis of it.[6]

2. The globalization and internationalization of business require public agencies to redefine their boundaries and cooperate across boundaries.[7] Organizations must cope with uncertainty and manage it well if they want to

be effective. Uncertainty increases the risk of failure of an organization's response and makes it difficult to compute the costs and probabilities associated with alternative decisions.

3. There is a growing shortage of public resources, which is leading to the rethinking of service delivery, the ways organizations function, and the degree of efficiency of the whole system.[8] Organizations are preoccupied with the lack of material and financial resources and with the need to ensure the availability of these resources.

4. Pressure from citizens is growing regarding the quality of services provided, combined with the widespread perception of inefficiency and backwardness of the public sector as a whole.[9]

Several empirical studies have shown the effects, expected or not, of public management reforms. In many cases, changes to regulations, structures, and processes have not led to the expected results.[10] In some cases the reforms have produced unintended consequences that have had a negative impact on maintenance of the basic values embodied by governments and the public sector. Public administrations have often imported tools and ideas for reform from the private sector or from other governments (for example, performance-related pay) while failing to bear in mind the national context or to consider the limits and weaknesses of these tools.[11]

Many countries continue to struggle to achieve the fundamental changes needed to respond to the unexpected effects of modernization initiatives. Such paradoxes seem to be a feature of public sector reforms, where we often witness the "indifference to careful evaluation of the consequences of action . . . particularly in domains of strong beliefs and ambiguous experiences."[12]

Especially in time of crisis we need to modernize the public sector and to focus on the relevance of "public value." So we need to explore the current status of government reform. After almost three decades of reforms, the role of the public sector has changed significantly. The expectations for government action have not decreased, but in fact have increased; meanwhile the nature of public policy problems faced by governments is still undergoing profound change.

Thus, there is a growing need to understand the dynamics of the public sector in general. The modernization of governments requires an understanding of the nature and dynamics of public administrations as a whole and how they work within the global society. Our volume title, "Reforming the Public Sector: How to Achieve Better Transparency, Service, and Leadership," states the challenge the public sector faces.

Sometimes with the benefit of hindsight we recognize patterns leading to the future. As noted, there is no doubt but that the public sector operates in an ever-changing and increasingly complex environment. An intricate array of drivers of change will influence the future—some of them known, some of them emerging, and some of them yet to appear on the horizon.

The ongoing reform process that most governments are undertaking demonstrates that public management reforms still represent a priority and offer an important opportunity for rethinking how to make changes effective and how to manage reforms. This recognition led to the idea for this book, whose aim is to contribute to the growing body of literature and develop this stream of research, to help practitioners and policymakers tackle the problems and challenges they face every day. It is hoped that this volume will

—Make possible a better understanding and discussion of the principles underpinning the ongoing reforms in the public sector

—Provide the community of practitioners with a scientific understanding of the main issues at stake in the reform processes

—Place the approach to public administration reform in a broader international context

—Identify the roadmap for public management

The priority of public sector reforms is also emphasized in this book. The contributors to this volume discuss some of the most relevant areas of modernization in the public sector in European countries: four imperatives that are coming together and forcing public sector managers, researchers, and policy experts to intensify and extend the agenda of public sector reforms.

1. *Enhancing transparency.* Enhanced transparency is regarded as a highly prized value, one often studied by academics and emphasized by practitioners. It is generally discussed as a tool for increasing government accountability, as a desirable principle for reducing corruption in public administration, and as a means for putting pressure on government performance.

2. *Boosting the motivation of public servants.* This can be done by focusing on the relevance of motivational factors of public employees, including not only material incentives and bureaucratic efforts to control actions but also the need to improve performance by managing the values that motivate public employees. The review of policies and motivation systems of human resources represents one of the areas of ongoing public reform.

3. *Improving leadership.* The need has emerged to strengthen leadership and enhance managerial responsibility in order to create a qualified cohort of civil servants capable of ensuring coherence, coordination, and continuity within the public sector. Reforms relating to leadership emphasize several concepts, such as the definition of the key skills of future leaders and the development of human resources departments for the recruitment of public leaders.

4. *Measuring performance.* The effective use of information on performance remains one of the most debated issues in the public sector today. Public sector organizations around the world face unprecedented pressure to improve the quality of their services while at the same time lowering their costs. The importance of strengthening the systems used to measure and assess performance has plainly increased in recent years.

The Structure of This Book

This volume has five parts, one each focusing on the four main challenges just described and a section on public sector reforms from an international perspective.

Part 1 introduces the issue of transparency in the public sector. Transparency is the focus of growing attention not only of governments but also of international organizations such as the World Bank and the Organization for Economic Cooperation and Development. Most studies agree on the universal underlying assumption that transparency in government is a critical ingredient for efficient and well-functioning economic and political markets. In more general terms, transparency is seen as a cornerstone of democracy. In fact, the call for a transparent government is embedded in the birth of the modern idea of democracy.[13] In chapter 2, Maria Cucciniello, Greta Nasi, and Raffaella Saporito provide an interesting definition of transparency, combining the different streams of research focusing on this subject: "Transparency is discussed as a tool to enhance governments' accountability, as a principle to activate for reducing public administration's corruption and as a means to diffuse government's performance information." This concept of transparency leads the three authors to suggest a model for measuring the degree of transparency in public organizations that is "based on the following four . . . dimensions: institutional, political, financial and service delivery." Irvine Lapsley, in chapter 1, offers a critical perspective on transparency, using the concept of the "Audit Society" proposed in 1994 by Michael Power.[14] As Lapsley states, "The diffusion of audit and the significant increase in the quantum of audit-like processes of checking and verification have given primacy to audit thinking and audit work across a wide range of contemporary society." Lapsley leads us toward an interesting investigation of the unexpected consequences of transparency in government: "The subtle shifts in the significance of audit activity in contemporary society may have deleterious effects as the audit view of the world may not capture the subtleties of complex service provision."

The focus in part 2 is on the relevance of public servants' motivation as a tool for boosting public sector productivity. One of the most popular managerial devices all over the world introduced by civil service reforms is performance-related pay schemes.[15] Pay-for-performance systems are tools borrowed from the private sector, designed to increase individual productivity. The impact on motivation of these incentives appears less strong in the public sector than in the private sector.[16] A growing body of evidence demands a rethinking of civil service reform policies and more exploration of the specific features of public service motivation (PSM).[17]

In chapter 3, James Perry describes the extensive diffusion and consolidation of PSM as a subject for public management study. Research on PSM is not just a good field for interesting intellectual challenges, where empirical evidence shows counterintuitive findings regarding the relationship between incentives and motivation; it can also become a very influential theory with inevitable effects on strategies and policies for human resources.

The issue of generalizability is also explored in chapter 4, by Wouter Vandenabeele and his coauthors. He found that the relationship between PSM and job satisfaction is moderated by country, suggesting that "with regard to individual civil servants, both the origins and the outcomes of individual PSM are subject to the institutional context in which they are situated." This work is also an important example of how comparative studies can help underpin public management research.

In chapter 5, Nicola Bellé and Paola Cantarelli provide a review of literature on the PSM construct and also present "the definitions of PSM along with details of the context where they were proposed. By making the contextual factors explicit, it is possible to achieve an understanding of the concerns that each definition was intended to address." The most interesting contribution to PSM literature by this article is its focus "on methodological issues related to the measurement of PSM." This chapter also looks at the generalizability of the construct of PSM across sectors and countries outside the United States, where the concept was originally introduced. Accordingly, the two authors grouped all the articles they analyzed according to the type of statistical relationship used.

Part 3 analyzes the role of leadership in public sector reforms since 1990. To effectively lead a new tide of public management reforms we can leverage on what has been done up until now. Christopher Pollitt, in chapter 6, tries in particular to highlight what can be learned from thirty years of public management reform, in order to act in this policy field in a more successful way. Moving from the past, he identifies three levels of learning: "The first kind is simply (or not so simply) learning *what has happened*. The second is *unlearning*, that is, learning what errors there were in some of the views that one held oneself—or that influential others held—in the past. We could call this correcting false impressions. The third kind of learning is finding explanations—identifying reasons and processes that help us understand *why* things happened as they did." Having identified ten key observations about the character of public management reform, on the basis of these three types of learning he offers seven main lessons on what can be learned from previous reforms.

Montgomery Van Wart in chapter 7 examines which leadership skills are related to reforms and focuses on the Italian context. Using the analysis by Paul Light, Van Wart divides the reform initiatives into four fundamental types and provides a description of different types of leadership according to Bernard M. Bass and the related skills that should be emphasized in order to achieve the different types of reform.[18] According to Van Wart, "Transactional skills are likely to be much stronger than transformational skills, but with less discipline than new Italian public law calls for. The new and critical transformational skills are likely to be largely deficient because of a lack of opportunity and practice." The author advises Italian governments that "transformational skills will therefore need to be bolstered at all levels of Italian government through extensive training programs, widespread investments in new education, and role modelling."

Mariannunziata Liguori, Mariafrancesca Sicilia, and Ileana Steccolini, in chapter 8, discuss "leadership" from an interesting point of view, investigating the emerging roles of administrators and politicians at the local government (LG) level. As a consequence of the waves of "modernization" in the public sector, "administrators are increasingly being asked to wear the hat of managers. . . . Politicians and administrators are seen as actors with separate functions, whereby the former are supposed to play a strategic role, deciding on broad policies and setting targets for managers, [and] the latter are expected to reach these targets in an efficient and effective manner." The authors offer several suggestions concerning the implementation of future reforms within LGs that are based on the Italian experience: policymakers should acknowledge the existence of the political, managerial, and professional dimensions within LGs and try to keep these balanced. "Emphasizing only one of the three (as often happens during processes of modernization) may foster organizational tension that may ultimately slow down the success of both the LG and the reform process itself," the authors conclude.

The chapters in part 4 discuss public sector performance and the possibility of managing governments by numbers. Governments are increasingly managed by numbers—that is, decisions are based on various types of statistics.

In chapter 9, Geert Bouckaert suggests that "this solves certain problems, not all, and creates new problems. This shift also helps to make legally defined responsibilities substantial and tangible, and substantiates accountability beyond a formal level." However, he argues that it is important to combine the logics of numbers with the logic of governmental systems (consequences and appropriateness) into logics of public management. To do this, it is important to look at the management of numbers "to guarantee a sufficiently large scope and depth of performance, to match supply and demand of numbers, and to choose trajectories by using numbers in a broader context."

In chapter 10, Denita Cepiku, Andrea Bonomi Savignon, and Luigi Corvo explore the status of strategic management in Italian ministries, highlighting the determinants of an implementation gap. They conclude that the results of the reform processes regarding strategic management in the Italian central government "have so far been unsatisfactory. Even in the most advanced cases, a formal compliance-oriented approach prevails." The authors emphasize the need to establish stronger links between public sector reforms and the processes of budgeting, performance management, and human resources. The focus of law and central policy guidance has been (and continues to be) on strategic documents, but the "actual use of the strategic management system has not been a priority, neither of the central actors nor of the ministries."

Part 5 provides an international perspective on public sector reforms. Michael Barzelay, in chapter 11, examines a crucial issue of public management studies: how to bridge the gap between theory and practice in public management and how to provide the community of public management practitioners with actionable knowledge. He introduces the "design science" approach to public management, a discipline that is a reference point for practitioners looking for solutions to their managerial problems: "A sensible practice for the study of public management is to target reference points, since their selection and use is an inherent feature of problem-solving and the devising of novel means within the world of practice. Since reference points are often presented as expert knowledge, they are liable to being put into question by arguments stemming from public management research." The approach proposed by Barzelay has important implications not just for the research community but also for public management education, especially for executive education: "In some institutional and cultural settings, studying public management as a practitioner is typically staged as acquiring skills, learning techniques, and internalizing professional values" rather than learning how to recognize and classify problems, in order to look for the best solutions. "Seeking to undermine the intellectual capital of the field would be counterproductive: not only would it tend to make the audience for this methodological argument less interested in considering what it being proposed, but reinventing conceptions of managerial challenges is entirely unnecessary."

Elaine Kamarck, in chapter 12, examines central aspects of government reform in the contemporary era, surveying and analyzing developments and patterns in four separate historical contexts: (1) the late-twentieth-century revolution in governance in advanced Information Age democracies; (2) the late-twentieth-century revolution in governance in the world's developing nations; (3) the postbureaucratic state in advanced, Information Age democracies; (4) the challenge of government capacity building in the developing world.

Mario Ianniello, Luca Brusati, and Paolo Fedele, in chapter 13, look at an increasingly popular practice: the inclusion of the principal stakeholders in decisionmaking. The approach of their case study is to identify the formal organizational factors affecting the results of the decisionmaking process. They found that inclusive decisionmaking processes possess a value per se, regardless of the effects and the quality of the decision: "Moreover, there is a confirmation that inclusive decisionmaking has a role in conflict reduction. . . . The higher the correspondence between the decisions taken and stakeholders' needs, the higher their satisfaction with the decision taken, even if they are not completely satisfied with the process itself." This conclusion has important consequences for decisionmaking settings in the public sector and for the traditional devices of political representation as a way to reach democratic decisions.

Finally, in the concluding chapter Giovanni Valotti suggests an interpretation of the agenda of public sector reforms and factors that could drive changes leading to better government in the future. To sum up, this book examines broad areas of the modernization of the public sector in European countries and the ways public managers can use the challenges listed earlier as a framework to intensify and extend their own reform agendas.

Notes

1. See, among others, Owen E. Hughes, *Public Management and Administration,* 3rd ed. (New York: Palgrave Macmillan, 2003); Christopher Hood, "The 'New Public Management' in the 1980s: Variations on a Theme," *Accounting Organization and Society* 20 (February–April 1995): 93–109; Michael Barzelay, *Breaking through Bureaucracy: A New Vision for Managing in Government* (University of California Press, 1992); Michael Barzelay, *The New Public Management: Improving Research and Policy Dialogue* (Berkeley and New York: University of California Press and Russell Sage Foundation, 2001);

Barry Bozeman, *Public Management and Policy* (New York: St. Martin's Press, 1979); Christopher Pollitt and Geert Bouckaert, *Public Management Reform: A Comparative Analysis* (Oxford University Press, 2000); David Osborne and Ted Gaebler, *Reinventing Government: How the Entrepreneurial Spirit Is Transforming the Public Sector* (Reading, Mass.: Addison-Wesley, 1993); Laurence E. Lynn Jr., *Public Management as Art, Science and Profession* (Chatham, N.J.: Chatham House, 1996); Laurence R. Jones, Kuno Schedler, and Stephen W. Wade, *International Perspectives on the New Public Management* (London: Jai Press, 1997).

2. See, among others, Nils Brunsson, *Reform as Routine: Organizational Change in the Modern World* (Oxford University Press, 2009); Shuan F. Goldfinch and Joe L. Wallis Jr., *International Handbook of Public Sector Reform* (Northampton, Mass.: Edward Elgar, 2009); Nils Brunsson and Kerstin Sahlin-Andersson, "Constructing Organizations: The Example of Public Sector Reform," *Organization Studies* 21, no. 4 (2000): 721–46.

3. Christopher Hood and Guy Peters, "The Middle Aging of New Public Management: Into the Age of Paradox?" *Journal of Public Administration Research and Theory* 14, no. 3 (2004): 268.

4. See, among others, Hughes, *Public Management and Administration*, p. 1; Giovanni Valotti, *Temi di management pubblico* [Themes in public management] (Milan: Egea, 2004); Stephen P. Osborne and Kerry Brown, *Managing Change and Innovation in Public Service Organizations* (London: Routledge, 2005).

5. Osborne and Brown, *Managing Change and Innovation in Public Service Organizations*, p. 4.

6. See, among others, Howard Aldrich, *Organizations and Environments* (Englewood Cliffs, N.J.: Prentice-Hall, 1979); Fred Emery and Eric Trist, "The Causal Texture of Organizational Environments," *Human Relations* 18, no. 1 (1965): 21–32.

7. Fiona Graetz, "Strategic Change Leadership," *Management Decision* 38, no. 8 (2000): 550–62.

8. Valotti, *Temi di management pubblico*, p. 4.

9. See, among others, Ian Alam, "Removing the Fuzziness from the Front-End of Service Innovations through Customer Interactions," *Industrial Marketing Management* 35 (May 2006): 468–80; David Albury, "Fostering Innovation in Public Services," *Public Money & Management* 25, no. 1 (2005): 51–56; Audit Commission (London), *Seeing the Light: Innovation in Local Public Services* (London: 2007).

10. See, among others, Organization for Economic Cooperation and Development, *Modernising Government: The Way Forward* (Paris: OECD Publications, 2005); Giovanni Valotti, Alex Turrini, and Daniela Cristofoli, *Da burocrati a manager: Una riforma a metà—primo rapporto sulla dirigenza Italiana* [From bureaucrat to manager: first white paper on public management in Italy], OCAP (Osservatorio sul cambiamento delle amministrazioni pubbliche [Observations on changes in public administration]), Collana white paper 1-2/2007 (Milan: Egea, 2007).

11. James L. Perry, Trent A. Engbers, and So Yun Jun, "Back to the Future? Performance-Related Pay, Empirical Research, and the Perils of Persistence," *Public Administration Review* 69 (January–February 2009): 39–51.

12. Hood and Peters, "Middle Aging of New Public Management"; James G. March and Johan P. Olsen, *Rediscovering Institutions: The Organizational Basis of Politics* (New York: Free Press/Macmillan, 1989).

13. Christopher Hood and David Heald, *Transparency. The Key to Better Governance* (Oxford University Press, 2006).

14. Michael Power, *The Audit Explosion* (London: Demos, 1994).

15. T. J. Lah and James L. Perry, "The Diffusion of the Civil Service Reform Act of 1978 in OECD Countries: A Tale of Two Paths to Reform," *Review of Public Personnel Administration* 28 (September 2008): 282–99.

16. Perry, Engbers, and Yun Jun, "Back to the Future?" p. 14; Edward P. Lazear, "Performance Pay and Productivity," *American Economic Review* 90 (December 2000): 1346–61.

17. James L. Perry and Lois Recascino Wise, "The Motivational Bases of Public Service," *Public Administration Review* 50 (May–June 1990): 367–73.

18. Paul C. Light, *The Tides of Reform: Making Government Work: 1945–1995* (Yale University Press, 1997); Bernard M. Bass, *The Bass Handbook of Leadership: Theory, Research, & Managerial Applications* (New York: Free Press, 2008).

PART I

Transparency: When the Auditor is the Society

IRVINE LAPSLEY

1

Shedding Light or Obfuscating? Audit in an NPM World

This chapter examines the significance of audit in contemporary society. The role of audit within the public sphere—and its role in what has come to be called New Public Management, or NPM—has become the subject of intense debate.[1] Specifically, this discussion focuses on the extent to which audit practices and audit work have become a dominant reference point in everyday lives of citizens as they go about their business, whether in a personal capacity or in the course of fulfilling workplace commitments. In this discussion the phenomenon of audit practice is scrutinized from the perspective of whether the tools and techniques of audit actually enhance or inhibit, or even negate, transparency in public finances and public administration.

This chapter has six sections. First there is an exploration of what NPM means and the role of audit and accounting within this phenomenon. Second, audit practices are examined from the perspective of the "Audit Explosion." Next there is a discussion of the impact of audit practices in shaping the development of the "Audit Society," a concept that builds on the idea of the Audit Explosion. The fourth section presents an examination of the practices and technologies of auditors, who operate within the sphere of public services. Fifth, there is a discussion of what transpires when the Audit Society meets the Risk Society. This section examines whether audit technologies and the context in which they are deployed actually aid transparency in public finances and public administration. Finally, I set forth my conclusions on the implications of the preceding discussions.

An NPM World

The idea of the NPM world was first advanced by Christopher Hood.[2] His initial reflections were based on policy developments in the United Kingdom in the 1980s.[3] Subsequently, he examined the variable diffusion of NPM ideas internationally.[4] These ideas advanced by Hood have proved to be immensely significant in understanding, studying, reflecting on, and analyzing public sector reforms. There is now an immense literature on the NPM phenomenon. The attributes identified by Hood remain hallmarks by which analysts can study the public sector. The key NPM components, according to Hood, are the following:

—Unbundling of the public sector into corporatized units organized by product

—More contract-based competitive provision, with internal markets and term contracts

—Stress on private sector management styles

—More stress on discipline and frugality in resource use

—Visible hands-on top management

—Explicit formal measurable standards and measurement of performance and success

—Greater emphasis on output controls

All of these dimensions of NPM enhance the significance of both accounting and auditing practices, particularly private sector practices in the oversight of public services. It is important to note that Hood's observations were exactly that—Hood reflected on what was happening in the United Kingdom in the 1980s and early '90s and that was the basis of his coining of the term NPM. This is not to be confused with advocacy of any or all of these reforms by Hood. However, the significance of NPM as a government policy, internationally, is beyond challenge. Regarding this particular study, one of the key authors in the field of audit located his concepts of Audit Explosion and Audit Society specifically within the sphere of the NPM.[5] These ideas are discussed next.

The Audit Explosion

In 1994 Michael Power observed that there was an Audit Explosion in the United Kingdom. He justified this observation by detailing the diffusion of audit: "financial . . . VFM . . . environmental . . . management . . . forensic . . . data . . . intellectual property . . . medical . . . teaching . . . technology. More recent examples include suggestions of "gender audit . . . religious audit."[6]

Power was criticized on the grounds that many of these examples of the Audit Explosion were inspections, not audit.[7] However, inspections of, for example, schools or social work now fall within the sphere of influence of regulatory audit bodies. Power highlights the manner in which "audit thinking" permeates inspection activities.[8] No one has challenged the basic assumption that the quantum of audit and inspections in public life has grown significantly in recent years.

Indeed, the volume and scale of audit activity continue to increase. For example, Irvine Lapsley identifies a number of recent examples from the United Kingdom's National Health Service.[9] The National Health Service has heavy inspection and audit with at least fifty-six bodies having the right to visit NHS hospitals and trusts. The sheer number of inspections standards, and the volume of information required to demonstrate compliance, makes it difficult to extract value from these processes and use them to improve patient services.

Indeed, the Health Commission's "Light Touch" annual health check has an overwhelming impact. It requires five hundred separate information topics to be addressed in a questionnaire so voluminous that managers doubted they could complete it. There is overlap with other audits and inspections. Lapsley cites the views of the NHS Confederation in 2007 in support of this.[10] Much of this Audit Explosion has had little to do with efficiency, and there is skepticism regarding the claims of value added that financial auditors promote.[11]

The Audit Society

In 1997 Power articulated the thesis that we now live in an Audit Society.[12] This builds and extends on the idea of the Audit Explosion. Power depicts a society in which audit practices dominate much of everyday life. Power identified a number of manifestations of the Audit Explosion that enhance the influence of audit on society. One feature of this was the use of formal audit documents outside their original context. An example of this would be a risk assessment of specific internal controls that is portrayed as a generic weakness at management meetings, especially at meetings of managers at some remove from the scene of the risk assessment. A further dimension of this is the manner in which the term "audit" brings up images, especially public images, of control. A consequence of this is a spread of "audit talk" in governance. One fundamental implication of this pervasive influence, according to Power, is that audit can *shape* the activities it controls. This outcome is affected by the nature of audit, which presents a "very particular" concept of accountability. This concept of accountability is based on a closed-loop, cybernetic concept of how organizations function—it is an instrumental view of organizational life, in which cause and effect can be determined with precision. However, Power argued that the spread of audit does not necessarily make matters of public finances or public administration more transparent and can actually *obscure* activities going on in organizations.[13] In particular, the audit process remains invisible to the wider public, commentators, and policymakers. Audit is only public when it "fails." A truly spectacular example of such public failure is the case of Enron and its aftermath.

The Audit Society thesis has been interpreted as having three strands: (1) legitimation and decoupling strategies, (2) colonization and culture change, and (3) displacement of core organizational activities.[14] Regarding the relationship of audits to legitimacy, the context of the Audit Society suggests that audits offer "comfort or organizational legitimacy" to the management of organizations. This may result in audit becoming a "rationalized ritual," as audit concerns itself with auditable form rather than substance. This has the distinct impact of creating a compliance, or "tick box," mentality, which is explored further in a later section. Power also suggested that a classic feature of legitimacy theory—the decoupling of audit from core activities—might emerge as an aspect of the Audit Society. The second strand of the Audit Society—colonization and culture change—may lead to challenges to the organizational power of professional groups. Within this dimension, the technology of VFM (value for the money) audit may become a vehicle for organizational change. The act of "compliance" with audit requirements may also result in the implanting of the values underlying the audit approach within organizations and society at large. In this sense, audit activity becomes a dominant reference point in everyday life, and the values of individual members of society and employees of organizations and their practices may change. However, although Power articulated the concept of colonization as a feature of the Audit Society, he also expressed the view that outright colonization is rarely successful. The third dimension of the Audit Society—displacement—is one of the dysfunctional impacts of audit. Displacement is the primacy of audit compliance over operational needs and tasks. It is one of the "side effects" that may undermine the performance of organizations. Through displacement, the impact of the Audit Society is profound. The fulfillment of audit needs and processes may reduce the time available for core organizational activities. This phenomenon can take on a number of manifestations—information overload, for example. This reliance on audit may reveal a decline in organizational trust. Power suggests that in presentations on audit that are given within organizations the view may be expressed that "audit works," even if it does not. Fundamentally, "auditable" performance becomes an end in itself—that is, performance that can be counted, what can be checked, with evidence of an audit trail more important than service outcomes. A triumph of bureaucracy over service needs.

The study and investigation of such a wide-ranging phenomenon as the Audit Society presents difficulties because of its sheer scale. However, examples of aspects of the Audit Society are evident in everyday life—in particular, the compliance mentality. A number of cases of this "tick box" compliance mentality were identified in the 2007 Police Confederation Annual Conference in Blackpool, England:

—Case 1. Police spent weeks doing door-to-door investigations to turn a single theft into 542 different cases to meet crime-fighting targets. The operation began after a child was accused of keeping £700 raised for Comic Relief through sponsorship. To beef up their number of targets, police officers were sent to talk to every person who had sponsored the child. They spent two weeks on door-to-door inquiries—community police officers thus investigated 542 crimes. Five hundred is better than one.

—Case 2. A Cheshire man was cautioned by police for being "found in possession of an egg with intent to throw."

—Case 3. A child in Kent who removed a slice of cucumber from a tuna mayonnaise sandwich and threw it at another youngster was arrested because the other child's parents claimed that it was an assault.[15]

All of these cases demonstrate the manner in which a compliance culture as part of the Audit Society may lead to perverse, absurd, illogical outcomes in public administration.

This discussion continues with a close scrutiny of the technologies deployed by auditors and an examination of these technologies' capacity to aid transparency in public affairs.

Audit Technologies: Illumination or Obfuscation?

The tool most frequently used by public sector auditors is VFM, or "value for money." The core idea of VFM is an expansion of the audit function from accounting and compliance to assessments of the efficacy of public expenditures. The VFM approach is concerned with the identification of economies and efficiencies in the provision of services, but also with the overall effectiveness of programs of expenditure. Within the United Kingdom this tool has developed into the Best Value audit. Where VFM is an approach that can be used for specific audit investigations, Best Value is a more holistic approach to public sector audit in which complete organizations are audited.

VFM Audit

Proponents of VFM audit exhibit a "can do" philosophy—any problems of practice can be overcome. Proponents also present VFM as a *market opportunity* for accountants and auditors. There is some evidence of professional firms "projecting" themselves as experts in this area. The overall thrust of professional institute publications is of a "received wisdom"—all is clear, self-evident. However, there are fundamental reservations over what VFM means, an issue that is glossed over by practitioners. In particular, the issue of quality of service is a major problem in VFM studies. Also, there are uncertainties over how auditors detect and demonstrate efficiency in a public sector context. Indeed, the level of skills required to undertake high-level VFM studies may be beyond the core competencies of professional auditors. Also, the public services are replete with services and organizations in which professional groups have a voice and influence. These powerful professional groups may be an impediment to VFM studies.

There is not a significant volume of evidence of VFM audit in practice. Given the sensitive nature of the subjects that may be subject to VFM audit, this scarcity of evidence should not be surprising. However, in a novel study Lapsley and C. K. M. Pong investigated the experiences of an expert group of VFM auditors.[16] Surprisingly, the study by Lapsley and Pong found that members of public sector organizations—from all professions—were generally positive about VFM, although initially they had been hostile. Within this group of professionals, the finance staff were most positive about VFM, which might be expected. However, the overall focus of VFM audits tended to be on operational rather than strategic benefits. Furthermore, the conduct of VFM audits presented major challenges for these VFM auditors. The view was expressed by them that they were not dealing with "text book situations." These VFM auditors experienced particular difficulties resulting from the ambiguity of what constituted "quality." They expressed concerns about the lack of robust measures of key variables that they wished to investigate. They also expressed reservations over the quality of evidence that they could gather. For example, one acute issue was the interdependence of service provision. VFM auditors found it difficult to disentangle the interactions of different services in their evaluations of a specific service. In short, the *easy VFM audits have been done.*[17] These findings suggest that the apparently self-evident outcome of transparency from VFM audits is misleading, given the operational difficulties of VFM and its potential for ambiguity in interpretation and implementation.

Best Value Audit

This form of audit was introduced as government policy in the United Kingdom in 1997. The policy of the previous Conservative administrations of introducing Compulsory Competitive Tendering (outsourcing) for a range of public services had been criticized as being overly focused on cost saving, with little attention paid to the quality of services offered. In 1997 the incoming Labour government proposed Best Value audit as an alternative to Compulsory Competitive Tendering. It did this by placing the entire process within the domain of government auditors. Thus the very act of introducing Best Value audit can be seen as an addition to the Audit Explosion. The aim of this new tool was to obtain Best Value by securing economic, efficient, and effective services.[18] Actually, the "three E's" of economy, efficiency and effectiveness are fundamental tenets of VFM as well. The difference between VFM and Best Value was that the latter approach was even more comprehensive, with auditors delivering verdicts on whether entire organizations were fit for purpose. The aim was to devise a general framework with considerable local discretion on resource use. The reality was a system that privileged audit as a function, which contributed to the Audit Explosion and also contributed to the expansion of the Audit Society.

In the implementation of Best Value, the definition of this new tool resonates with the ideas of the Audit Society. Specifically, one government policy statement described Best Value as "a process rather than a product . . . a process of change and *progress. . . . It promotes changes in attitude, culture and management style within councils*" (emphasis added). Best Value audit requires constant reflection on the measurement of successes and on shortcomings found and actions taken to improve.[19]

In practice, Best Value has attracted criticisms. Concerns have been expressed about the bureaucratic burden and the displacement effect of Best Value.[20] In one study, concerns were expressed about the nature, scale, and scope of the Best Value regime, and there was also evidence of the displacement of resources from frontline services to compliance with the requirements of the Best Value audit process, including the preparation of reports, discussions with staff members, and the collation of performance statistics to demonstrate staff were effective.[21] Although this study did find top management support for Best Value, the authors found that interviewees expressed concern over the extent to which Best Value had penetrated all parts of the organization. In their study, Michela Arnaboldi and Lapsley found that there was skepticism among managers over ideas underpinning Best Value such as "continuous improvement."[22] This study also found evidence of legitimacy. Not the "loose coupling" envisaged by Power, but clear evidence of the "tick box" society. These manifestations of the Audit Society undermine transparency by creating an illusion that all is well, when there may be deep-seated issues that are not being addressed by managers and administrators of public services.

Audit Society Meets Risk Society

In contemporary society a new phase has appeared within the idea of the Audit Society—the introduction of ideas of "risk" and the manner in which risk must be addressed by auditors. This dimension of the Audit Society adds a new lexicon, a new layer of complexity, all of which intensifies the issues of legitimacy, colonization, and displacement as exemplified by the Power critique.[23] I discuss this development in three stages: first, the most recent developments with the specific technique of Best Value audit; second, in terms of the Power critique of how risk is managed in contemporary society; third, I explore instances of the unintended consequences of the Risk Society meeting the Audit Society.[24]

In the preceding discussion I noted that the Best Value audit could be seen as a clear example of the Audit Society in action. The government auditor responsible for the conduct of Best Value audits in Scotland has undertaken a major consultation exercise to review the effectiveness of this form of audit.[25] The new variant of this form of audit is called BV2. The key elements of BV2 include a variety of tests by which auditors exercise judgment as to whether the public sector organization is capable of fulfilling its mission. The BV2 includes an assessment of the vision and strategic direction of the public sector organization. This includes an appraisal of the leadership and culture of the organization being audited. It also includes an evaluation of planning and resource alignment, performance management and improvement, use of resources and governance, and accountability at the audited organization. This evaluation is rounded off by an evaluation of the partnership working and community leadership shown by the auditee. These key dimensions of BV2 are *remarkably similar to those of BV1*. One significant difference is the approach, which is deemed to be "more proportionate": specifically, risk management technologies will be deployed in assessing the need for BV2 audits. Will this addition of risk management make these audits more proportionate and eliminate the downside of displacement of core activities by the need to demonstrate compliance with the requirements of Best Value? Or will this addition to audit technologies intensify the effects of the Audit Society? These are empirical questions for which we do not have answers at this time. However, there are pertinent reflections in the Power critique of risk management.

Power's critique of risk management identifies a number of unintended consequences of its widespread application.[26] There is quantitative expansion of risk management, but also there are important qualitative changes in the alignment of risk management with "good governance." The state sector has imported and implemented risk management ideas and blueprints from the private sector. In the public sector, risk management is a "reputation management strategy." The growth of risk management involves an intensified focus on process and on auditable trails and documentation. Risk management systems "hardwire" defensiveness in organizations. Risk management threatens to imprison organizational thinking. Power contends that *the risk of risk management* is that it will consume organizational life.

This thesis by Power on risk management in organizations needs to be substantiated through empirical research. However, it is possible to identify specific cases of the collision between the Risk Society and the Audit Society and the corrosive effect of such influences on professional judgments, with audit instincts and compliance given primacy over common sense in situations of perceived risk.

—Case 1. On a handful of occasions each year we serve a glass of wine with lunch on the yacht charters we organize. Legislation enacted by the last government forced us to obtain an alcohol license, requiring a four-day course, a £180 application fee, a £180 annual fee, and submission of ten copies of a forty-page form.

Our stocks (four bottles of white wine) were inspected separately by the police, fire, and rescue service, the Health and Safety Executive (which has overall responsibility for compliance with all legislation on health and safety matters in the United Kingdom), the district council, and the licensing officer. We subsequently allowed our license to lapse (out of common sense) but now after three further visits by the council have been threatened with prosecution for noncompliance with relevant legislation. We start again at base zero with another four-day course.[27]

—Case 2. A tourist tried to board a flight to Canada from Gatwick Airport with a nine-inch model soldier in her hand luggage. A scanner showed that the soldier was holding a plastic "firearm" and officials said it would have to be disarmed. The tourist had to snap the rifle from the model's hands and post it to her home in Toronto. The plastic rifle was three inches long with no moving parts and no trigger. Security officers at Gatwick were quoted as saying, "Rules are rules."[28]

—Case 3. Alison Hume, forty-four, died in July 2008 after falling down a sixty-foot mineshaft on her way home. She was trapped for six hours and died of a heart attack. The firefighters arrived within thirty minutes of the accident. One firefighter was lowered into the mineshaft by ropes. The firefighters on the scene were willing to attempt a rescue, but they were told they were not allowed to use their safety equipment to help members of the public. After five hours police mountain rescue arrived. After forty minutes, Mrs. Hume was hauled to safety, but had developed hypothermia and died of a heart attack shortly afterward.[29] The head of Strathclyde Fire Service said health and safety rules were "having the cumulative effect of putting the firefighters in a position where they are more fearful of the legislation than they are of risking their lives."[30]

—Case 4. In March 2011 emergency workers were told not to pull a charity shop worker from a waist-deep boating lake, in case they "compromised their safety." Staff from two fire engines, two police cars, two ambulances, and an air ambulance stood by as Simon Burgess, forty-one, was left lying face-down in the shallow water, twenty-five yards from the edge of the lake. He drowned.[31]

These cases reveal how the Audit Society copes with risk: a preoccupation with compliance, a neglect of the safety of members of the public, and a defensive-minded attitude that hides behind rules and regulations. The Audit Society meets the Risk Society, and the winner is a compliance mentality and the losers are unfortunate citizens in distress. It might be said that these are extreme cases, and that they are not representative. However, many other similar examples could be cited in this discussion. There is a definite phenomenon—an intermingling of ideas of audit, control, and compliance and a fear of how to cope with risks in everyday life that strengthens the audit mentality within the ranks of officials within public services. This phenomenon is counter to the very idea of transparency. These cases have come to light because of fatal accident inquiries, exasperated citizens, and the occasional investigative journalist. The cumulative effect of this force for risk minimization is the creation of reports for the public that present a picture of orderliness and tidiness, even though this may not be the case. This is obfuscation, not transparency.

Conclusion

This discussion has explored the concept of transparency in public affairs, specifically by focusing on the role and impact of public sector audit. The objective of transparency is to achieve openness, by shedding light on dark areas and making all parts of public finance and public administration open to scrutiny by citizens. The government audit may be seen as a natural component of this process, with auditors providing attestations of the merits or otherwise of public institutions, their finances, and the effectiveness of their services. The impartiality of auditors can be seen as providing trust and confidence to the citizens.[32]

However, this discussion has also explored the unintended and dysfunctional effects of audit processes. In particular, the emergence of an Audit Explosion has changed expectations regarding audit.[33] The diffusion of audit and the significant increase in the quantum of audit-like processes of checking and verification has given primacy to audit thinking and audit work across a wide spectrum of contemporary society. This phenomenon has taken hold so firmly that we can now speak of an Audit Society.[34] The actual tracking and identification of such effects in society is a mammoth task, but there certainly are a whole series of events in which audit thinking has become extremely influential.[35]

A major feature of this particular state of affairs is the nature of audit technologies such as VFM and Best Value audit, which are not methodologically as robust as they might appear, as these technologies do not provide clear-cut guidance for action. Furthermore, the operationalizing of these techniques has led to significant challenges. In particular, VFM and Best Value auditors have issues regarding the quality of data and the ability to extract from them meaningful interpretations of complex situations. These features of government audit have resulted in a compliance mentality in many contexts, in which checking off the appropriate box may be regarded as a sufficient act rather than ensuring that the best outcome has been obtained for services being audited. This may be counter to the very idea of transparency if it misleads citizens into thinking that all is well, when there may in fact be deep-seated problems that are not being addressed. This checklist kind of thinking may lead to actions based on presenting organizational or managerial legitimacy rather than achieving genuine transparency.

I have also reflected here on the intermingling of audit thinking as captured in the concept of the Audit Society with ideas of risk as encapsulated in ideas of the Risk Society. Empirical research is needed to determine the impact of the development of the connection between these two bodies of thought. But the case studies presented do support the contention that a defensive-minded attitude might prevail as a consequence of the perceived need to eliminate risks in society.[36]

In conclusion, on one level government audit reports can be seen as beneficial to citizens and as promoting an open society based on transparency in policymaking and policy appraisal. But the subtle shifts in the significance of audit activity in contemporary society may have deleterious effects as the audit view of the world may not capture the subtleties of complex service provision. This may result in an *appearance* of transparency that is accepted by many citizens as transparency per se. This raises questions about the privileging of the audit function as a body of expertise and of auditors who sit in judgment of public services, organizations, and the members of these organizations. Audit may add to transparency in public affairs, but it may not. And it may lead to behaviors that run counter to the best interests of citizens.

Notes

1. Irvine Lapsley and Jeremy Lonsdale, "The Audit Society: Helping to Develop or Undermine Trust in Government?" in *Administrative Justice in Context*, edited by Michael Adler (Oxford, UK: Hart Publishing, 2010).

2. Christopher Hood, "A Public Management for All Seasons?" *Public Administration* 69 (Spring 1991): 3–19; Christopher Hood, "The New Public Management in the 1980s: Variations on a Theme," *Accounting Organizations and Society* 20 (February–April 1995): 93–109.

3. Hood, "Public Management for All Seasons?" p. 2.

4. Hood, "New Public Maanagement in the 1980s."

5. Michael Power, *The Audit Explosion* (London: Demos, 1994); Michael Power, *The Audit Society: Rituals of Verification* (Oxford University Press, 1997), p. 183; Michael Power, "The Audit Society—Second Thoughts," *International Journal of Auditing* 4 (March 2000): 111–19; Michael Power, "In Defence of the Audit Society: A Reply to Maltby," *Ephemera: Theory and Politics in Organization* 8 (November 2008): 399–402.

6. Irvine Lapsley, "New Public Management: Cruellest Invention of the Human Spirit?" *Abacus* 45 (March 2009): 1–21.

7. Mary Bowerman, Helen Raby, and Christopher Humphrey, "In Search of the Audit Society: Some Evidence from Health Care, Police and Schools," *International Journal of Auditing* 4 (March 2000): 71–100.

8. Power, "The Audit Society—Second Thoughts.".

9. Lapsley, "New Public Management."

10. Ibid.

11. Power, "The Audit Society—Second Thoughts."

12. Power, *The Audit Society.*

13. Ibid.

14. Michela Arnaboldi and Irvine Lapsley, "Making Management Auditable: The Implementation of Best Value in Local Government," *Abacus* 44 (March 2008): 22–47.

15. Lapsley, "New Public Management."

16. Irvine Lapsley and C. K. M. Pong, "Modernization versus Problematization: Value for Money Audit in Public Services," *European Accounting Review* 9 (December 2000): 541–67.

17. Ibid.

18. Department of the Environment, Transport and Regions, *Modernising Local Government: Improving Local Services through Best Value* (London: DETR, 1998).

19. Scottish Office Development Department, "Best Value Task Force: Report to Secretary of State and COSLA" (Edinburgh: 1997), and SODD Circular 22/97, letter sent July 25, 1997, to chief executives of Scottish local authorities (for both documents see http://mars.northlan.gov.uk/xpedio/groups/public/documents/report/060317.pdf, pp. 5–10).

20. Paul Higgins, Philip James, and Ian Roper, "Best Value: Is It Delivering?" *Public Money and Management* 24 (August 2004): 251–58; Steve Freer, "Comprehensive Performance Assessment in Local Government," *Public Money and Management* 22 (June 2002): 5–6.

21. Amanda Ball, Jane Broadbent, and Cynthia Moore, "Best Value and the Control of Local Government: Challenges and Contradictions," *Public Money and Management* 22 (June 2002): 9–16.

22. Arnaboldi and Lapsley, "Making Management Auditable," pp. 3–42.

23. Power, *The Audit Society*.

24. Michael Power, *Risk Management* (London: Demos, 2004); Michael Power, *Organised Uncertainty: Designing a World of Risk Management* (Oxford University Press, 2007).

25. Audit Scotland, "Best Value 2 Characteristics" (Edinburgh: Audit Scotland, 2010).

26. Power, *Risk Management*; Power, *Organised Uncertainty*.

27. Quoted in R. Ward "Red Tape Blues," *The Times*, Letters to the Editor, March 12, 2011.

28. "Airport Security Staff Disarm Pocket-Sized Insurgent," *The Times*, January 28, 2011.

29. T. Campbell, "We Could Have Helped Alison," *The Scotsman*, February 22, 2011.

30. Claire Smith, "Health and Safety Rules Prevent Us Saving Lives, Complains Fire Chief," *The Scotsman*, March 2, 2011.

31. Quoted in BBC News, "Safety Fear Stopped Police Pulling Man from Lake," March 11, 2011 (www.bbc.co.uk/news).

32. Lapsley and Lonsdale, "The Audit Society."

33. Power, *The Audit Explosion*.

34. Power, *The Audit Society*.

35. Power, "In Defence of the Audit Society."

36. Power, *Risk Management*; Power, *Organised Uncertainty*.

MARIA CUCCINIELLO, GRETA NASI,
AND RAFFAELLA SAPORITO

2 *Making Transparency Transparent: An Assessment Model for Local Governments*

Transparency in government is a highly regarded value, often studied by academics and emphasized by practitioners. In the literature, transparency is discussed as a tool to enhance governments' accountability, as a principle to activate for reducing public administration corruption, and as a way to distribute information on government's performance.

Despite these different concepts, most studies operate on a common underlying assumption: that transparency in government is a critical ingredient for efficient and well-functioning economic and political markets. More generally, transparency is seen as a cornerstone of democracy. In fact, the claim for the need for a transparent government was embedded in the modern idea of democracy at its birth.[1]

Many countries, including Italy, refer to transparency in their constitutions and emphasize its application—mainly in terms of free access to information and openness—as underlying principles of their legal systems. However, according to David Heald, "Transparency is widely canvassed as a key to better governance, increasing trust in public office holders. But transparency is more often preached than practised, more often referred to than defined, and more often advocated than critically analysed."[2] This thought finds support in literature where different studies present and discuss theoretical models and practical findings that focus on single dimensions of transparency.[3]

In this chapter we construct an assessment framework aimed at measuring the degree of transparency in government on the basis of the multiple dimensions that can be analyzed, using primarily information published on the governments' websites. For this purpose we review literature about transparency in government and focus on studies from different disciplines and fields that describe transparency's meaning and applications in the public sector.

The framework has been tested on a purposive sample consisting of the twenty-one Italian regional capitals. The results show that these municipalities tend to distribute mainly information that they are required to publish to comply with the requirements of the law. They also seem to be more interested in publishing information about their functioning than about their performance.

This chapter is organized into six sections. Section 2 describes the literature about transparency in government, section 3 presents the assessment model, section 4 describes the methods, and the last two sections present and discuss findings, draw some conclusions, and make recommendations.

Literature Review: Theories and Previous Studies

The principle of transparency is regarded as having great value in government as a means to enhance and reinforce the relationship between public administrations and their external stakeholders. Many researchers have been focusing on this topic, adopting different disciplinary approaches and investigating different streams of research. Some main considerations derive from a review of the growing body of literature about transparency in government.

First, despite the existence of a few important efforts to provide unambiguous terminology concerning transparency, there is a great variety of studies that use different definitions and meanings of this principle.[4]

Second, in recent years, many studies have focused on the relationship between the use of information and communication technologies by governments as tools to enhance the level of transparency in government. These studies assume that these technologies—especially the websites of public administrations—reduce all barriers to government accessibility, including time and spatial ones.[5]

Third, some studies attempt to understand the degree of transparency in different types of government, presenting both theoretical frameworks and empirical evidences.[6] Most of them focus on single dimensions of transparency, mainly on the degree of information accessibility about mission-related tasks and services, or on their use of resources and the degree of financial accountability. However, a common point is that all of these studies focus on assessing websites, which they consider to be the main tool to evaluate the level of transparency of public administrations.

Here we identify and discuss the main branches of the literature on transparency, in order to construct our own assessment framework.

What Is Transparency?

More information allows better analysis, better monitoring, and evaluation of events, all of which are significant to people's economic and social well-being.[7]

It is a fact that information is a key factor for all types of organizations. Private organizations consider it a strategic variable to maintain and enhance their innovation capacity, which is considered crucial for surviving in markets.[8] For public administrations, information is a crucial element to improve their functioning, enhance their capacity to fulfill citizens' and businesses' requirements, and to enhance their trustworthy relationship with all their stakeholders.[9]

In order to support organizations' goals, information has to be shared among the relevant internal and external stakeholders.[10] The degree of information sharing is described in the literature as openness and transparency.

But openness and transparency are fairly different, even if they have been sometimes used as synonyms. In fact, according to Patrick J. Birkinshaw, both openness and transparency, although similar in meaning, convey something wider than access to government information.[11] Birkinshaw defines openness as "concentrating on processes that allow to see the operations and activities of government at work, subject . . . to necessary exemptions." Transparency goes beyond openness, meaning that "lawmaking and public process should be made as accessible as possible" while taking into consideration several constraints and obstacles, such as complexity and disorder.[12]

Furthermore, as Alisdair Roberts points out, openness without transparency might be detrimental to citizens.[13] It is difficult for citizens to extract information that has not been edited with citizens in mind. This is especially the case now, when, thanks to new communication technologies, the quantity of information available and the difficulty of navigating it may actually contribute to greater confusion and an overall reduction of transparency.[14] This view of transparency can be defined as actionable openness, also shared by Heald,[15] which means that the openness is designed for and accessed by citizens and stakeholders.[16]

The most relevant definitions, starting from a technical definition, are as follows. The *Oxford Dictionary of Economics* defines transparent policy measures as "policy measures whose operation is open to public scrutiny. Transparency includes making it clear who is taking the decisions, what the measures are, who is gaining from them, and who is paying for them." According to Jonathan Koppell, transparency is a critical tool and also an end in itself.[17] Several studies show that an open and transparent government strengthens democracy by providing a defense against forms of bad government, denouncing abuses of power, offering greater protection to minorities through the provision of equal citizenship rights, and providing more opportunities for popular participation. As noted by James Madison about two centuries ago, "A popular Government without popular information or the means to acquire it is only the prologue to a farce, tragedy or perhaps both."[18] The driving force behind all systems of accountability is the democratic imperative for government organizations to respond to demands from elected representatives and the wider public.[19] Many government policies seeking greater transparency explicitly recognize the ways these measures improve the democratic process. Some countries have gone further, recognizing that an open government is necessary (though not sufficient) to strengthen democracy.

Vicente Pina, Lourdes Torres, and Basilio Acerete offer a specific and narrow definition, describing transparency as a component of accountability.[20] In fact, according to both Linda Deleon and Richard Mulgan, accountability encompasses issues concerned with the external control exercised by the audit offices—financial accountability—together with others such as how voters can make elected representatives answer for their policies.[21]

Other authors describe transparency as a tool to enhance government effectiveness as perceived by their stakeholders.[22] Robert D. Putnam argues that public satisfaction with government is a function of both public expectation and perception of governmental performance.[23] As a consequence, the more transparent an organization is, the better its stakeholders can monitor its performance.[24] Some authors also state that an organization with transparent decisionmaking processes can vastly increase citizen participation and, eventually, improve the functioning of democracy.[25]

Heald also argues that transparency allows an organization to perform its mission and periodically to release performance-relevant information that assessment will actually or potentially be based on.[26]

Finally, some authors as well as many reports about transparency published by international organizations discuss the role of transparency as a tool to prevent and reduce government corruption.[27]

In conclusion, there are several manifestations of transparency in an organization. Heald groups them in four types, arguing that transparency can be described as a means to control the conduct of the agent or subordinate in a hierarchical relationship as well as the capacity of the ruled organization to be able to observe the conduct of its rulers and assess their needs.[28] However, it can also be expressed as the capacity of an organization to monitor the habitat and the conduct of external competitors and, finally, as a means to allow outside monitoring of what happens inside the organization (related to freedom of information legislation).

This review shows a lack of comprehensive models to assess transparency as a tool for enhancing better government. Thus, there is no one commonly shared framework of transparency: narrower and wider definitions can be found, as well as unclear and missing definitions.[29]

Information Technologies as a Tool to Enhance Government Transparency

All these lines of thought fall squarely into line with the use of information and communication technologies (ICT) to enhance transparency. In fact, ICT provides promising tools to increase the transparency of government, establishing the connection between e-government and transparency.

Helen Margetts offers a more specific framework for thinking through the notion of transparency, suggesting three key ways in which digital government could be more transparent than government in the predigital era.[30] She notes that information technology can

—Aid implementation of Freedom of Information legislation

—Provide better information (for example, by linking decisions to their legal context)

—Provide better access to information

Furthermore, the availability of information represents a crucial factor in a democratic society because it allows all citizens to have approximately equal access to information. This point is emphasized by Pippa Norris, who argues that the marriage of information technology and government might produce several positive consequences for different aspects of democracy.[31]

E-government applications play a critical role in strengthening the linkages between policymakers and the poor and between the poor and service providers as well as between policymakers and service providers. Daniel Kaufmann explores this concept and argues that transparency mechanisms through the use of Internet help in implementing complementary measures to reduce incentives for bribery abroad.[32] He maintains that transparency "is supposed to discipline institutions and their office-holders by making information about their performance more public. Publicity is taken to deter corruption and poor performance, and to secure a basis for ensuring better and more trustworthy performance."

Thomas H. Davenport maintains, further, that the informational transparency of government organizations increases because digital systems generally register more information about their (internal) business processes.[33]

Some other scholars point out that governments, through their own web sites, should make use of several transparency and accountability features to enhance the level of public trust and legitimacy.[34] According to Valentina Ndou, if websites are designed carefully and openly, they can be valuable resources for transparency, for citizens, businesses, and other stakeholders should be able to see political and governmental information, rules, and policies.[35] Darrell M. West, by analyzing e-government usage and the exposure of managers to e-government questions, found that those who visited federal government websites experienced a significant increase in their belief that government is effective.[36] This study suggests that in some respects, e-government has the potential to transform service delivery as well as citizens' attitudes.

Frameworks to Assess Transparency

However, many researches, using measures to assess the degree of website transparency, only partially explain its impact on stakeholders (citizens, businesses, and so forth) who daily interact with local governments.[37]

Pina, Torres, and Acerete argue that transparency of websites refers to the extent to which an organization makes available information about its internal processes, decision processes, and procedures available.[38] They conducted several empirical studies about the improvements made by e-government of transparency, openness, and accountability, focusing on financial information. One of these studies focused on analyzing the websites of the regional or other subnational administrative levels and of the five biggest cities of each of the fifteen EU countries.[39] Based on this analysis they discovered that citizens would not be able to hold their government accountable if they did not know what it is doing and had no channel for interacting with it. As long as public organizations are ultimately accountable to the citizens, transparency and interactivity will be two critical elements for the accountability function of government. Moreover, they conducted another study in 2010 with the aim of assessing the extent to which e-government enables transparency and accountability in local governments. They conducted this analysis on seventy-five European local government websites (of the four biggest cities plus the capital of each of the first fifteen EU countries). In particular, they used a framework of analysis based on a checklist of specific financial information to be searched in government websites, in order to measure the level of *financial accountability*.

Some other empirical studies have attempted to define criteria for the evaluation of sites of public administration, by using the level of accessibility and usability as a synonym for institutional transparency. The research group called Cyberspace Policy Research Group (CyPRG), founded by the National Science Foundation in collaboration with the University of Arizona, conducted a comparative analysis of public sector websites focusing on two key elements: accessibility and transparency of administrative action. The CyPRG study suggests that greater openness and transparency of the site is associated with greater accountability.[40]

Other models have been focused on analyzing the level of transparency in health care organizations; one such example is the work conducted by the Leapfrog Group, which defined a set of indicators for evaluating the transparency of hospital websites that can be generalized to other contexts.

Lasse Berntzen proposed a transparency framework based on Norwegian legislation dealing with aspects of transparency.[41] The model proposed identified different types of transparency: document transparency, benchmarking transparency, meeting transparency, disclosure transparency, and decision-maker transparency. For each of these variables Berntzen defined specific items needed to measure the level of transparency achieved.

Some other international organizations have developed frameworks and models, focusing on country perspective or on specific types of transparency. For example, the World Bank carried out a comparative study that shows that "in contexts with high levels of transparency, efficient parliamentary control and high ethical standards, there is a higher growth rate of GDP, compared with countries that settled at lower levels."[42]

Our Assessment Model

On the basis of our literature review, we drafted some considerations that led to the definition of a comprehensive assessment framework.

As stated in the literature, governments publish information mainly about their institutional mission and the use of financial resources. In some countries they might be required to make public certain types of information about their functioning and performance.[43]

However, we also took into account the evidence from other studies showing that transparency of government operations and performance might contribute to higher trust in government and, eventually, to a more participatory democracy.[44] As a consequence, we drafted a framework to monitor the degree of transparency, one based on four different dimensions: institutional, political, financial, and service delivery.

The institutional dimension captures the degree of transparency about the mission and the functioning of governments, their mandatory activities and the information they are legally required to publish.

The service delivery dimension assesses the degree of transparency about the performance of governments in delivering services to citizens and businesses.

The political dimension captures the degree of accessibility of information about the political representatives such as the council members—their political mandate and activities, along with other information such as their degree of absenteeism at the different councils' meetings and their salaries.

Figure 2-1. *The Four Dimensions of Transparency*

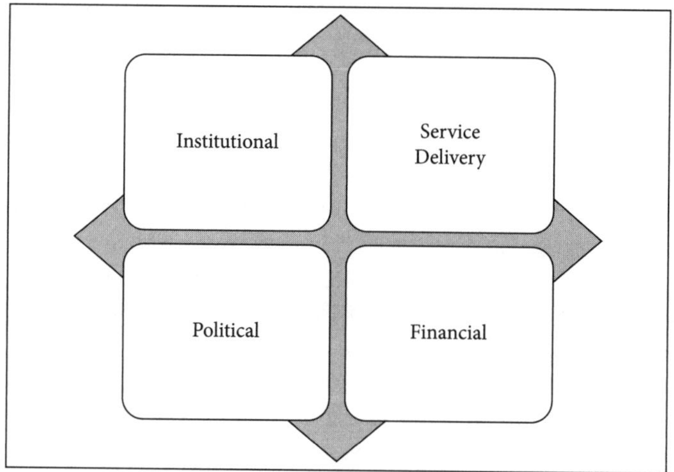

Source: SDA Bocconi School of Management, 2010.

The financial dimension assesses the degree of transparency regarding the use of financial resources, governments' financial solvency, and other financial issues.

The assessment model has been designed in particular to measure government transparency on the basis of the information published on governments' websites.

Description of the Four Dimensions of the Model

Each dimension of the assessment framework is articulated into different variables that are described in this section. Each of them has been selected in order to allow its applicability to different institutional contexts and types of governments (see figure 2-1).

The institutional dimension contains items grouped in three variables: ownership of site content (including information about the agency's involvement with site), contact information (concerning people inside the organization), and organizational information (in the Italian context this includes the new legal requirements concerning transparency stated by the public sector reform of 2009, launched by the minister of public administration, Renato Brunetta. For this variable we have used some items included in the checklist produced by the CyPRG in their Web Site Attribute Evaluation System (WAES) by adapting them to our purposes: we have introduced new items concerning the specific Italian context and the new Italian legislation in terms of transparency.

The service delivery dimension assesses the level of transparency of the information about service delivery and activities performed. This dimension comprises five variables, moving from the simplest to the more complex level. In designing the items included in this variable we referred to nursery school service delivery online (we will further explain this choice in the next section). It includes general information about the service (office details), activities delivered (including information about activities and specific services provided), activities measurement (such as statistics on users), and performance information (which analyzes the level of performance concerning the service selected, in terms of how the supply matches the demand for that service). The last group of items for this variable investigates the existence of feedback concerning the performance of services, in terms of explanations of such data.

The political dimension comprises three variables: profile of political representatives (for example, mayor, cabinet, and council), political activities (for example, information about the mayor's priorities), and political accountability (for example, information about how to contact the mayor, the members of the cabinet, and others).

For the financial dimension we used the model proposed by Pina, Torres, and Acerete by adding some items and reducing some others, in order to better adapt the model to organizations of different dimensions (in terms of number of inhabitants, employees, budget, and thus of complexity).[45] The final version of this dimension contains items concerning economic and financial information and a more general variable concerning qualitative characteristics and comprehensibility of financial and economic information.

Stages of Transparency

Our intention is for the model we are developing not only to check whether or not the website is transparent but also to ask and answer the question "How transparent is it?" In doing this we identified three different stages that organization websites could reach (or have already reached), which reflect the degree of transparency of the organization regarding the four dimensions (see figure 2-2):

—Stage 1. Basic level of information (mandatory information by law)

—Stage 2. Availability of information concerning the performance for each of the four dimensions identified

—Stage 3. Availability of information about feedback and explanations related to performance

Figure 2-2. *Stages of Transparency*

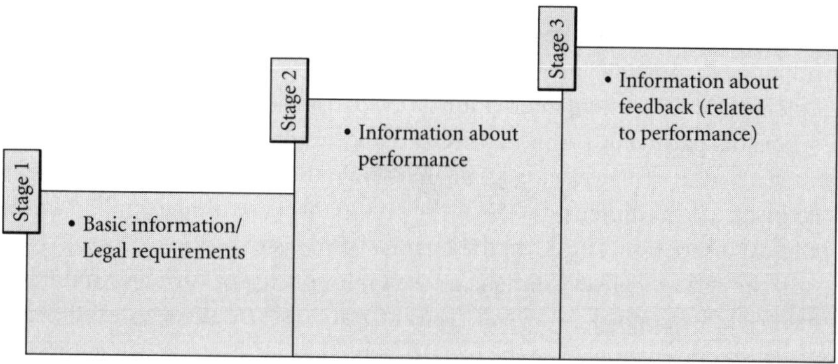

Source: SDA Bocconi School of Management, 2010.

Research Method

In this study we conduct an empirical analysis of the level of transparency in Italian municipalities.

The research sample is made up of the websites of the regional capitals of the twenty-one Italian regions.[46] In conducting this pilot analysis, we defined a purposive sample, which is a nonprobability sampling, but it helps to pick subjects on the basis of specific characteristics.[47] In fact, we identified as criteria for purpose selection of the sample the following:

—Dimension of the pilot sample: small

—Geographical distribution: the whole country (all the regions)

—Size of municipalities (number of inhabitants): medium-large[48]

Using these criteria, we decided to investigate as a pilot sample the Italian regional capitals.

Each Italian region has a regional capital, which in eighteen of twenty one regions also is the largest city. The exceptions are Abruzzo, whose capital is L'Aquila while the most populous city is Pescara, and Calabria, whose capital city is Catanzaro while the largest city is Reggio di Calabria. With the exception of the autonomous region of Valle d'Aosta, which is not divided into provinces, the regional capitals are also provincial capitals.

The reason for using a purposive sample is to achieve a symbolic representation. Purposive samples are designed to be as diverse as possible, including all key groups and constituencies. Units are selected on the basis of their potential contribution to theory development. In this case the sample does not need to be large enough to support statements of prevalence or incidence.[49]

According to this purpose, even if this sample is not statistically representative of the entire country, the analysis can lead to some interesting and useful hints for extending the study—for example, to all the 183 Italian municipalities with more than 40,000 inhabitants (including all the 21 regional capitals already explored), or for making international comparisons.

For this particular study we conducted a comprehensive content analysis of twenty-one websites using a 121-item evaluation checklist: 34 items are in the institutional dimension, 29 in the service delivery dimension, 20 in the political dimension, and 37 in the financial dimension.

In the service delivery dimension we built up a list of variables and items that could be applied to several types of public services. As an example of service to citizens we chose the nursery school, since it is one of the top services delivered by local governments (according to the results of a 2009 study conducted by a research group of the Ministry of Public Administration).

All websites were assessed in May and June 2010.

The scores show the frequencies with which the different items analyzed appear on the websites evaluated. All the items identified were given a score of 1 if they appeared in the websites and 0 if they did not.

Since the scope of this pilot analysis is to test the model, in order to check its validity and to extend its usage in further analysis, our focus is on discussing preliminary results, based on descriptive statistics and a frequency table. We will provide a deeper analysis of the correlation between certain results and the characteristics of our sample when the sample is more significant.

Findings and Discussion

The analysis of the websites of twenty-one Italian municipalities that are also capital regions shows that the municipalities are more transparent in the institutional and the political dimensions. This could have also been hypothesized since these two dimensions include most of the variables and measures that refer to information that public administrations are legally required to publish.

However, it is interesting to note that not all items that legally must be published on the websites can actually be found on them. For example, the new national regulation about Italian municipality transparency states that all the expenses for external professionals or consultants have to be published on the municipalities' websites, to enhance the accountability of the appointment system. But we found that almost 25 percent of the sample were not yet complying with this legal requirement. We got the same results concerning information about senior civil servants' compensation. The recent reform requires inform-

Figure 2-3. *Overall Results for the Four Dimensions*

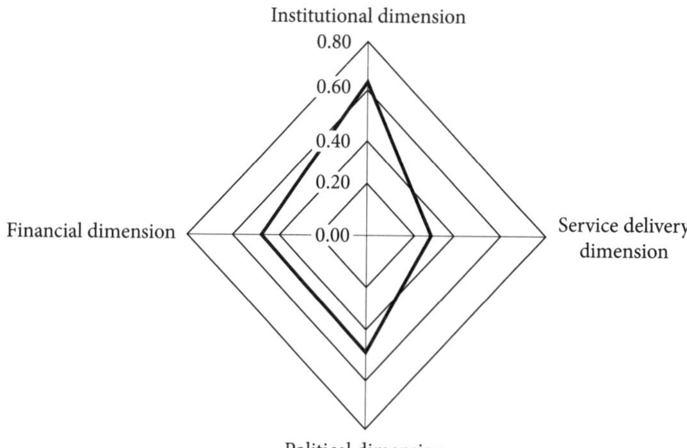

Source: SDA Bocconi School of Management, 2010.

ing citizens via the government website of the amount of bonuses paid each year, but 25 percent of the municipalities we analyzed failed to do so (see figure 2-3).

A general overview to the data shows that the dimension with the highest score is the institutional one, followed by the political dimension, the financial dimension and, bringing up the rear, the service delivery dimension.

Now we take a closer look at the data for each dimension.

The Institutional Dimension

What does it mean that the municipalities are more transparent on their institutional dimension? As already explained in the model's description, the institutional dimension provides various types of information about local governments. The first level of information is very basic: the organizational structure, the description of the main activities, and the different ways to get access to the organization (see table 2-1).

Included in the thirty-four items used to measure this dimension is specific institutional information whose inclusion became mandatory at the beginning of 2011 in accordance with the recent reform of the public sector. Going deeper into the third variable (organizational information and accountability) we can observe the level of compliance of our sample with the legal requirements. The organizational information in this variable could be categorized as mandatory, nonmandatory, and forthcoming mandatory starting in 2011 (see table 2-2).

Table 2-1. *Institutional Dimension*
Percent

Institutional dimension (average)	*0.69*
Ownership	0.62
Accessibility	0.66
Organization information and accountability	0.47
Information on organizations' issues	0.84
Citizen feedback	0.84

Source: SDA Bocconi School of Management, 2010.

Referring to the three stages identified earlier (basic, performance, and feedback), which reflect the degree of transparency of the organization, for this dimension we can affirm that the results are very good for stage 1, the basic level of information, concerning basic organizational information, even though they are not yet mandatory.

For stage 2, the results seem to reflect legal requirements. For example, information about civil servants' efforts, which we consider to be characteristic of stage 2 transparency, is quite frequent, present in almost 66 percent of the sample, because it is a mandatory one. Yet information about other standards of performance are completely absent (stage 2), and no feedback information (stage 3) is provided up until the point when the results were analyzed. It will be interesting to repeat the data collection when these aspects have become mandatory.

The Service Delivery Dimension

The second dimension aims at exploring the level of transparency concerning the performance of governments in delivering services to citizens and businesses (see table 2-3). In order to collect comparable data, we chose a service covered by all the organizations in our sample, the nursery school service, as already explained.

As previously stated, the service delivery dimension is the one with the lowest score. This could be due to the fact that this dimension explores very advanced content in terms of transparency, which is related to specific service delivery. In our research we checked the level of transparency, but we did not have any information about the management of services. In other words, on the basis of our analysis we can hypothesize that some types of information are not provided on the website because the organization, for various reasons, has not yet collected them—for example, because collecting this kind of infor-

Table 2-2. *Level of Municipalities' Compliance with Legal Transparency Requirements, as Percentage of Municipalities Providing Information Type*

Type of information provided on organization and accountability	*Mandatory*	*Nonmandatory*	*Forthcoming mandatory*	*Score*[a]
Mission statement and various activities of agency		x		0.86
Senior officials' background (résumé, previous experience)	x			0.86
Senior officials' experiences or vision for future for organization		x		0.86
Civil servants' work attendance or absence	x			0.81
Staff collaboration with consultants or interns	x			0.76
Civil servants' level of pay, bonus, incentives	x			0.76
Diagram of organizational structure		x		0.48
Amount of personnel incentive fund			x	0.24
Collective agreements			x	0.19
Variations of collective agreements			x	0.10
Individual civil servants' performance			x	0.00
Feedback about individual civil servants' performance			x	0.00

Source: SDA Bocconi School of Management, 2010.
a. Percentage of municipalities providing this information on their websites.

mation takes a lot of time and requires organizational efforts and skills, resources, informatics systems, and so forth. In further studies it would be interesting to verify whether the level of transparency of this dimension is consistent with the presence of information, planning and control, and quality systems.

Table 2-3. *Service Delivery Dimension*
Percent

Service delivery dimension (average)	*0.30*
General information	0.55
Activities delivered	0.48
Activities measurement	0.18
Performance, social, and environmental information	0.15
Feedback	0.10

Source: SDA Bocconi School of Management, 2010.

As was the case for the institutional dimension, the quality of the scores decreases as one moves from the basic stage 1 of information (general information, information about activities delivered) to stage 2, which includes information about activities measurement and performance, and are very low at stage 3, about performance feedback.

The Political Dimension

The variable that scores the highest percentage on the political dimension is the one concerning information about political representatives, followed by the variables that show the level of transparency concerning their activities and performance (see table 2-4).

Taking a closer look at the information available for political representatives, we find that mayors provide more information than do municipal councils and their members (see table 2-5).

This makes sense in terms of the electoral system of municipalities that we investigated: citizens vote for the mayor directly, and he leads a group of council members, who are less visible than the mayor, not just during the political campaign but also during the entire mandate. This could explain a very high level of information provided by the mayor on the municipality's website, when compared to the information level provided by the council and the council members. This difference in terms of visibility seems to correspond to a difference in political power.

Table 2-4. *Political Dimension*
Percent

Political dimension (average)	*0.49*
Profile of the representatives	0.76
Political activities	0.39
Political accountability	0.36

Source: SDA Bocconi School of Management, 2010.

Table 2-5. *Profile of the Representatives*
Percent

Profile of the representatives (average)	*0.76*
Name of the mayor	0.95
Names of members of the cabinet	0.90
Names of members of the city council	0.81
Information about the mayor (such as a curriculum vitae, previous political responsibilities, personal information)	0.90
information about the members of the cabinet	0.62
information about members of the city council	0.38

Source: SDA Bocconi School of Management, 2010.

A methodological clarification: the municipality of Bologna got low scores on the political dimension because, owing to a political crisis in the ruling majority, there was no political board governing the city during the period of data collection, and so no information about this dimension could be found online.

The Financial Dimension

The financial dimension of transparency is crucial, since the disclosure of how resources are allocated is one of the most important factors of accountability of any public body. Looking at the results, the values for the two variables considered, economic and financial information and qualitative characteristics' understandability, are both around 47 percent (see table 2-6).

Concerning the economic and financial variable, at least 66 percent of the sample shows very basic financial information on its institutional website, such as a statement of income. Fewer municipalities, around 50 percent, provide more sophisticated information such as classification of expenditure by function or by object.

In accordance with our understanding of the three stages of transparency (see figure 2-2), we can say that the financial information items just described

Table 2- 6. *Financial Dimension*
Percent

Financial dimension (average)	*0.47*
Economic and financial information	0.47
Qualitative characteristics—understandability	0.47

Table 2-7. *Financial Indicators and Feedback*
Percent

Provides economic performance indicators	0.05
Provides feedback about efficiency-productivity-performance indicators	0.05
Provides efficiency-productivity-performance indicators	0.00
Provides effectiveness performance indicators	0.00
Provides feedback about performance indicators	0.00

represent the first stage of transparency: basic information and or compliance with legal requirements.

Moving to a higher degree of transparency, the items concerning the transparency on financial indicators (stage 2) or comments on financial results (stage 3) register very low scores (see table 2-7).

Ranking the Sample

In this study we focus on descriptive analysis because of the size and the representative power of our sample do not allow any significant correlation between municipalities' characteristics and the data gathered. However, we can order the municipalities of our sample on the basis of the results obtained. This is another type of analysis that our model allows us to discuss. We can rank the twenty-one municipalities on the basis of the sum of each regional capital's scores (see figure 2-4).

Conclusion

In this chapter we present an assessment framework whose purpose is to measure the degree of transparency in government, based on the multiple dimensions that can be analyzed. The literature analysis leads us to verify that there is no one common definition of transparency: narrower and wider definitions can be found, as can unclear or incomplete definitions.[50]

The literature review does reveal the existence of a number of models for assessing transparency. Their limits, in our understanding of the subject, are that they focus just on very specific and narrow interpretation of the concept of transparency in governments. Hence, the purpose of this chapter is to try to craft a comprehensive assessment model that can widen the concept of transparency vis-à-vis the models that have been used in research till now. In this chapter we also present a pilot study of our assessment model. Some

Figure 2-4. *Municipalities Ranked by Level of Transparency*

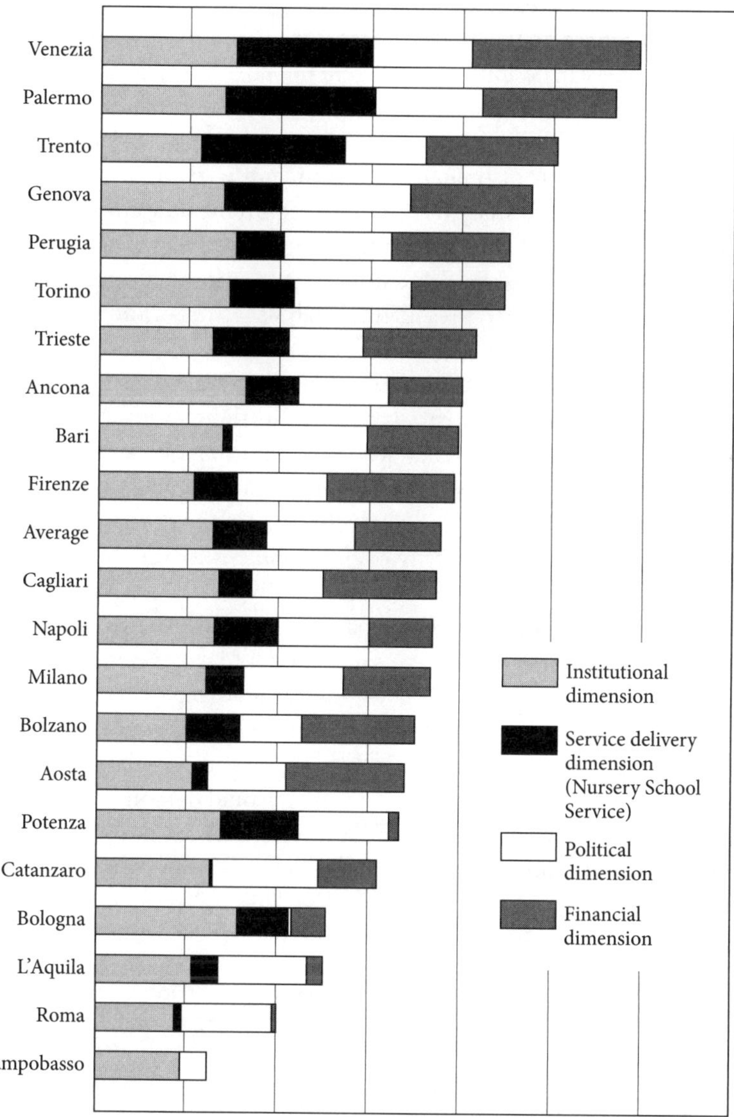

Source: SDA Bocconi School of Management, 2010.

inferences that can be drawn from this preliminary analysis provide interesting hints for further research.

A first comment on the model concerns the types of data that can be gathered. The model can be applied to different public organizations, contexts, and time frames. The time could be a crucial aspect in order to introduce dynamics in this analysis: the data set underlining our model allows data gathering over different periods of time, in order to identify trends and patterns. For instance, we saw in this study that the legal requirements seemed to affect the degree of transparency. This suggests that to increase the level of transparency, a key role may be played by mandatory, legally enforceable prescriptions—though this conclusion requires further analysis for verification. A longitudinal analysis will be a good way to verify this dynamic.

This model investigates not just whether a website is transparent but also how high the level of transparency is. We identify three stages of transparency: stage 1 (basic level of transparency, with basic information), stage 2 (advanced level of transparency, with performance information), and stage 3 (very advanced level of transparency, with feedback). This first application of our model confirms that the majority of our sample is mainly transparent at a basic level and the number of municipalities registering high transparency scores decreases as the degree of transparency increases. The same conclusions arose from the application of the same model to a larger sample (capital provinces) and to a different level of government (regional government).[51] However, further studies will allow us to verify whether we are dealing with a Guttman scale, which is unidimensional, ordinal, and cumulative. This would have important policy implication, because it would demonstrate that transparency concerning information about performance cannot be provided absent clear information at the basic level.

Notes

1. James Madison, "Letter to W. T. Barry, August 4, 1822," in *The Writings of James Madison*, volume 9, edited by Ian G. Hunt (New York: G. P. Putnam's Sons, 1910), pp. 790–93.

2. Christopher Hood and David Heald, eds., *Transparency: The Key to Better Governance* (Oxford University Press, 2006), p. 3.

3. Chris C. Demchak, C. Friis, and Todd M. La Porte, "Democracy and Bureaucracy in the Age of the Web: Empirical Findings and Theoretical Speculations," paper presented at the International Political Science Association meetings, Québec City, Canada, August 2000; Todd M. La Porte, Chris C. Demchak, and Martin De Jong, "Democracy and Bureaucracy in the Age of the Web: Empirical Findings and Theoretical Speculations," *Administration & Society* 34 (September 2002): 411–46; Vicente

Pina, Lourdes Torres, and Sonia Royo, "Are ICTs Improving Transparency and Accountability in the EU Regional and Local Governments? An Empirical Study," *Public Administration* 85 (June 2007): 449–72; Tara Vishwanath and Daniel Kaufmann, "Towards Transparency in Finance and Governance," Finance 0308009, EconWPA (2003) (http:// econpapers.repec.org/paper/wpawuwpfi/0308009.htm).

4. Summarized in Hood and Heald, *Transparency*.

5. John M. Stevens and Robert P. McGowan, *Information Systems and Public Management* (New York: CBS Educational and Professional Publishing, 1985).

6. Ibid., p. 3.

7. Roumeen Islam, "Do More Transparent Governments Govern Better?" Policy Research Working Paper 3077 (Washington: World Bank, 2003).

8. Michael Porter, "The Five Competitive Forces That Shape Strategy," *Harvard Business Review*, January 2008, pp. 86–104.

9. Greta Nasi, *Innovazione e cambiamento nelle aziende del settore pubblico* [Innovation and change in public agencies] (Milan: Egea, 2008).

10. Ibid.

11. Patrick J. Birkinshaw, "Freedom of Information and Openness: Fundamental Human Rights?" *Administrative Law Review* 58 (Winter 2006): 177–218.

12. Ibid., pp. 189, 191.

13. Alasdair Roberts, *Blacked Out: Government Secrecy in the Information Age* (Cambridge University Press, 2006).

14. Helen Margetts, "Transparency and Digital Government," in *Transparency: The Key to Better Governance?* edited by Hood and Heald.

15. Hood and Heald, *Transparency*.

16. Ibid., p. 27.

17. Jonathan Koppell, "Pathologies of Accountability: ICANN and the Challenge of Multiple Accountabilities Disorder," *Public Administration Review* 65 (January–February 2005): 94–108.

18. Madison, "Letter to W. T. Barry."

19. Barbara S. Romzek and Melvin Dubnick, "Issues of Accountability in Flexible Personnel Systems," in *New Paradigms for Government*, edited by Patricia Ingraham and Barbara S. Romzek (San Francisco: Jossey-Bass, 1994).

20. Vicente Pina, Lourdes Torres, and Basilio Acerete, "Are ICTs Promoting Government Accountability? A Comparative Analysis of E-Governance Developments in 19 OECD Countries," *Critical Perspectives on Accounting* 18 (July 2007): 583–602.

21. Linda Deleon, "Accountability in a 'Reinvented' Government," *Public Administration* 76 (Autumn 1998): 539–58; Richard Mulgan, "Accountability: An Ever-Expanding Concept?" *Public Administration* 78 (Autumn 2000): 555–73.

22. Darrell M. West, "E-Government and the Transformation of Service Delivery and Citizen Attitudes," *Public Administration Review* 64 (February 2004): 15–27.

23. Robert D. Putnam, *Capitale sociale e individualismo: Crisi e crescita della cultura civica in America* [Social capital and individualism: Crisis and growth of civic culture in America] (Bologna: Il Mulino Saggi, 2000).

24. Christoph Reichard, "The Impact of Performance Management on Transparency and Accountability in the Public Sector," in *Ethics and Accountability in a Context of Governance and New Public Management*, edited by Annie Hondeghem (Amsterdam: IOS Press, 1998).

25. David S. Stodolsky, "Computer Network Based Democracy: Scientific Communication as a Basis for Governance," in *Home-Oriented Informatics, Telematics & Automation*, edited by Kresten Bjerg and Kim Borreby (Copenhagen: Oikos, 1994), pp. 51–58.

26. Ibid., p. 2.

27. Subhash Bhatnagar, "Transparency and Corruption: Does E-Government Help?" draft paper prepared for the compilation of "OPEN SESAME: Looking for the Right to Information in the Commonwealth," CHRI 2003 Report (New Delhi: Commonwealth Human Rights Initiative, 2003) (www.iimahd.ernet.in/~subhash/pdfs/CHRIDraftPaper2003.pdf); Roumeen Islam, "Do More Transparent Governments Govern Better?" Policy Research Working Paper 3077 (Washington: World Bank Institute, June 2003); Organization for Economic Cooperation and Development, "Public Sector Modernisation: Open Government," OECD Policy Brief (Paris: OECD, 2005); United Nations, "Global E-government Readiness Report 2005. From E-government to E-inclusion" (New York: United Nations, 2005).

28. Organization for Economic Cooperation and Development, "Public Sector Modernisation: Open Government," p. 2.

29. Eric E. Otenyo and Nancy S. Lind, "Faces and Phases of Transparency Reform in Local Government," *International Journal of Public Administration* 27, no. 5 (2004): 287–307.

30. Helen Margetts, "Transparency and Digital Government," in *Transparency. The Key to Better Governance,* edited by Hood and Heald, pp. 197–207.

31. Pippa Norris, "Deepening Democracy via E-Governance," draft of chapter for the *United Nations World Public Sector Report* (Harvard University, 2004) (www.hks.harvard.edu/fs/pnorris/Acrobat/World Public Sector Report.pdf).

32. Daniel Kaufmann, "Transparency Matters: The 'Second Generation' of Institutional Reform," special report on public sector transparency (Washington: World Bank, 2005).

33. Thomas H. Davenport, *Process Innovation: Reengineering Work through Information Technology* (Boston: Harvard Business School Press, 1993).

34. Diana Burley Gant and Jon P. Gant, "Web Portals: The Key to Enhancing State Government E-Service" (New York: PricewaterhouseCoopers Endowment for the Business of Government, 2002).

35. Valentina Ndou, "E-Government for Developing Countries: Opportunities and Challenges," *Electronic Journal on Information Systems in Developing Countries* 18, no. 1 (2004): 1–24.

36. West, "E-Government and the Transformation of Service Delivery and Citizen Attitudes," pp. 15–27.

37. La Porte, Demchak, and De Jong, "Democracy and Bureaucracy in the Age of the Web," p. 3.

38. Ibid., p. 20; Pina, Torres, and Acerete, "Are ICTs Promoting Government Accountability?" p. 3.

39. Pina, Torres, and Acerete, "Are ICTs Promoting Government Accountability?" p. 3.

40 Demchak, Friis, and La Porte, "Democracy and Bureaucracy in the Age of the Web," p. 3.

41. Lasse Berntzen, "E-Transparency: The Use of Information Technology to Increase Government Transparency," in EGOV 2006, *Communication Proceedings* (Linz, Austria: Trauner Verlag, 2006).

42. Vishwanath and Kaufmann, "Towards Transparency in Finance and Governance."

43. Ibid., p. 2.

44. Ibid., p. 34.

45. Pina, Torres, and Acerete, "Are ICTs Promoting Government Accountability?" p. 3.

46. We considered the two provinces of Bolzano and Trento as regions, because their functions and powers are comparable with those of the regions.

47. Alan Bryman, *Social Research Methods* (Oxford University Press, 2008).

48. According to the classification provided by the Italian National Statistic Institute.

49. Jane Ritchie and Jane Lewis, eds., *Qualitative Research Practice: A Guide for Social Science Students and Researchers* (London: Sage, 2003).

50. Ibid., p. 29.

51. Maria Cucciniello, G. Nasi, and R. Saporito, "E-Government and Transparency: The Degree of Interactivity and Openness of Italian Municipalities," in *Managing E-Government Projects: Concepts, Issues and Best Practices*, edited by Stephen Aikins (University of South Florida: IGI Global, forthcoming in 2012); Maria Cucciniello, G. Nasi, and R. Saporito, *Trasparenza nel settore pubblico: quale divario tra il dichiarato e il desiderato?* [Transparency in the public sector: What is the difference between the stated aims and the desired ones?] (Milan: EGEA, forthcoming 2012).

PART II

Public Service Motivation: The Other Side of the Public Sector Productivity

JAMES L. PERRY

3

Does Making a Difference Make a Difference? Answers from Research on Public Service Motivation

In a classic contribution to our insights about administrative reform, James March and Johan Olsen remind us that administrative reform typically entails two contrasting, but equally important, rhetorics.[1] One is orthodox administrative rhetoric; it speaks of the design of administrative structures to facilitate the efficiency and effectiveness of bureaucracy and is mainly prescriptive in orientation. The second is the rhetoric of realpolitik, which speaks of reform in terms of a political struggle among contending interests. Political interests seek access, representation, and policy benefits, and organizational reforms reflect which interests are victorious and what mechanisms are in place for these interests' future dominance.[2] The realpolitik rhetoric sometimes drowns out the voice of the orthodox administrative rhetoric. On other occasions, realpolitik shapes the messages of administrative rhetoric, changing its tone and validity.

In this chapter I make a case for an alternative administrative rhetoric for reform. I begin by defining public service motivation and discussing two contending perspectives about human nature. Next I review some of the accumulating research about motivations for public service, focusing on three outcomes: membership, ethical behavior, and performance. I conclude by discussing how what we are learning about public service motivation could be applied to change governance and administrative infrastructures.

This research was supported by the World Class University program through the National Research Foundation of Korea and was funded by Korea's Ministry of Education, Science and Technology (grant number R32-20002).

Building Reform on the Right Fundamentals

The quest for greater public efficiency and responsiveness, whose most recent manifestation began in the 1970s but has been a recurring theme in democratic societies since early in the twentieth century, is rooted in legitimate concerns about governmental performance. The administrative rhetoric surrounding the most recent cluster of interventions dating to the 1970s has a name, New Public Management (NPM). NPM speaks in the language of efficiency, private business practices, and markets. The values and rhetoric of NPM have been repeatedly reinforced by imperatives of political control, the realpolitik rhetoric.

As popular as the complementary administrative and realpolitik rhetorics have been since the 1970s, they are receiving greater scrutiny as a result of experience, changing worldviews about the role of knowledge and technology in modern societies, and new research that calls into question premises of the dominant rational choice models, which gave NPM reforms intellectual legitimacy.[3] The relational glue that once bound government and nonprofit institutions to their stakeholders and the general public—the social contract—is being replaced, critics contend, by partnerships based in principal-agent contracts, where responsibilities of the parties are formally enumerated and exchanges are primarily pecuniary. Patrick Dunleavy and Christopher Hood negatively characterize the new regime of cross-sectoral partnerships (for example, between state governments and private, profit-making corrections firms) as "a chain of low-trust principal/agent relationships (rather than fiduciary or trustee-beneficiary ones), a network of contracts linking incentives to performance."[4] They worry that citizen trust and confidence in government will get marginalized in the process of opaque negotiations, dealmaking, and compliance monitoring, thus decreasing the legitimacy of government. Critics are questioning logics of consequence, that is, a reliance on utilitarian rules and reasoning, as the primary or sole foundation for administrative reform.

An emerging alternative to traditional administrative theory and rhetoric—at least with respect to motivational foundations for administrative reform—has its roots in research on altruism, sociobiology, evolutionary and developmental psychology, prosocial behavior, and public service motivation.[5] This new thinking rests on logics of appropriateness that involve individuals assessing situations and making choices on the basis of rules and their identity.[6] In the next section I discuss a particular foundation for a logic of appropriateness—public service motivation.

Public Service Motivation and Its Analogues

In the two decades since 1990, public service motivation research has grown significantly.[7] Public service motivation originates in beliefs that individuals engaged in public service are predisposed to respond to "motives grounded primarily or uniquely in public institutions and organizations."[8] The definition sought to emphasize motives, such as civic duty, compassion, and self-sacrifice, that historically have been associated with public service. Over time, scholars have come to refer to public service motivation in terms of motives and actions in the public domain that are intended to do good for others and shape the well-being of society.[9]

Public administration definitions of public service motivation invoke the concepts of both self-sacrifice and altruism—"other-regarding motives" and behaviors, which emphasize concern for the well-being of others.[10] Thus, research about altruism is directly relevant to research about public service motivation.[11] Economists sometimes use the rhetoric of altruism and public service motivation interchangeably.[12]

Another stream of related research is prosocial behavior, which encompasses a broad category of other-regarding behaviors. Some have argued that the meaning of prosocial behavior is tied to an actor's motives. Adam Grant, for example, defines prosocial motivation as simply "the desire to expend effort to benefit other people."[13]

This brief summary of public service motivation and related constructs suggests that the phenomena emphasize an *other* orientation that accords with our long-held understandings of a public service ethic. The boundaries placed on the scope of public service motivation suggest that it is a particular form of altruism or prosocial motivation that is animated by specific dispositions and values arising from public institutions and missions. Given the blurring of boundaries between sectors and differences in the location of the functions of government, public service motivations are not unique to government organizations, but they are grounded in the tasks of public service provision.

The Nature of Human Nature

The motivational underpinnings associated with public service are part of an enduring debate in the social sciences concerning basic assumptions we make about human nature. The central assumption about human nature in early management theory was what Douglas McGregor later popularized under the label Theory X, which was that people disliked their work and responsibility and opted for security.[14] Beginning with intellectual landmarks such as Anthony Downs's *Inside Bureaucracy* and William Niskanen's *Bureaucracy and Representative Government*, bureaucrats were consistently assumed to be both rational and self-interested.[15] Given these assumptions, bureaucrats were depicted as budget maximizing self-aggrandizers incapable of discerning and pursuing the public will.

Scholarship about the depiction of bureaucrats as self-aggrandizers was challenged with the publication of Charles Goodsell's *The Case for Bureaucracy*.[16] Goodsell rejected criticisms of bureaucratic performance. His general point was that, at least with respect to the American situation, public organizations were far more efficient and effective and bureaucrats more "ordinary" than the public and scholarly critics acknowledged.

About the same time as Goodsell's counterattack on the criticisms of bureaucracy, other scholars contributed alternative perspectives about fundamental human orientations.[17] Amitai Etzioni argued that social and behavioral science research was at least as strongly supportive of what he called a "we" perspective as it was of the "I" perspective popularized by rational choice economics. Theoretical and empirical research about non-self-interested motivations has accelerated in the past decade.

Participants in the debate about human nature tend to align themselves as adherents associated with logics of consequence, or with logics of appropriateness. Public service motivation fits with the latter perspective. I envision public service motivation as being better suited as both an explanatory and normative foundation for public administrative design and reform than frameworks grounded in logics of consequence. Empirical research that supports public service motivation as an explanatory foundation for public reform is discussed next.

Taking Stock of What We Know

The volume of research relating to public service motivation has grown substantially during the last decade, and reviewing it comprehensively is beyond the scope of this chapter. I will highlight some inferences that can be drawn from the body of accumulating evidence. I organize the summary around three behaviors that public organizations must elicit to be effective: membership; ethical behaviors; and performance.[18]

Membership

James L. Perry and Lois R. Wise, building upon research by David Knoke and Christine Wright-Isak, reasoned that individual behavior would be influenced by the magnetic effects between individual identities and organization characteristics.[19] Individuals who are high in public service motivation would seek out contexts compatible with their predispositions, and the contexts to which they would likely be attracted were organizations that satisfied their higher prosocial and altruistic orientations.

Research about links between public service motivation and attraction, selection, and retention is limited, but generally supportive of this view.[20] In a formative study on public service motivation, Hal G. Rainey found that public managers valued meaningful public service more highly than private managers, and the preference for public service was significantly related to job satisfaction.[21] In an analysis of U.S. General Social Survey (GSS) data from 1989 and 1998, Gregory B. Lewis and Sue A. Frank found significant positive associations between a desire to help others and be useful to society and preferences for government jobs.[22] They suggested that these relationships might be stronger for college graduates and younger employees, and in specific employment classifications such as education. Wouter Vandenabeele, using a sample of 1,714 advanced master's degree students in Flemish universities, found that public service motivation positively correlated with student preferences for prospective employers in the public sector.[23] The association of student preferences was stronger for government organizations classified as characterized by high, in contrast to low, publicness, where publicness was defined as the extent to which an organization's mission embodied public values and pursued uniquely public missions. An analysis of a large Dutch data set showed that public sector workers had higher levels of public service motivation than private sector workers.[24] Interestingly, private sector workers with high levels of public service motivation were more likely to be looking for public sector jobs.

Research about attrition from government organizations also supports a link with public service motivation. Philip E. Crewson found public service motivation associated empirically to higher organizational commitment and lower turnover.[25] Using data from the Merit Principles Survey (MPS) of 1997, a large, representative survey of federal employees conducted at about three-year intervals, Katherine C. Naff and John Crum found a positive association between public service motivation and intent to remain in the job.[26] Bram Steijn's study of a sample of more than 4,100 employees of public administration, education, defense, and public security entities and academic hospitals in the Netherlands showed that workers with high public service motivation fit are more satisfied and less inclined to leave their jobs and the organization they work for than workers without such motivation.[27]

Recent research using the British Household Panel Survey (BHPS) supports the public service motivation–membership link. Paul Gregg and his colleagues studied donated labor (unpaid overtime) in caring industries in the United

Kingdom.[28] They found that people with high public service motivation in caring industries are more likely to move to public sector or nonprofit organizations. A study by Yannis Georgellis, Elisabetta Iossa, and Vurain Tabvuma used data from the first fourteen waves of BHPS, covering the period from 1991 to 2004.[29] Their analysis focused on 747 transitions from the private to the public sector within the BHPS data. They concluded that a significant share of individuals move to the public sector because of the higher likelihood there of fulfilling their public service motivations.

Recent studies by Bradley E. Wright and Robert K. Christensen suggest nuances in how public service motivation affects membership behaviors that are relevant for future research and applications.[30] They found that a strong interest in social service and helping others did not predict the employment sector of a lawyer's first legal job, but it did increase the likelihood of his or her holding subsequent jobs in the public sector. The authors suggested that both initial sector choices and retention were affected by other factors that moderated the influence of public service motivation. They concluded that the key question for research is when and under what conditions public service motivation affects employee attraction and retention.

Research from public administration and economics holds out the near-term prospect of creating usable knowledge for improving the recruitment, selection, and retention in public organizations.

Ethical Behaviors

Scholars have looked at discrete variables that could be classified as ethical behaviors, behaviors such as blowing the whistle that are viewed as appropriate for people engaged in public service. Gene A. Brewer and Sally Selden concluded that public service motivation was positively related to propensity to blow the whistle.[31] Two more recent studies, one based in Korea and the other in the United States, found positive associations between public service motivation and organizational citizenship behavior.[32] Using the GSS, Houston found that government employees are more likely to volunteer for charity and to donate blood than employees of for-profits.[33]

Performance

Perry and Wise relied on two premises in positing that public service motivation positively influenced performance.[34] The first premise was that public jobs would be intrinsically motivating for individuals with high public service motivation because these individuals would embrace work characterized by attributes such as high task significance, that is, work perceived as having a positive impact on other people. Second, public service motivation is likely to affect positively organizational commitment, which influences prospects for reliable role behaviors and innovative activities, both of which are critical for high individual performance.

Several studies test the link between public service motivation and performance using self-reported measures of individual performance.[35] In an early study, Naff and Crum found a positive relationship between public service motivation and self-reported performance appraisals among U.S. federal employees.[36] In a subsequent study of federal employees with data from the 1991 Survey of Federal Employees and the 1996 MPS, Pablo Alonso and Gregory B. Lewis used job performance ratings and grade to measure performance.[37] Using a different model specification for the 1996 data than Naff and Crum, Alonso and Lewis were able to replicate Naff and Crum's findings that public service motivation had a positive impact on performance ratings.[38] Alonso and Lewis were unable, however, to find a relationship between valuing service to others and higher ratings in the 1991 data set. Public service motivation also had no association with grade level in 1996, and valuing service to others was negatively related to grade level in 1991. Alonso and Lewis acknowledged that differences in key measures across the data sets could account for differences in their results from previous findings.

Three studies that used self-reports of performance incorporated mediators into their models. Leonard Bright used self-reported performance as the dependent variable in a model that tested person-organization fit as a mediator of the relationship between public service motivation and performance.[39] He found indirect effects of public service motivation mediated by the fit measure, but no independent direct effects in a sample of 205 public health care workers representing three states and three levels of government. In a study of a large sample of Flemish civil servants, Vandenabeele concluded that there was a positive and significant relationship between public service motivation and self-reported performance.[40] In contrast to Bright, Vandenabeele found support for both direct and indirect effects on performance.[41] The indirect effects on the motivation-performance relationships were mediated by job satisfaction and normative and affective commitment. Leisink and Steijn analyzed the effects of public service motivation on three performance-related outcome variables—commitment, willingness to exert effort, and perceived job performance—among 4,130 Dutch public employees from all levels and varieties of public services.[42] The hypothesis that person-organization fit mediates the relationship between public service motivation and the outcome variables was rejected. The effects of public service motivation and fit on the outcome variables were independent.

Two studies tested multidimensional models in which public service motivation is one of three types of motivation (public service, task, and mission motivation) that are the proximate determinants of organizational effectiveness in government. The first of these studies, using data from the 1996 MPS, found a positive and significant relationship between public service motivation and perceived organizational effectiveness.[43] Sangmook Kim, analyzing responses from 1,739 full-time public employees in nine central government, five provincial, and twenty-six lower-level local government agencies in Korea, found that public service motivation was a significant positive influence on perceived organizational effectiveness, which replicated the Brewer and Selden results.[44]

Further evidence for ties between public service motivation and performance originate in economics. Francois's "'Public Service Motivation' as an Argument for Government Provision," for example, acknowledges that economists have not taken seriously the claims of public administration scholars about a public service ethic.[45] Using formal mathematical modeling, Francois demonstrates that when public service motivation exists, conditions can be created for government bureaucracy to better obtain effort from employees than a standard profit-maximizing firm.

How We Can Use the Research for Administrative Reform

The promising results of public service motivation research raise a question for reformers: Can the research findings serve as the basis for an alternative reform rhetoric, one that is grounded in logics of appropriateness rather than consequence? I believe the answer is yes. As Paul Light argues in *A Government Ill Executed*, building infrastructures must "involve the right motivations for service."[46] Indeed, public leaders and executives have given some attention to the motivational equation and the unique call of public service. The U.S. Office of Personnel Management (OPM) includes public service motivation among its list of six fundamental competencies for federal senior executives. OPM defines public service motivation as follows: "Shows a commitment to serve the public. Ensures that actions meet public needs; aligns organizational objectives and practices with public interests."[47] I foresee public leaders making progress in the course of the next decade toward enhancing and aligning public service values across organizational systems. Research on altruism, public service motivation, and prosocial behavior has begun to make headway in suggesting how infrastructures can be modified to strengthen reinforcement of other- and public-regarding motivational orientations.[48] The evolving research has begun to identify a number of infrastructure changes that might put governments in a better position to reap the power of public service. Among them are:

—Assessing applicants' past public service behaviors in selecting employees, to improve fit with public service values and accountability

—Providing formal opportunities for newcomers during on-boarding and early socialization experiences to learn about organizational values and expectations related to public service values[49]

—Developing performance appraisal and performance monitoring systems that include observations of behaviors that signal public service motivation

—Identifying beneficiaries of jobs, establishing opportunities for direct contact between employee and beneficiary, and providing clear channels for service beneficiaries to provide feedback

—Interpreting organization goals in ways that allow employees to connect their work tasks to broad, positive public service missions

—Designing compensation systems to emphasize long-term attractiveness to employees and avoid extrinsic incentives, such as merit pay, that crowd out intrinsic motivations

Three areas—human resource management policy, mission, and values—serve to illustrate the potential ways that public service motivation can be used by leaders and built into administrative infrastructures to promote public performance. They are discussed in more detail in the next sections.

Human Resource Management Policy

Public organizations have a variety of tactics they can pursue with regard to human resource management policy to enhance and reinforce public service motivations.[50] Two of these policies, employee recruitment and selection and financial compensation, are discussed here.

RECRUITMENT AND SELECTION. Recruiting and selecting individuals who are attracted to public service because of their interest in serving others and the larger public interest is a direct means to enhance public service motivation. Lewis and Frank write: "No one is suggesting that governments should recruit only among those who prefer public service. . . . Still, recruiting that targets people who are favorably predisposed to government service should yield greater success."[51] Recruitment and selection processes facilitate organizations' communicating the incentives they offer and individuals' discerning and matching their predispositions to organizational incentives.[52] Exchanges during recruitment and selection help both organization and individual determine fit between applicant values and organization practices.[53]

Face-to-face interviews offer opportunities to discern values and preferences and to identify characteristics that mesh with those of the organization. Interviews should be supplemented with multiple screens, including personality tests; interviews with human resource personnel, coworkers, and other employees; situational tests; and realistic job previews.[54] Situational judgment tests that present difficult but realistic situations people may face on the job and ask what the applicant might do in each situation may be useful in learning more about an applicant's values. Similarly, descriptions of past behavior may provide important indicators of public service motivations, on the assumption that past behavior is a likely indicator of future behavior. Kerry D. Carson and others recommend seeking out individuals who have previously engaged in activities that reflect high levels of public service, such as volunteering in the community, and that demonstrate altruism or identification with the organization's mission.[55]

FINANCIAL COMPENSATION SYSTEMS. Financial compensation systems constitute one of an organization's most important incentive systems, both literally and symbolically. Public organizations must be able to pay enough to attract, hire, and retain productive and the highest-performing workers. It is an important way of rewarding individual and group effort and performance. Well-designed compensation systems may also facilitate cooperative activity within the organization.

Although the optimal design for financial incentives in public-serving organizations is hard to specify, the evidence suggests that compensation systems that offer low-powered incentive pay (small monetary rewards that are distributed quite widely, which may have more honorific than financial value) are most effective for rewarding public service.[56] Performance-related pay may crowd out individuals' intrinsic motivations by shifting focus from internal motivators, like pride in one's work, to external ones.[57] An external reward of extra pay may signal that "doing one's duty without extra pay is not socially appropriate."[58] By clearly specifying behaviors that will be rewarded, financial incentives run the risk of discouraging desirable behaviors that are not explicitly rewarded. In a study of public utility employees, John R. Deckop, Robert Mangel, and Carol C. Cirka found that for employees with low levels of value commitment, performance-related pay reduced instances of extra-role behavior—something not required in the job description.[59]

Performance-related pay systems may, however, be effective to the extent that they encourage and promote employee public service motivations. In a study of school-based incentive systems in three U.S. school systems, Carolyn Kelley found that pay-for-performance systems that are linked to school-wide performance may enhance teacher performance by creating intrinsic rewards such as goal accomplishment and professional collaboration.[60] Performance-related pay (in contrast to pay linked to promotions) may also positively influence employee behavior when it is part of group-based incentive plans, such as profit sharing and gain sharing.[61]

David Marsden suggests that performance-related pay systems that incorporate opportunities for goal setting and appraisal provide line managers with the opportunity to engage in dialogue with employees about goals, and thus serve as the strategic link in "translating abstract objectives of change into everyday tasks that individual public servants undertake."[62] It is also important to note that performance-related pay often falls short as an incentive because of the lack of commitment of sufficient budgetary resources to the new incentives.[63] Incentives must also be large enough to be meaningful and significant to employees.

Mission

Since the turn of the new century, public organizations have increasingly been pushed to develop formal mission statements that describe the purpose of the organization and its vision. In contrast to work goals, compelling missions are broad, qualitative statements about the organization's purpose, rather than quantifiable production or financial measures. Mission statements that energize employees express common values that flow from employees' deeper values and beliefs.[64] For example, during the closure of the Rocky Flats Nuclear Weapons Plant, employees were motivated by a clear vision of a positive future that extended well beyond each employee's tenure with the organization. Employees were motivated to work toward closing the plant, even though it meant losing their jobs, by a compelling vision of a clean and safe landscape with no nuclear contamination.[65] Employees respond to organizational mission statements and other strategic communications only to the extent that such documents communicate values that fall within employees' "zone of existing values."[66]

Public service values are communicated not just through formal mission statements but also via informal channels, such as organizational stories, myths, and symbols.[67] In describing how leaders infuse day-to-day behavior with meaning and purpose, Philip Selznick describes the "elaboration of socially integrating myths" that use the language of "uplift and idealism" to describe what is distinctive about the "aims and methods" of the organization.[68] Steven Maynard-Moody and Michael Musheno describe how case reviews in staff meetings provided the context for social work staff and supervisors to use storytelling to discuss dilemmas and experiences in ways that heightened the possibility for "responsible action."[69] During the closure of the Rocky Flats Nuclear Weapons Plant, leaders used visual images to make the goal of safe closure of the nuclear facility come alive. Organizational leaders produced a before-and-after rendition of their closed plant to motivate employees. In addition, they used specific actions, such as the demolition of key buildings, to symbolize their mission of a closed facility.[70] John J. DiIulio describes the more mundane practice of using logos and symbols on T-shirts, ball caps, and mugs as ways to communicate the mission of the organization and motivate employees.[71]

Values

Selznick was one of the first to link institutions, values, and leadership.[72] In *Leadership in Administration* he writes: "The art of the creative leader is the art of institution building, the reworking of human and technological materials to fashion an organism that embodies new and enduring values."[73] Institutional leadership involves discerning, articulating, and modeling values that flow from and shape institutions. Values-based models of leadership involve processes by which leaders communicate values that raise followers' consciousness about idealized goals and then get followers to transcend their own self-interest for the sake of larger goals. Leaders communicate high expectations and inspire followers to become part of larger goals, stimulating followers not only to change their own belief systems but also to be creative problem solvers.[74] The theory of transformational leadership has its origins in the study of U.S. presidents, a quintessential public role.[75]

Values-based leaders communicate goals and values and model behaviors that are consistent with public service values. They raise their followers' consciousness about idealized goals by articulating high standards of moral and ethical conduct, and they are role models for prosocial behavior. In addition, values-based leaders lead by example, modeling "transparent decision making, confidence, optimism, hope and resilience, and consistency between their words and deeds."[76] Values-based leadership requires that organizations select individuals for positions of leadership who exhibit values that transcend individual self-interest, values such as social justice, equality, and benevolence.

Conclusion

In this chapter I have built a case for an alternative administrative rhetoric for future reform, grounded in logics of appropriateness rather than logics of consequence. Reform grounded in a rhetoric of public service is promising because of a growing body of behavioral and social science theory and empirical research. Research on public service motivation, altruism, and prosocial behavior points to advantages associated with institutions and administrative infrastructures that promote public values and reinforce public service ideals. The performance of governance and administrative systems grounded in public values and public service will have greater fidelity to their framers and the public interest.

Regardless of the promise associated with administrative reforms grounded in public service, public officials and reformers confront a wide gulf between "knowing" and "doing." Administrative change and reform are infrequently based on evidence and most certainly not evidence alone. Champions of an alternative administrative rhetoric, receptive political actors, and windows of opportunity will need to materialize before we can experience significant reform based on public values and public service ideals. Although evidence alone will not lead to reform, continued research on other-regarding motivation will make it more difficult to ignore alternative designs for future administrative and governance systems.

Notes

1. James G. March and Johan P. Olsen, "Organizing Political Life: What Administrative Reorganization Tells Us about Government," *American Political Science Review* 77 (June 1983): 281–96.

2. Terry Moe, "The Politics of Bureaucratic Structure," in *Can the Government Govern?* edited by John E. Chubb and Paul E. Peterson (Brookings, 1989): 267–329.

3. Barry Bozeman, *Public Values and Public Interest: Counterbalancing Economic Individualism* (Georgetown University Press, 2007).

4. Patrick Dunleavy and Christopher Hood, "From Old Public Administration to New Public Management," *Public Money & Management* 14 (July–September 1994): 9.

5. Jane A. Piliavin and Hong-wen Chang, "Altruism: A Review of Recent Theory and Research," *Annual Review of Sociology* 16 (1990): 27–65; Michael Koehler and Hal G. Rainey, "Interdisciplinary Foundations of Public Service Motivation," in *Motivation in Public Management: The Call of Public Service,* edited by James L. Perry and Annie Hondeghem (Oxford University Press, 2008).

6. James G. March and Johan P. Olsen, "Logics of Appropriateness," ARENA Working Papers 04/09 (University of Oslo, Centre for European Studies, 2004).

7. James L. Perry, Annie Hondeghem, and Lois R. Wise, "Revisiting the Motivational Bases of Public Service: Twenty Years of Research and an Agenda for the Future," *Public Administration Review* 70 (September–October 2010): 681–90.

8. James L. Perry and Lois R. Wise, "The Motivational Bases of Public Service," *Public Administration Review* 50 (May–June 1990): 368.

9. James L. Perry and Annie Hondeghem, "Editors' Introduction," in *Motivation in Public Management* (Oxford University Press, 2008).

10. Perry and Wise, "Motivational Bases of Public Service"; James L. Perry, "Measuring Public Service Motivation: An Assessment of Construct Reliability and Validity," *Journal of Public Administration Research and Theory* 6 (January 1996): 5–22; Hal G. Rainey and Paula Steinbauer, "Galloping Elephants: Developing Elements of a Theory of Effective Government Organizations," *Journal of Public Administration Research and Theory* 9 (January 1999): 1–32.

11. Piliavin and Chang, "Altruism," pp. 27–65.

12. Patrick Francois, "'Public Service Motivation' as an Argument for Government Provision," *Journal of Public Economics* 78 (November 2000): 275–99; Julian LeGrand, *Motivation, Agency and Public Policy: Of Knights, Pawns and Queens* (Oxford University Press, 2003).

13. Adam Grant, "Does Intrinsic Motivation Fuel the Prosocial Fire? Motivational Synergy in Predicting Persistence, Performance, and Productivity," *Journal of Applied Psychology* 93, no. 1 (January 2008): 49.

14. Douglas McGregor, *The Human Side of Enterprise* (New York: McGraw Hill, 1960).

15. Anthony Downs, *Inside Bureaucracy* (Boston: Little, Brown, 1967); William Niskanen, *Bureaucracy and Representative Government* (Chicago: Aldine-Atherton, 1971).

16. Charles Goodsell, *The Case for Bureaucracy*, 2nd ed. (Chatham, N.J.: Chatham House, 1985).

17. John Brehm and Scott Gates, *Working, Shirking, and Sabotage: Bureaucratic Response to a Democratic Public* (University of Michigan Press, 1999); Amitai Etzioni, *The Moral Dimension: Toward a New Economics* (New York: Free Press, 1988); Kristen Monroe, *The Heart of Altruism* (Princeton University Press, 1998).

18. Daniel Katz, "The Motivational Basis of Organizational Behavior," *Behavioral Science* 9 (April 1964): 131–46.

19. Perry and Wise, "Motivational Bases of Public Service"; David Knoke and Christine Wright-Isak, "Individual Motives and Organizational Incentive Systems," *Research in the Sociology of Organizations* 1 (1982): 209–54.

20. Bradley E. Wright and Adam M. Grant, "Advancing Public Service Motivation Research: Research Designs for Key Questions about Emergence and Effects," *Public Administration Review* 70 (September 2010): 691–700.

21. Hal G. Rainey, "Reward Preferences among Public and Private Managers: In Search of the Service Ethic," *American Review of Public Administration* 16 (December 1982): 288–302.

22. Gregory B. Lewis and Sue A. Frank, "Who Wants to Work for Government?" *Public Administration Review* 62 (July–August 2002): 395–404.

23. Wouter Vandenabeele, "Government Calling: Public Service Motivation as an Element in Selecting Government as an Employer of Choice," *Public Administration* 86 (December 2008): 1089–1105.

24. Bram Steijn, "Person-Environment Fit and Public Service Motivation," *International Public Management Journal* 11, no. 1 (2008): 13–27.

25. Philip E. Crewson, "Public-Service Motivation: Building Empirical Evidence of Incidence and Effect," *Journal of Public Administration Research and Theory* 4 (October 1997): 499–518.

26. Katherine C. Naff and John Crum, "Working for America: Does Public Service Motivation Make a Difference?" *Review of Public Personnel Administration* 19 (Fall 1999): 5–16.

27. Steijn, "Person-Environment Fit."

28. Paul Gregg and others, "How Important Is Pro-Social Behaviour in the Delivery of Public Services?" *Journal of Public Economics* 95 (August 2011): 758–66.

29. Yannis Georgellis, Elisabetta Iossa, and Vurain Tabvuma, "Crowding Out Intrinsic Motivation in the Public Sector," *Journal of Public Administration Research and Theory* 21, no. 3 (July 2011): 473–93.

30. Bradley E. Wright and Robert K. Christensen, "Public Service Motivation: A Longitudinal Study of the Job Attraction-Selection-Attrition Model," *International Public Management Journal* 13, no. 2 (2010): 155–76; Robert K. Christensen and Bradley E. Wright, "The Effects of Public Service Motivation on Job Choice Decisions: Disentangling the Contributions of Person-Organization Fit and Person-Job Fit," *Journal of Administration Research and Theory* 21, no. 4 (October 2011): 723–43.

31. Gene A. Brewer and Sally C. Selden, "Whistle Blowers in the Federal Civil Service: New Evidence of the Public Service Ethic," *Journal of Public Administration Research and Theory* 8 (July 1998): 413–39.

32. Sangmook Kim, "Public Service Motivation and Organizational Citizenship Behavior," *International Journal of Manpower* 27, no. 8 (2006): 722–40; Sanjay K. Pandey, Bradley E. Wright, and Donald P. Moynihan, "Public Service Motivation and Interpersonal Citizenship Behavior in Public Organizations: Testing a Preliminary Model," *International Public Management Journal* 11, no. 1 (2008): 89–108.

33. David J. Houston, "'Walking the Walk of Public Service Motivation': Public Employees and Charitable Gifts of Time, Blood, and Money," *Journal of Public Administration Research and Theory* 16 (January 2006): 67–86.

34. Perry and Wise, "Motivational Bases of Public Service."

35. Naff and Crum, "Working for America"; Pablo Alonso and Gregory B. Lewis, "Public Service Motivation and Job Performance: Evidence from the Federal Sector," *American Review of Public Administration* 31 (December 2001): 363–80; Leonard Bright, "Does Person-Organization Fit Mediate the Relationship between Public Service Motivation and the Job Performance of Public Employees?" *Review of Public Personnel Administration* 27 (December 2007): 361–79; Peter Leisink and Bram Steijn, "Recruitment, Attraction, and Selection," in *Motivation in Public Management*, edited by Perry and Hondeghem, pp. 118–35; Wouter Vandenabeele, "The Mediating Effect of Job Satisfaction and Organizational Commitment on Self-Reported Performance: More Robust Evidence of the PSM–Performance Relationship," *International Review of Administrative Sciences* 75 (March 2009): 11–34.

36. Naff and Crum, "Working for America."

37. Alonso and Lewis, "Public Service Motivation and Job Performance."

38. Naff and Crum, "Working for America."

39. Bright, "Does Person-Organization Fit Mediate the Relationship between Public Service Motivation and the Job Performance?"

40. Vandenabeele, "Mediating Effect of Job Satisfaction and Organizational Commitment on Self-Reported Performance."

41. Bright, "Does Person-Organization Fit Mediate the Relationship Between Public Service Motivation and the Job Performance?"

42. Leisink and Steijn, "Recruitment, Attraction, and Selection."

43. Gene A. Brewer and Sally C. Selden, "Why Elephants Gallop: Assessing and Predicting Performance in Federal Agencies," *Journal of Public Administration Research and Theory* 10 (October 2000): 685–711.

44. Sangmook Kim, "Individual-Level Factors and Organizational Performance in Government Organizations," *Journal of Public Administration Research and Theory* 15 (April 2005): 245–61; Brewer and Selden, "Why Elephants Gallop."

45. Francois, "'Public Service Motivation' as an Argument for Government Provision."

46. Paul Light, *A Government Ill Executed: The Decline of the Federal Service and How to Reverse It* (Harvard University Press, 2008), p. 233.

47. U.S. Office of Personnel Management, Senior Executive Service, "Recruitment and Selection: Fundamental Competencies" (www.opm.gov/ses/recruitment competencies.asp).

48. Laurie Paarlberg, James L. Perry, and Annie Hondeghem, "From Theory to Practice: Strategies for Applying Public Service Motivation," in *Motivation in Public Management*, edited by Perry and Hondeghem, pp. 268–93.

49. Partnership for Public Service, *Getting on Board: A Model for Integrating and Engaging New Employees* (Washington: Partnership for Public Service, 2008).

50. Paarlberg, Perry, and Hondeghem, "From Theory to Practice," pp. 268–93; Donald Moynihan, "The Normative Model in Decline? Public Service Motivation in the Age of Governance," in *Motivation in Public Management*, edited by Perry and Hondeghem, pp. 247–67.

51. Lewis and Frank, "Who Wants to Work for Government?" p. 402.

52. Knoke and Wright-Isak, "Individual Motives and Organizational Incentive Systems."

53. David E. Bowen, Gerald E. Ledford Jr., and Barry R. Nathan, "Hiring for the Organization, Not the Job," *Academy of Management Executive* 5, no. 4 (1991): 35–51.

54. Ibid.

55. Kerry D. Carson and others, "Structured Interview Questions for Selecting Productive, Emotionally Mature, and Helpful Employees," *Health Care Manager* 24 (July–September 2005): 209–15.

56. Simon Burgess and Marisa Ratto, "The Role of Incentives in the Public Sector: Issues and Evidence," *Oxford Review of Economic Policy* 19 (Summer 2003): 285–300; Moynihan, "Normative Model in Decline?"

57. Edward Deci, Richard Koestner, and Richard M. Ryan, "A Meta-Analytic Review of Experiments Examining the Effects of Extrinsic Rewards on Intrinsic Motivation," *Psychological Bulletin* 125 (November 1999): 627–68.

58. Bruno S. Frey and Margi Osterloh, "Yes, Managers Should Be Paid like Bureaucrats," *Journal of Management Inquiry* 14 (March 2005): 96–111.

59. John R. Deckop, Robert Mangel, and Carol C. Cirka, "Getting More Than You Pay For: Organizational Citizenship Behavior and Pay-for-Performance Plans," *Academy of Management Journal* 42 (August 1999): 420–28.

60. Carolyn Kelley, "The Motivational Impact of School-Based Performance Awards," *Journal of Personnel Evaluation in Education* 12, no. 4 (1999): 309–26.

61. Deckop, Mangel, and Cirka, "Getting More Than You Pay For."

62. David Marsden, "The Role of Performance-Related Pay in Renegotiating the 'Effort Bargain': The Case of the British Public Service," *Industrial and Labor Relations Review* 57 (April 2004): 351.

63. James L. Perry, "Making Policy by Trial and Error: Merit Pay in the Federal Service," *Policy Studies Journal* 17 (December 1988): 389–405.

64. Robert B. Denhardt, *The Pursuit of Significance: Strategies for Managerial Success in Public Organizations* (New York: Harcourt Brace, 1993).

65. Kim S. Cameron and Marc Lavine, *Making the Impossible Possible* (San Francisco: Berrett-Koehler, 2006).

66. Laurie E. Paarlberg and James L. Perry, "Values Management: Aligning Individual Values and Organizational Goals," *American Review of Public Administration* 37 (December 2007): 387–408.

67. John J. DiIulio Jr., "Principled Agents: The Cultural Bases of Behavior in a Federal Government Bureaucracy," *Journal of Public Administration Research and Theory* 4 (July 1994): 277–318.

68. Philip Selznick, *Leadership in Administration: A Sociological Interpretation* (University of California Press, 1957), p. 151.

69. Steven Maynard-Moody and Michael Musheno, *Cops, Teachers, Counselors: Stories from the Front Line of Public Service* (University of Michigan Press, 2003).

70. Cameron and Lavine, *Making the Impossible Possible.*

71. DiIulio, "Principled Agents."

72. Selznick, *Leadership in Administration.*

73. Ibid., pp. 152–53.

74. Bernard M. Bass, *Leadership and Performance beyond Expectations* (New York: Free Press, 1985).

75. James McGregor Burns, *Leadership* (New York: Harper & Row, 1978).

76. Bruce J. Avolio and William L. Gardner, "Authentic Leadership Development: Getting to the Root of Positive Forms of Leadership," *The Leadership Quarterly* 16 (June 2005): 326.

4

WOUTER VANDENABEELE, BRAM STEIJN, PETER LEISINK, FRANCESCO CERASE, ISABELL EGGER-PEITLER, GERHARD HAMMERSCHMID, RENATE MEYER, AND ADRIAN RITZ

Public Service Motivation and Job Satisfaction in Various European Countries: A Tale of Caution and Hope

The motivation of public servants in general and public service motivation (PSM) in particular have become important issues in public administration and public management research in recent years.[1] Whereas the former refers to motivation in general, the latter refers to the motivation people have to contribute to society and is therefore a specific dimension of the broader general motivation. The discussion will hereafter focus on PSM. Much of the research has been concerned with PSM as an independent variable, trying to explain its consequences, but recent research has also examined the question of its origins.[2] This latter type of studies often, implicitly or explicitly, resorts to institutions and the differences among them as an explanation for variations in PSM. From an institutional theory perspective, PSM can be understood as an expression of institutional-level values manifested at the level of the individual. The concept of PSM can be fitted into the idea of the "logic of appropriateness," that is the drive to behave according to a normative standard applicable to certain institutions, which is opposed to the more calculative "logic of consequence" involving self-interested utility maximization as a driving force.[3] Therefore, the link between PSM and institutions is evident and researchers often rely on the institution, seen as a value-based, structured interaction, as an explanatory variable for variation in PSM.[4]

Institutions are partly country-specific in the sense that both the type of institution and its character differ between countries. According to the literature, national institutions have a defining power with respect to which values are considered important in a national society.[5] This observation has obvious relevance to PSM research. Empirical research of PSM reported differences between the United States, where the concept originated, and Europe, where other dimensions or a different clustering of dimensions is found.[6] This situation has given a new impulse to research on PSM. First, interest has increased in developing a conceptualization and measurement instrument that can lay the basis for solid comparative research by building on the different ways in which researchers have attempted to adapt the concept of PSM to their national circumstances.[7] Second, various researchers, making use of such comparative data that are currently available and that approximate PSM, have established that there are differences in PSM between countries and have provided explanations to account for these differences.[8] In this chapter we attempt to make a contribution to this research by studying whether national differences also impact on the relationship between PSM and job satisfaction, and by developing a theoretical explanation that combines institutional theory with insights from person-environment fit theory applied to PSM, job satisfaction, and public management reform. The scientific relevance of this study is that it moves beyond the recognition that the scores on PSM dimensions differ between countries and examines whether national differences also moderate the relationship between PSM and its consequences. We focus on job satisfaction as a consequence of PSM because job satisfaction as well as PSM have been found to influence employee behavior and to increase (public service) performance in a variety of ways.[9]

The structure of our contribution is as follows. In the first section, we have framed the central issue of the chapter. The following section presents a discussion of the theoretical concepts, an overview of the relevant literature, and the elaboration of the theoretical argument underlying the hypothesis that national differences in the relationship between PSM and job satisfaction are to be expected. Also, the countries included in this study are briefly described. In the "Methodology" section we describe the data collection, and some measurement issues are discussed. The last three sections present results and analysis, discussion, and, finally, our conclusions.

Theoretical Framework

In this section we provide a theoretical framework that enables us to analyze the issue at hand in terms of the existing literature and the present state of the art. We explore the ramifications of the concepts of PSM, job satisfaction, and person-environment fit and the relationships among these concepts, thus trying to build on preexisting knowledge.

Public Service Motivation

PSM refers to the motivation individuals have to contribute to the public interest, or to society at large, disregarding their own interests. PSM was first defined by James Perry and Lois Wise as "an individual's predisposition to respond to motives grounded primarily or uniquely in public institutions."[10] However, other authors have applied their own definitions, focusing on particular elements of the concept.[11] Moreover, other concepts, such as public service ethos or "l'éthique du bien commun," have been developed to describe similar or related phenomena.[12] This multitude of similar concepts has hampered empirical research. In order to ground this study we apply an encompassing definition of PSM: "the belief, values, and attitudes that go beyond self-interest and organizational interest, that concern the interest of a larger political entity and that motivate individuals to act accordingly whenever appropriate."[13]

PSM is known to differ from country to country, but caution is required, because elaborate instruments covering all the dimensions of PSM have not been used in comparative research so far. However, Wouter Vandenabeele and Steven Van de Walle were able to make an international comparison of PSM in thirty-eight countries on the basis of the International Social Survey Program, which combines internationally comparative survey datasets on a varied set of social issues such as the role of government, work, or religion.[14] They found differences between the regional scores for PSM, and these scores did not display the same pattern for all dimensions of PSM. Restricting ourselves to the countries in our study, we note that four countries—Austria, Belgium, the Netherlands, and Switzerland—belong to the group of western European countries that score average on the PSM dimension of compassion, low to middle on that of self-sacrifice, and lowest on attraction to politics and policy. Italy belongs to the group of southern European countries that score relatively high on compassion and self-sacrifice and score in the middle on attraction to politics and policy.

The research on PSM has grown substantially since 2000, and this interest has also generated studies in the outcomes of PSM such as job satisfaction, organizational commitment, and performance.[15] However, Sanjay Pandey and Edmund Stazyk observe correctly that "it is not possible to mount definitive evidence and arguments on the nature and direction of a causal relationship on the basis of extant research," and they therefore denote job satisfaction as a "correlate" of PSM.[16] The notion of job satisfaction being a consequence of PSM is theoretically accounted for by the idea that the work situation in the public sector offers employees the opportunity to satisfy their individual need to help others or to do something for society.[17] Empirical evidence for the positive relationship between PSM and job satisfaction comes from a number of studies.[18]

However, Leonard Bright argues that inconsistencies in the PSM literature, such as the finding of a negative relationship between PSM and tenure in public organizations, are due to a failure to consider the fit between individuals and organizations (understood as the direct congruence between respondents and their organization).[19] He claims that PSM has no direct impact on job satisfaction (and turnover), but rather that person-organization fit is the primary cause. Thus, individuals who are compatible with the characteristics of their organization will have higher job satisfaction, and PSM will likely increase the compatibility between individuals and public organizations, but not with any and every public organization.[20] A survey of 205 public employees from various public organizations allowed Bright to demonstrate that PSM had no significant relationship with job satisfaction when person-organization fit was taken into account. Bright concludes that PSM offers benefits to public organizations when it increases person-organization fit, but that environments ill-suited to the needs and values of public employees with high levels of PSM will leave them significantly less satisfied and more prone to leave.[21]

There is also empirical evidence for the hypothesis that job satisfaction mediates the relationship between PSM and individual performance.[22] Vandenabeele observes that the idea that positive feelings toward a work situation or organizational setting mediate the effects of PSM on performance in a public sector context more or less resonates with earlier work by Timothy Judge and others about the relationship between job satisfaction and job performance.[23] Vandenabeele also suggests that in a public sector context the presence of PSM will improve the person-environment fit and this will in turn generate feelings of satisfaction. Consequentially, one may also assume that PSM's capacity to generate feelings of satisfaction is affected by changes in the public sector environment that disturb or undermine the person-environment fit. This is where new public management–inspired reforms and their effects are relevant to be included in the analysis.

Job Satisfaction

Job satisfaction is a widely researched subject. According to the Social Science Citation Index, no less than 4,336 articles related to job satisfaction were published in the 2000–09 period. For many years, the research on job satisfaction has been dominated by the works of Frederick Herzberg, and later by the Job Diagnostic Survey of Richard Hackman and Greg Oldham.[24] A general definition of job satisfaction is provided by Edwin Locke: "a pleasurable or positive emotional state resulting from the appraisal of one's job or job experiences."[25] According to many studies, greater job satisfaction is related to better organizational and individual performance, increased productivity, lower absenteeism, and lower employee turnover.[26]

An important issue in the literature is how to explain differences in job satisfaction. According to several studies, individual characteristics like age or gender play only a marginal role in level of job satisfaction.[27] Factors related to job and organizational characteristics appear to be much more important.[28] In this vein many studies have built on the now classic studies of Hackman and Oldham, who have focused on the design of work in relation to the satisfaction and motivation of workers.[29] In addition to the design of the job, a number of other organizational characteristics such as pay, promotion, job security, supervision, work-group characteristics, participation, and organizational structure and climate are held responsible for differences in the level of job satisfaction.[30]

Several studies have also looked at the effect of institutions on job satisfaction.[31] There are clear differences in the level of job satisfaction between countries. Within Europe the level of job satisfaction is higher in northern and western countries, and lower in southern and eastern countries.[32] The question is, how to explain these differences. Florian Pichler and Claire Wallace point to two different lines of reasoning.[33] In the first one, these differences are explained by differences in the *composition of the workforce*. A higher job satisfaction in country A than in country B can for example be explained by the fact that within country A there are more higher-paid jobs or more workers with a permanent contract. The second explanation looks at more "structural" institutional explanations. These are sometimes based on Esping-Anderson's typology of welfare regimes, but Pichler and Wallace use more specific measures of institutional characteristics of European countries, including the GDP-level, the degree of inequality, and the degree of unionization.[34] They argue, for instance, that a country with better economic conditions is more likely to tend toward a post-industrialized labor market providing better jobs and higher rewards.

Duncan Gallie found that cross-national differences in job satisfaction are much more the outcome of differences in the workforce composition than of "true" structural or institutional conditions based on various welfare regimes.[35] Pichler and Wallace have come to a similar conclusion in their comparison of job satisfaction in twenty-seven EU countries. They conclude that "the same things [such as share of higher occupations, prevalence of various types of contracts, varying involvement in life-long learning] affect job satisfaction across

Europe, but they are more or less prevalent in different countries."[36] Nevertheless, their findings also point to a limited effect of "real" institutional factors. In their view, some countries have in comparison to other countries a "country premium" with respect to job satisfaction; others have a "country penalty." Countries with such an "institutional" premium include Denmark, Austria, and Romania; countries with a penalty include France and the Netherlands.

The findings regarding the determinants of job satisfaction hold for job satisfaction in the public sector as well.[37] In general, studies on job satisfaction in the public sector come to similar results with respect to its determinants. In addition, PSM is seen as an additional determinant of job satisfaction in a public service environment.[38]

Person-Environment Fit and Institutional Theory

The factors that are assumed to have an effect on job satisfaction are regarded by some studies as independent variables that have a direct effect. Following person-environment fit theory, however, job satisfaction may be assumed to be dependent on the extent to which individual needs are met by the job or the organization.[39] For example, the job satisfaction of a worker who does not assign much value to having an enriched job will be less negatively affected by doing a simple job than a worker who does value having an enriched job. Thus, in this example it is the person-job fit instead of the job characteristics as such that influences an employee's job satisfaction. In fact, there is evidence that person-job fit as well as person-organization fit have a positive effect on a range of employee attitudes and behaviors.[40] Combining the person-environment fit theory with institutional theory suggests how national differences may impact the relationship between PSM and satisfaction.

Vandenabeele and others have demonstrated that PSM varies among countries and that country accounts for up to 11 percent of the variation in PSM levels.[41] They suggest that the countries differ in national values in general and administrative culture in particular. Differences in national values have been described using the work by Geert Hofstede and by Ronald Inglehart and Christian Welzel.[42] Differences in administrative cultures have been described by Christopher Pollitt and Geert Bouckaert, who suggest a continuum ranging from a *Rechtsstaat* model (in which the state is the central integrating force in society and in which laws and bureaucratic rules are the focal concern) to a public interest model (which accords the government a less dominant role and where the main focus is on seeking the public's consent for measures devised in the public's interest).[43] Vandenabeele and others suggest that from an institutional perspective these differences in national and administrative cultures account for differences in PSM between countries.[44]

Therefore, we expect that there will be country-specific differences in the relationship between PSM and job satisfaction. This explanation is based on the idea that levels of PSM and the extent of public management reforms differ from country to country and that this translates into different levels of person-environment fit. We assume that the impact of reforms inspired by New Public Management (NPM) will result in changes in job and organizational characteristics (more emphasis on outputs, on measurements, on deployment of market-type mechanisms, on service quality and consumers), that provide less opportunity for employees to fulfill their PSM and will negatively impact on the job satisfaction of employees with high levels of PSM.[45] However, countries differ in the extent to which they are open to such NPM-inspired reforms and governments differ in the extent to which they have the capacity to implement such reforms.[46] Therefore, we expect that the relationship between PSM and job satisfaction will be moderated by country.

Institutional environments are multidimensional. National cultural differences and differences in administrative cultures interact with other institutional differences. For instance, religion is an important institution in southern European countries such as Italy, whereas secularization has been especially strong in northern and western European countries such as the Netherlands.[47] Thus, given this multidimensional character of institutional environments and taking into account the individual-level determinants of and compositional effects on job satisfaction as demonstrated by Pichler and Wallace, we recognize that a comprehensive theoretical explanation for actual differences in the relationship between PSM and job satisfaction between the countries in this study will be difficult if at all possible.[48] However, the theoretical insights and the results of previous research that we have reviewed justify testing the following hypothesis: *The relationship between the average levels of the various dimensions of PSM and job satisfaction will be moderated by country.*

Methodology

Testing our hypothesis on a quantitative basis will involve the use of various statistical techniques. As they are not frequently used in public administration studies, some elements will be highlighted to make the analyses more accessible to readers with a less strong statistical background. However, before we tackle this, the data collection and the measures used in this study are discussed.

Description of the Cases and Data Collection

The study examines the relationship between PSM and job satisfaction across five different countries: Belgium, Austria, Italy, the Netherlands, and Switzerland. We use aggregate comparative data on these cases, which, however, have been gathered for different purposes, using different methods of data collection. Therefore, we present an overview of the case and the data collection.

The data on Belgium were collected at the level of the Flemish government. Belgium's administrative culture can be characterized as a *Rechtsstaat* tradition. Government at the state level is strongly developed in Belgium, so many important competencies are covered by the state governments.[49] The only competencies not present at this level are defense, foreign affairs, and taxation (although some counterparts are present, except for defense). The data were collected in spring 2005, by means of a web-based e-mail survey; the response rate was 33 percent.[50]

Austria, not unlike Germany, is characterized by a strong *Rechtsstaat* tradition, what Max Weber called a rational legal form of authority, and a related specific *Beamtenethos* (civil servant ethos) grounded in ideas of neutrality, impartiality, public interest, legal security, and a tenured civil service status.[51] The source of our data was an online survey among employees of the city of Vienna. Vienna has a special role in Austria as it is both the capital city and a state (*Bundesland*) and executes a broad variety of city and state functions as well as some delegated to it by the federal government. The survey conducted in spring 2006 covers a sample of 1,890 public sector employees (response rate 39 percent) from fourteen departments in different policy fields.

Italy has a *Rechtsstaat* tradition, but recently it has been moving to a more majoritarian system while simultaneously devolving authority to the regions.[52] The data on Italy come from an online survey, conducted in the first half of 2006, of Italian Revenue Agency personnel.[53] The Revenue Agency seemed a very appropriate case as it had recently been subjected to major public management reform.[54] The response to the survey was 1,258 employees out of a total of 36,799.

Originally the Netherlands had a *Rechtsstaat* tradition with a very legalistic orientation, but this has shifted, moving between a pluralistic-consensual and a public interest orientation. The Dutch Ministry of the Interior and Kingdom Relations has conducted a biannual survey of public sector employees since 1999. In the 2006 survey the respondents were asked whether they were prepared to take part in regular short surveys to be held by the ministry. In total, 17,277 were willing to do so. After a representative weighting procedure, 9,440 employees were invited to take part in this online survey on PSM. The response rate was 4,156, or 44 percent, but to make the data comparable to other data sets, only civil servants working at the national level were retained in the data set used for this paper. This resulted in data for 351 respondents at the Dutch national level who occupy various types of positions in all ministries.

Switzerland used to have a *Rechtsstaat* tradition, but New Public Management–inspired reforms have had a strong impact on the administrative culture.[55] The Swiss data were collected within the framework of the 2007 employee survey of the Swiss federal administration.[56] On the basis of the responses and the statistical indices of the 2005 personnel survey, one representative random sampling per unit was taken, which was additionally examined according to the representative distribution of sociodemographic features (language, sex, age, salary). A total of 26,774 persons were given the questionnaire. The response rate was 51 percent of those surveyed (13,532 responses).

Combining the Data Sets

Some integrating actions were taken to combine the data into one data set that can be analyzed comparatively. First, the data were standardized to an answer scale of five points. Some of the cases used a different response scale (a six- or seven-point instead of the five-point scale) and therefore the scores were recoded to metric values with 1 as its minimum and 5 as its maximum. For the remainder of the analysis, the entire data set will therefore be treated as being metric rather than ordinal. Second, also for some of the control variables, the data set needed to be recoded in order to make it comparable. Where categories were used for age and tenure (in the Austrian and the Swiss cases), the middle between the two ends of the category score (for example, an age category of sixty to sixty-five) was used as a metric value of the variable.

These operations resulted in a data set that certainly has its flaws, but can be used comparatively, as the scores have approximately the same meaning throughout the set. However, one should still be careful when interpreting results, since we have no information as to whether the positions that are occupied by the respondents are comparable, and we therefore cannot distinguish between national institutional effects and other confounding effects such as person-job fit effects.

Statistical Techniques

To investigate the hypothesis, the use of some specific statistical techniques is necessary. To assess the effect of PSM on job satisfaction, taking the possibility of a differential effect in the various countries into account, moderated multiple regression combined with subgroup correlation comparison can be an appropriate technique.

Regression analysis is the most appropriate method for examining the relation between a set of independent variables and a single dependent variable.

Multiple ordinary least squares (OLS) regression is probably the most widely used variant of regression analysis. A number of points are of particular interest when interpreting OLS regression results. First, in the case of nominal independent variables, dummy variables are used. This entails the existence of a reference group to which the other categories are compared.[57] Second, it is important to consider the problem of multicollinearity. If two independent variables highly correlate, regression results become spurious and results are not clearly attributable anymore.[58] In particular, product-terms as used in MMR are prone to this phenomenon.

In order to test the hypothesis, the analysis should be able to incorporate interactive effects. More specifically, when testing for the effect of PSM on job satisfaction, the analysis should be capable of assessing this effect for different levels of the moderator variables, in this case the country in which the survey was done. An obvious methodology would be interactive or moderated multiple regression (MMR) using product-terms of the independent and the moderator variables.[59]

However, in comparison to experimental settings, MMR is often underachieving in detecting moderator variables in survey data, although a compelling theoretical reason for such a relationship exists. Although the general model statistics (Model F, R^2) are in these cases reliable, the estimates of the regression parameters (βs and standard errors) are especially prone to unreliability, due to the joint distribution of the data.[60] As cross-products are highly correlated with both independent variables, the risk of multicollinearity is substantial. Even mean-centering, a strategy proposed for reducing multicollinearity, does not alleviate these problems.[61] As a consequence, MMR is not always capable of specifying the direction of the interaction (positive or negative). Furthermore, the statistical power of MMR is also sometimes very low because of the joint variable distribution.[62]

Therefore, other ways of detecting interactions should be added to supplement MMR. One of these possible approaches is the comparison of subgroups (subgroup correlation comparison, or SCC). Although the statistical power of SCC is lower than that of MMR, it suffers less from multicollinearity, as no product-terms are involved.[63] In particular, SCC enables the investigation of the direction of the alleged interaction effect by comparing sizes of correlation coefficients. In order to compare subgroups, the null-hypothesis of equal correlations between the subgroups (one for each country) needs to be tested by means of the Q-statistic. This statistic is based upon Fisher's Z-scores of the correlations of the different subgroups, and it is approximately distributed as a chi-square with k-1 degrees of freedom.[64]

Box 4-1. Public Service Dimensions and How Public Service–Motivated Workers Feel about Them

Politics: "I do not care much about politicians." (reverse coded)
Public interest: "Meaningful public service is very important to me."
Compassion: "I have little compassion for people in need who are unwilling to take the first step to help themselves." (reverse coded)
Self-sacrifice: "Making a difference in society means more to me than personal achievements."

Source: Based on James L. Perry, "Measuring Public Service Motivation: An Assessment of Construct Reliability and Validity," *Journal of Public Administration Research and Theory* 6, no. 1 (1996): 5–23.

Dependent, Independent, and Control Variables

The core variable used in this analysis is PSM, being an independent variable in our hypothesis. James Perry originally conceived it to be a multidimensional twenty-four-item measurement construct having four dimensions: interest in politics and policymaking, public interest, compassion, and self-sacrifice.[65] Although replication of the model has not always proved to be possible by using the original items, most of the replication studies confirmed the factorial structure (although sometimes adding or removing a dimension).[66]

As our goal is to compare PSM levels in various countries, we decided to stick with the original four dimensions of the concept as suggested by Perry, but restrictions in the questionnaires mean that there are some limitations. We were able to include each original dimension in the data set, but each dimension is only measured by one item (see box 4-1).[67] Each of these four items represents the dimension it belongs to in the original measurement scale and has been recoded to make the scores comparable.[68]

A number of control variables are also included in this analysis. First, these are dummy variables of gender (male is the reference group) and supervisory position (being in a nonsupervisory position is the reference group). Second, age and organizational tenure, both measured in years, have been included as additional controls. Third, dummy variables for country (a dummy with Belgium being the reference group) are included.

Following Pichler and Wallace it would have been advisable to include a number of variables (such as job characteristics, occupational class, and contract type) indicating the composition of the workforce, so that individual-

Table 4-1. *Descriptive Statistics of the Variables*

Variable	*N*	*Mean*	*Standard deviation*	*Minimum*	*Maximum*
Politics	22,539	3.42	1.20	1	5
Public interest	22,445	3.76	1.01	1	5
Compassion	9,069	3.27	1.21	1	5
Self-sacrifice	22,386	3.36	1.00	1	5
Satisfaction	19,883	3.67	1.04	1	5
Age	21,863	42.32	10.59	17	66
Tenure	21,889	16.06	11.58	0	45
Gender	21,889	0.35	0.48	0	1
Supervisory position	21,859	0.34	0.48	0	1
Belgium	22,658	0.15	0.36	0	1
Austria	22,658	0.08	0.28	0	1
Italy	22,658	0.05	0.23	0	1
Netherlands	22,658	0.02	0.12	0	1
Switzerland	22,658	0.60	0.49	0	1

Source: Authors.

level effects, effects grounded in a different composition of the public sector workforce, and institutional-level effects could be distinguished. However, such variables were not available.[69]

Job satisfaction has been used as a dependent variable. Respondents were asked to what extent they were satisfied with their current job. Again, the scores were recoded where necessary to fit a five-point measurement scale.

Analysis and Results

The descriptives in table 4-1 show that scores of the main variables (PSM dimensions and job satisfaction) are all above midpoint of the scale. The respondents on average agree with the statements on PSM (thus finding that it is rather important) and they also agree (again on average) that they are rather satisfied than dissatisfied with their jobs. When looking at the mean scores for each country, the Netherlands score highest (with 4.15), closely followed by Belgium (4.10) and Austria (4.05). Italy (3.68) and Switzerland (3.50) score substantially lower (see appendix table 4-A1).

Inspection of the correlation matrix (table 4-2) shows that, due to a large sample size, even very small correlations are statistically significant. One can observe a significant correlation of three dimensions of PSM (politics, public interest. and self-sacrifice) with job satisfaction.

Table 4-2. Correlation Matrix of Variables (Missing Included)

	1	*2*	*3*	*4*	*5*	*6*
1 Job satisfaction	1.00					
2 Politics	–0.03***	1.00				
3 Public interest	0.25***	0.14***	1.00			
4 Compassion	0.01	0.03**	0.04***	1.00		
5 Self-sacrifice	0.13***	0.13***	0.41***	0.18***	1.00	
6 Age	–0.04***	0.13***	0.03***	0.03**	0.11***	1.00
7 Tenure	–0.08***	0.02***	0.02**	0.04***	0.06***	0.63***
8 Gender	0.08***	–0.14***	0.06***	0.03**	–0.02**	–0.22***
9 Supervisory position	0.03***	0.10***	0.11***	–0.10***	0.04***	0.16***
10 Belgium	0.19***	–0.04***	–0.01	–0.03**	0.06***	–0.01*
11 Netherlands	0.07***	0.07***	0.07***	0.02*	0.03***	0.01
12 Italy	0.00	0.00	0.11***	–0.03**	0.20***	0.01
13 Austria	0.10***	–0.04***	0.28***	–0.24***	–0.02*	–0.02***
14 Switzerland	–0.23***	0.23***	–0.30***	N.A.***	–0.16***	0.09***

Source: Authors.
*** $p < .001$; ** $p < .01$; * $p < .05$; N.A. = Not available.

Two sets of statistical tests provide insight into the possible moderating effect of country on the relationship between PSM and job satisfaction. First, an MMR-model is developed, trying to uncover a moderating relationship. Second, a series of SCCs are performed to assess the direction of this moderating relationship.

Table 4-3 shows the results of the MMR, which has been developed in six steps. The first step demonstrates that gender (when comparing females to males) has on average a positive influence on job satisfaction throughout the five countries. Organizational tenure has a negative influence on job satisfaction. Although the model is statistically significant, it explains only 1.4 percent of job satisfaction. The second step adds three dimensions of PSM (compassion is not entered into the equation because no data are available for the Swiss case). Adding these variables increases the explained variance to 8 percent, which is a statistically significant increase, as can be read from the *F*-ratio. Where politics has a negative influence on job satisfaction, both public interest and self-sacrifice have a positive influence. The standardized regression parameters show that the impact of public interest is the most important parameter for explaining variation in job satisfaction. The third step adds the dummy variables for the countries (with Belgium being the reference group). These data further increase the R^2 to 11.2 percent, a statistically significant

7	*8*	*9*	*10*	*11*	*12*	*13*	*14*
1.00							
–0.20***	1.00						
0.20***	–0.21***	1.00					
–0.19***	0.12***	–0.08***	1.00				
–0.02**	0.01	–0.04***	–0.05***	1.00			
–0.02*	0.06***	–0.06***	–0.10***	–0.03***	1.00		
0.07***	0.08***	0.24***	–0.13***	–0.04***	–0.07***	1.00	
0.10***	–0.21***	0.01	–0.52***	–0.15***	–0.29***	–0.37***	1.00

increase. In steps 4 to 6, the moderator variables are added. First, the product terms of country and politics are added. The analysis of the *F*-ratio indicates a moderator effect, but when looking at the increase in R^2, the additional R^2 is very small (only .1 percent). Nevertheless, it indicates a significant moderated relationship. Second, when entering the product terms of country and public interest, the *F*-ratio also indicates a moderator effect. Although it is bigger than the previous one, it still is very small (.4 percent). Finally, the product terms of country and self-sacrifice are added. Although the *F*-ratio shows a statistical increase of the R^2, it is only marginal (less than 0.1 percent). Nevertheless, the results indicate that country has a significant moderating effect on the relationship between PSM and job satisfaction.

According to the literature, in an interaction effect one should not only take the unique explained variance of interaction (in this case just over 0.5 percent) into account, but also the main effect, so the total effect of the interaction amounts to almost 10 percent of the variance.[70]

In a second series of tests, the differences between the correlation of PSM and job satisfaction is assessed individually. These tests (SCC) enable us to assess both the direction and the size of the moderator effect (as the parameter estimates from the MMR could be unreliable). First, a first test (table 4-4) shows the direction of the relationship and the size. Second, the tests in table 4-5 (A and

Table 4-3. *Moderated Multiple Regression Analysis of Job Satisfaction (Standardized Parameters)*

	Step 1	*Step 2*	*Step 3*	*Step 4*	*Step 5*	*Step 6*
	B (*SE*)	*B* (*SE*)	*B* (*SE*)	*B* (*SE*)	*B* (*SE*)	*B* (*SE*)
Gender	0.08*** 0.02	0.05*** 0.02	0.03*** 0.02	0.03*** 0.02	0.03*** 0.02	0.02*** 0.02
Age	0.02 0.00	0.01 0.00	–0.01 0.00	–0.01 0.00	–0.01 0.00	–0.01 0.00
Tenure	–0.09*** 0.00	–0.08*** 0.00	–0.04*** 0.00	–0.04*** 0.00	–0.04*** 0.00	–0.04*** 0.00
Supervisory position	0.06*** 0.02	0.03*** 0.02	0.03*** 0.02	0.03*** 0.02	0.03*** 0.02	0.03*** 0.02
Politics		–0.08*** 0.01	–0.06*** 0.01	–0.02 0.01	0.00 0.01	–0.01 0.01
Public interest		0.25*** 0.01	0.23*** 0.01	0.23*** 0.01	0.12*** 0.02	0.10*** 0.02
Self-sacrifice		0.03*** 0.01	0.03*** 0.01	0.03*** 0.01	0.02*** 0.01	0.07*** 0.02
Netherlands			0.00 0.06	–0.01 0.23	–0.02 0.37	0.01 0.39
Italy			–0.12*** 0.03	–0.15*** 0.09	–0.13*** 0.17	–0.15** 0.20
Austria			–0.06*** 0.04	–0.08** 0.10	–0.02 0.28	0.01 0.28
Switzerland			–0.22*** 0.02	–0.11*** 0.06	–0.34*** 0.09	–0.28*** 0.10
Poltics X Netherlands				0.01 0.06	0.01 0.06	0.01 0.06

Politics X Italy				0.03	0.02	0.02
				0.03	0.03	0.03
Politics X Austria				0.01	0.00	0.01
				0.03	0.03	0.03
Politics X Switzerland				–0.12***	–0.17***	–0.16***
				0.02	0.02	0.02
Public interest X Netherlands					0.02	0.04
					0.07	0.08
Public interest X Italy					0.00	0.00
					0.04	0.04
Public interest X Austria					–0.02	0.01
					0.06	0.06
Public interest X Switzerland					0.28***	0.32***
					0.02	0.02
Self-sacrifice X Netherlands						–0.05
						0.06
Self-sacrifice X Italy						0.01
						0.04
Self-sacrifice X Austria						–0.07*
						0.03
Self-sacrifice X Switzerland						–0.11**
						0.02
N	19,090	18,780	18,780	18,780	18,780	18,780
Adjusted R^2	0.014	0.080	0.112	0.113	0.117	0.117
F-model	109.37***	234.22***	215.39***	160.6***	131.51***	109.37***
F-ratio		446.86***	166.89***	7.93***	18.58***	3.19*

Source: Authors

*** $p < .001$; ** $p < .01$; * $p < .05$.

Table 4-4. *Subgroup Correlation Comparison Table of Public Service Motivation and Job Satisfaction, by Country*

	Belgium		*Netherlands*		*Italy*		*Austria*		*Switzerland*		*Average*	
	r	*Z1*	*r*	*Z2*	*r*	*Z3*	*r*	*Z4*	*r*	*Z5*	*Z'*	Q
Politics	.01	.01	.03	.03	.03	.03	.01	.01	–.01	–.01	.00	3.96
Public interest	.13***	.13	.12***	.12	.09**	.09	.05	.05	.27***	.27	.22	131.73***
Self-sacrifice	.11***	.11	.02	.02	.09**	.09	.00	.00	.13***	.13	.11	26.14***
N	3,412		347		1,237		1,444		13,091		19,531	

Source: Authors.

*** $p < .001$; ** $p < .01$; * $p < .05$.

Table 4-5A. *Pairwise Q-Tests for Statistical Difference of Correlations between Public Interest and Job Satisfaction*

	Belgium	*Netherlands*	*Italy*	*Austria*
Netherlands	0.00			
Italy	1.50	0.37		
Austria	6.20*	1.54	0.94	
Switzerland	56.67***	7.41*	451.22***	64.56***

Source: Authors.
*** $p < .001$; ** $p < .01$; * $p < .05$.

B) investigate which countries differ significantly in their pairwise correlations between PSM and job satisfaction.

The analysis in table 4-4 demonstrates that the main moderating effect can be found for the relationship between job satisfaction and, respectively, public interest and self-sacrifice (the analysis does not render a significant Q for politics; this lack of moderating relationship is probably due to the lower statistical power of the Q-test). Z indicates the standardized correlation with job satisfaction for the entire dataset, whereas Z1 to Z5 demonstrate the country-specific correlations. The analysis shows that the size of the correlations differ considerably, with correlations for public interest ranging from 0.05 (nonsignificant) to 0.27 and correlations for self-sacrifice ranging from 0.00 (nonsignificant) to 0.13. These different correlations illustrate the size and the nature of the moderator effect of country. On the face of it, the correlation between PSM and job satisfaction is much stronger in Switzerland than it is in the rest of the countries, and this despite the fact that average job satisfaction levels are substantially lower in Switzerland than in the other countries (see table 4-3).

Table 4-5B. *Pairwise Q-tests for Statistical Difference of Correlations between Self-Sacrifice and Job Satisfaction*

	Belgium	*Netherlands*	*Italy*	*Austria*
Netherlands	2.60			
Italy	0.52	1.20		
Austria	13.75***	0.18	5.68*	
Switzerland	0.63	3.81	1.74	22.53***

Source: Authors.
*** $p < .001$; ** $p < .01$; * $p < .05$.

However, only a pairwise comparison of the correlation can statistically test whether these correlations are different (only for public interest and self-sacrifice; as politics is not a significant moderator in the SCC). Table 4-5 (A and B) shows that with regard to the correlation between public interest and job satisfaction, there is a difference between the nonsignificant Austrian correlation (the lowest) and every other correlation except for the Italian and the Dutch and between the Swiss correlation (the highest) and every other correlation. For the correlation between self-sacrifice and job satisfaction, there is a statistical difference between the highest-scoring group (Belgium, Switzerland, and Italy) and the Austrian correlation (the lowest), whereas the Dutch correlation cannot be distinguished from either of those extremes.

Discussion

The findings on job satisfaction match the general findings of the European Quality of Life Survey, as also indicated by Pichler and Wallace.[71] The Netherlands, Belgium, and Austria score rather high on job satisfaction, whereas Italy scores lower (Switzerland was not included in the aforementioned sample). These results have been replicated in other studies that included part of our sample. Hans De Witte and Katharina Naswall find that Belgium and the Netherlands score higher than Italy on job satisfaction, but Alfonso Souza-Poza and Andrés Souza-Poza observe that the Netherlands score higher than Italy in their comparative study.[72] This suggests that our data relating to public servants mirror those relating to the general workforce. Regarding the Swiss data (which were not included in any of these studies), one would assume that, on the basis of the composition of the workforce, they would score higher than they do in our sample. Unemployment rates, social inequality, and average national wages indicate that the Swiss can be expected to score rather high on job satisfaction, whereas in our survey they score substantially lower, thus not mirroring the general population.

The analysis of the entire sample demonstrates that, in general, one can find an effect of PSM on job satisfaction. So in general, these results suggest that government employees experience higher job satisfaction when they are public service–motivated. This corresponds with earlier findings in previous studies investigating the PSM-job satisfaction relationship. It suggests that job satisfaction is indeed a function of the individual characteristics, of which, for public sector employees, PSM is a very prominent one. This makes the relationship one of the most consistently found outcomes of PSM. This finding could also suggest a person-environment fit effect as stated in the theoretical framework, but absent any ability to fully test for this, one can only observe that PSM apparently correlates with job satisfaction.

With regard to our hypothesis, which predicted a moderation effect for the correlation between PSM and job satisfaction, the analysis shows that this hypothesis can be corroborated. The MMR demonstrated a significant moderator effect of all three available dimensions of PSM, whereas the SCC showed a moderator effect for both public interest and self-sacrifice, but not for politics, possibly owing to a lower statistical power and a reversed effect for Switzerland. The analysis of the SCC also shows that where in most countries at least one dimension of PSM correlates significantly with job satisfaction, this is not the case in Austria. This finding alone merits the moderator analysis, as an assumed universal outcome of PSM appears not to be so universal after all.

Concerning the effect of public interest on job satisfaction, roughly three categories can be discerned. First, in Switzerland, the correlation between the public interest dimension and job satisfaction is much stronger than in the other countries. In light of the relatively low average job satisfaction score, one can conclude that civil servants who are more public interested than other civil servants are substantially more satisfied and that the presence of PSM thus can make up for the low satisfaction scores by focusing on employees' furthering of the public interest. Civil servants who are less public service–motivated have less reason to be satisfied. Bearing in mind that job satisfaction is mainly determined at the institutional level, this might suggest that Swiss civil servants have severely suffered from the extensive management reforms that have taken place in the last few years.[73] Second, another category of countries (Belgium, Italy, and the Netherlands) demonstrates a lower correlation, which is still significant (although the Dutch correlation cannot be statistically distinguished from the next lowest category, owing to a lack of statistical power of the limited Dutch sample). In Belgium and the Netherlands, where the job satisfaction scores are relatively high, PSM contributes to the individual job satisfaction of public servants, but other elements are also likely to contribute to this job satisfaction. For Italy, given the lower satisfaction score, these other elements may play a less important role than in Belgium and the Netherlands (this finding conforms to the general findings in other surveys, which attribute it to the composition effect for job satisfaction). However, PSM plays a smaller role in these two countries than in Switzerland. Third, the final category, Austria, shows no correlation between public interest and job satisfaction. However, the extremely high scores on public interest (4.71) and a low standard deviation (0.51; see appendix table 4-A1) mean that this could be due to a plateau effect, which occurs when independent variables show high means and low variation, causing them not to correlate with dependent variables. This matter should be further investigated.

Distinctions between countries are smaller with regard to the relationship of self-sacrifice to job satisfaction among civil servants. One group of countries (Belgium, Italy, and Switzerland, the correlation group) shows a relative weak effect, and the remainder of the countries do not display any effect of the self-sacrifice dimension on the job satisfaction of their civil servants. In Austria and the Netherlands (the no-correlation group), self-sacrifice does not lead to high job satisfaction, and in the correlation group it only has a weak effect. Interpreted from a person-environment fit perspective, this could imply that in the no-correlation countries, self-sacrifice is not required for employees' to feel job satisfaction in public sector jobs. Public sector jobs are designed so that public servants are not expected to sacrifice themselves, in terms of effort, pay and other common benefits, or time. Conversely, in the correlation countries (Belgium, Italy, Switzerland), public servants are implicitly or explicitly expected to sacrifice something, and so those who have a positive attitude to self-sacrifice would have more positive experiences in the job and higher job satisfaction. However, further investigation is necessary before we can draw definite conclusions concerning this issue.

All in all, it remains very hard to explain the moderator effects that were found in this analysis, because so many factors influence job satisfaction. This analysis makes it still difficult to assess whether something is an individual effect, a composition effect, or an institutional effect. However, some elements point to an institutional explanation in a broad sense, as institutions are designed to devote little or much attention to both public service values and other elements that can explain job satisfaction by means of person-environment fit. It is this element that makes his analysis particularly interesting and instructive. Institutions are just as much national macro-level systems of government as meso- or micro-level arrangements such as organizations or subsystems of particular organizations. The makeup of these institutions also determines the levels of job satisfaction or lack of it, as can be derived from this analysis. Therefore one cannot and must not assume that public service motivation impacts job satisfaction positively before actually testing this assumption, whether the institution under investigation is a national system or a small organization. Institutions and the values on which they are based might act as moderators, so caution is warranted. The analysis provided here might prove a useful tool in further investigations.

Conclusion

This chapter investigates the possible moderator effect of national institutional differences on the relationship between PSM and job satisfaction. A moderator effect of country on the relationship between PSM and job satisfaction was found. These results indicate that with regard to individual civil servants, both the origins and the outcomes of individual PSM are subject to the institutional context in which they are situated. This finding should encourage researchers and practitioners to consider both the possible presence of PSM and its motivational effect in the particular institutional settings in which researchers and practitioners operate.

Despite these interesting findings, several limitations of this study should make one cautious in interpreting these results. First, the analysis is cross-sectional, which may pose a threat to the internal validity of the data. Second, although efforts were made to make the data of different countries comparable, the initial samples were not conducted with the aim of comparison in mind. Thus, it may be that Italy's Revenue Agency, which had just been subjected to major public management reform, is not representative of Italy's public sector employees, and that municipal employees (as in Austria, although Vienna is hardly a typical municipality) differ from state employees (as in Belgium) and national government employees (as in the Netherlands and Switzerland). Therefore, further research based on a true comparative design should be done to corroborate or amplify the findings that were obtained in this study. Third, only single items that were translated from the original PSM-measurement scale developed by Perry are used in this study. Single items are in general less reliable in capturing the dimensions of PSM than a more elaborated instrument. In addition, translation issues could further threaten the validity of the items in measuring similar concepts. Fourth, due to a lack of appropriate variables this study was unable to differentiate properly between composition effects and "real" institutional effects.[74]

We took all feasible measures to deal with and counterbalance these problems and believe that the conclusions of this study are valid, despite the methodological caveats. As such, this chapter offers a substantial contribution the body of knowledge concerning PSM in general and the institutional dependence of the concept in particular. Clearly, further research remains necessary to study in more detail the questions investigated in this study. A genuinely comparative design, with balanced subsamples and the application of a more elaborated instrument for measuring PSM, would eliminate from future results some of the shortcomings that can be found in the presented study.

Appendix Table 4-A1. *Means of the Variables, by Country*

	Mean (SDT)				
	Belgium	*Netherlands*	*Italy*	*Austria*	*Switzerland*
Politics	3.32 1.25	3.90 1.07	3.42 1.31	3.27 1.18	3.65 1.07
Public interest	3.73 0.91	4.16 0.88	4.22 0.87	4.71 0.51	3.51 1.01
Compassion	3.22 1.13	3.38 1.26	3.18 1.24	2.69 1.15	N.A. N.A.
Self-sacrifice	3.49 0.87	3.54 1.07	4.18 0.97	3.31 1.05	3.23 0.95
Job satisfaction	4.10 0.90	4.15 0.90	3.68 1.31	4.05 0.96	3.50 1.01

Source: Authors.
N.A. = Not available.

Notes

1. R. D. Behn, "The Big Questions of Public Management," *Public Administration Review* 55, no. 4 (1995): 313–24; James L. Perry and Annie Hondeghem, eds., *Motivation in Public Management: The Call of Public Service* (Oxford University Press, 2008).

2. James L. Perry, "Antecedents of Public Service Motivation," *Journal of Public Administration Research and Theory* 7, no. 2 (1997): 181–97; James L. Perry, "Bringing Society In: Toward a Theory of Public Service Motivation," *Journal of Public Administration Research and Theory* 10, no. 2 (2000): 471–88; Wouter Vandenabeele, "Toward a Public Administration Theory of Public Service Motivation: An Institutional Approach," *Public Management Review* 9, no. 4 (2007): 545–56; James L. Perry and Wouter Vandenabeele, "The Behavioral Dynamics of Public Service Motivation," in *Motivation in Public Management*, edited by Perry and Hondeghem, pp. 56–79; Sanjay J. Pandey and E. C. Stazyk, "Antecedents and Correlates of Public Service Motivation," in *Motivation in Public Management*, edited by Perry and Hondeghem, pp. 101–17; Donald P. Moynihan and Sanjay K. Pandey, "The Role of Organizations in Fostering Public Service Motivation," *Public Administration Review* 67, no. 1 (2007): 40–53; L. DeHart-Davis, J. Marlowe, and Sanjay J. Pandey, "Gender Dimensions of Public Service Motivation," *Public Administration Review* 66, no. 6 (2006): 873–87; E. Camilleri, "Antecedents Affecting Public Service Motivation," *Personnel Review* 26, no. 3 (2007): 356–77.

3. J. G. March and J. P. Olsen, *Rediscovering Institutions* (New York: Free Press, 1989); J. G. March and J. P. Olsen, *Democratic Governance* (New York: Free Press, 1995).

4. Perry and Vandenabeele, "Behavioral Dynamics of Public Service Motivation"; Perry, "Bringing Society In"; Vandenabeele, "Toward a Theory of Public Service Motivation."

5. W. R. Scott, *Institutions and Organizations* (Thousand Oaks, Calif.: Sage, 2001); Jos C. N. Raadschelders, *Government: A Public Administration Perspective* (Armonk, N.Y.: M. E. Sharpe, 2003).

6. James L. Perry and Lois R. Wise, "The Motivational Bases of Public Service," *Public Administration Review* 50, no. 3 (1990): 367–73; Wouter Vandenabeele, "Development of a Public Service Motivation Scale: Corroborating and Extending Perry's Measurement Instrument," *International Public Management* 11, no. 1 (2008): 143–67; Wouter Vandenabeele, "Government Calling: Public Service Motivation as an Element in Selecting Government as an Employer of Choice," *Public Administration* 86, no. 4 (2008): 1089–105; S. Castaing, "The Effects of Psychological Contract Fulfilment and Public Service Motivation on Organizational Commitment in the French Civil Service," *Public Policy and Administration* 21, no. 1 (2006): 84–98.

7. Sangmook Kim and Wouter Vandenabeele, "A Strategy for Building Public Service Motivation Research Internationally," *Public Administration Review* 70, no. 5 (2010): 701–09.

8. Pippa Norris, "Is There Still a Public Service Ethos? Work Values, Experience, and Job Satisfaction among Government Workers," in *For the People: Can We Fix Public Service*? edited by John D. Donahue and Joseph S. Nye Jr. (Brookings, 2003), pp. 72–89; Wouter Vandenabeele and S. Van de Walle, "International Differences in Public Service Motivation," in *Motivation in Public Management*, edited by Perry and Hondeghem, pp. 223–44; Wouter Vandenabeele and others, "Comparing Public Service Motivation within Various European Countries: Do Institutional Environments Make a Difference?" paper presented at the International Public Service Motivation Research Conference, Bloomington, Indiana, June 7–9, 2009.

9. Sangmook Kim, "Individual-Level Factors and Organizational Performance in Government Organizations," *Journal of Public Administration Research and Theory* 15, no. 2 (2005): 245–61; Wouter Vandenabeele, "The Mediating Effect of Job Satisfaction and Organizational Commitment on Self-Reported Performance: More Robust Evidence of the PSM-Performance Relationship," *International Review of Administrative Sciences* 75, no. 1 (2009): 11–34.

10. Perry and Wise, "Motivational Bases of Public Service," p. 368.

11. Gene A. Brewer and Sally C. Selden, "Whistle Blowers in the Federal Civil Service: New Evidence of the Public Service Ethic," *Journal of Public Administration Research and Theory* 8, no. 3 (1998): 413–39; Hal G. Raine and Paula Steinbauer, "Galloping Elephants: Developing Elements of a Theory of Effective Government Organizations, *Journal of Public Administration Research and Theory* 9, no. 1 (1999): 1–32.

12. R. A. Chapman, "Ethics in Public Service for the New Millennium," in *Ethics in Public Service for the New Millennium*, edited by R. A. Chapman(Aldershot, UK: Ashgate, 2000), pp. 217–31; D. Woodhouse, *In Pursuit of Good Administration: Ministers, Civil Servants and Judges* (Oxford: Clarendon Press, 1997); J.-F. Chanlat, "Le managérialisme et l'éthique du bien commun: la question de la motivation au travail dans les services publics" [Managerialism and the ethic of the public good: The question of motivation

to work in the public sector], in *La motivation au travail dans les services publics* [Motivation to work in the public sector], edited by T. Duvillier, J.-L. Genard, and A. Pireaux (Paris: Editions L'Harmattan, 2003), pp. 51–64.

13. Vandenabeele, "Toward a Public Administration Theory of Public Service Motivation," p. 549.

14. Vandenabeele and Van de Walle, "International Differences in Public Service Motivation."

15. Perry and Hondeghem, *Motivation in Public Management.*

16. Pandey and Stazyk, "Antecedents and Correlates of Public Service Motivation," p. 101.

17. Perry and Wise, "Motivational Bases of Public Service."

18. Katherine C. Naff and John Crum, "Working for America: Does Public Service Motivation Make a Difference?" *Review of Public Personnel Administration* 19, no. 4 (1999): 5–16; S. M. Park and Hal G. Rainey, "Antecedents, Mediators, and Consequences of Affective, Normative, and Continuance Commitment: Empirical Tests of Commitment Effects in Federal Agencies," *Review of Public Personnel Administration* 27, no. 3 (2007): 197–226; J. Taylor, "The Impact of Public Service Motives on Work Outcomes in Australia: A Comparative Multidimensional Analysis," *Public Administration* 85, no. 4 (2007): 931–59; J. Taylor, "Public Service Motivation and Work Outcomes: The Effects of Organizational Rewards and Work Relations," *International Public Management Journal* 11, no. 1 (2008): 67–88; Bram Steijn, "Person-Environment Fit and Public Service Motivation," *International Public Management Journal* 11, no. 1 (2008): 13–27; Kim, "Individual-Level Factors and Organizational Performance in Government Organizations."

19. Leonard Bright, "Does Public Service Motivation Really Make a Difference on the Job Satisfaction and Turnover Intentions of Public Employees?" *American Review of Public Administration* 38, no. 2 (2008): 149–66; Moynihan and Pandey, "Role of Organizations in Fostering Public Service Motivation."

20. Bright, "Does Public Service Motivation Really Make a Difference?"

21. Ibid.

22. Vandenabeele, "Mediating Effect of Job Satisfaction"; Park and Rainey, "Antecedents, Mediators, and Consequences of Affective, Normative and Continuance Commitment."

23. Vandenabeele, "Mediating Effect of Job Satisfaction"; T. A. Judge and others, "The Job-Satisfaction Performance Relationship: A Qualitative and Quantitative Review," *Psychological Bulletin* 127, no. 3 (2001): 376–407.

24. M. M. Gruneberg, *Job Satisfaction* (Basingstoke, UK: Macmillan, 1976); J. R. Hackman and G. R. Oldham, "Development of the Job Diagnostic Survey," *Journal of Applied Psychology* 60, no. 2 (1975): 159–70; J. R. Hackman and G. R. Oldham, *Work Redesign* (Reading, Mass.: Addison-Wesley, 1980).

25. Cited in M. M. Gruneberg, *Understanding Job Satisfaction* (Basingstoke, UK: Macmillan, 1979), p. 3.

26. M. T. Iaffildano and P. M. Muchinsky, "Job Satisfaction and Job Performance: A Meta-Analysis," *Psychological Bulletin* 97 (1985): 251–73.

27. Y. Ting, "Determinants of Job Satisfaction of Federal Government Employees," *Public Personnel Management* 26, no. 4 (1997): 313–34; M. D. Reiner and J. Zhao, "The Determinants of Job Satisfaction among United States Air Force Security Police," *Review of Public Personnel Administration* 19, no. 3 (1999): 5–18; Bram Steijn, "HRM and Job Satisfaction in the Dutch Public Sector," *Review of Public Personnel Administration* 24, no. 1 (2004): 291–303.

28. P. E. Spector, *Job Satisfaction: Application, Assessment, Causes, and Consequences* (Thousand Oaks, Calif.: Sage, 1997).

29. Hackman and Oldham, "Development of the Job Diagnostic Survey"; Hackman and Oldham, *Work Redesign.*

30. Hal G. Rainey, *Understanding and Managing Public Sector Organizations* (San Francisco: Jossey-Bass, 2004).

31. F. Pichler and C. Wallace, "Job Satisfaction across Europe," *European Sociological Review* 25, no. 5 (2009): 535–49.

32. C. Wallace, F. Pichler, and B. Hayes, *First European Quality of Life Survey: Quality of Work and Subjective Life Satisfaction in Europe* (Luxembourg: European Foundation for the Improvement of Living and Working Conditions/Office for Official Publications of the European Communities, 2007).

33. Pichler and Wallace, "Job Satisfaction across Europe."

34. G. Esping-Andersen, *The Three Worlds of Welfare Capitalism* (Cambridge: Polity Press, 1990); D. Gallie, "Welfare Regimes, Employment Systems and Job Preference Orientations," *European Sociological Review* 23 (2007): 279–93; Pichler and Wallace, "Job Satisfaction across Europe."

35. Gallie, "Welfare Regimes, Employment Systems and Job Preference Orientations."

36. Pichler and Wallace, "Job Satisfaction across Europe."

37. Rainey, *Understanding and Managing Public Sector Organizations*; Bright, "Does Public Service Motivation Really Make a Difference?"

38. Perry and Wise, "Motivational Bases of Public Service"; Pandey and Stazyk, "Antecedents and Correlates of Public Service Motivation."

39. A. L. Kristof-Brown, R. D. Zimmerman, and E. C. Johnson, "Consequences of Individuals' Fit at Work: A Meta-Analysis of Person-Job, Person-Organization, Person-Group, and Person-Supervisor Fit," *Personnel Psychology* 58, no. 2 (2005): 281–320; A. F. Kristof, "Person-Organizational Fit: An Integrative Review of Its Conceptualizations, Measurement, and Implications," *Personnel Psychology* 49, no. 1 (1996): 1–49.

40. Steijn, "Person-Environment Fit and Public Service Motivation"; P. Peter Leisink and Bram Steijn, "Public Service Motivation and Job Performance of Public Sector Employees in the Netherlands," *International Review of Administrative Sciences* 75, no. 1 (2009): 35–52; Lynn Bright, "Does Person-Organization Fit Mediate the Relationship between Public Service Motivation and the Job Performance of Public Employees?" *Review of Public Personnel Administration* 27, no. 4 (2007): 361–79;

Bright, "Does Public Service Motivation Really Make a Difference?"; Kristof-Brown and others, "Consequences of Individuals' Fit at Work."

41. Pichler and Wallace, "Job Satisfaction across Europe."

42. G. Hofstede, *Culture's Consequences* (Newbury Park, Calif.: Sage, 1980); R. Inglehart and C. Welzel, *Modernization, Cultural Change and Democracy* (Cambridge University Press, 2005).

43. Christopher Pollitt and Geert Bouckaert, *Public Management Reform: A Comparative Analysis,* 2nd ed. (Oxford University Press, 2004).

44. Vandenabeele and others, "Comparing Public Service Motivation within Various European Countries."

45. Christopher Pollitt, *The Essential Public Manager* (Maidenhead, UK: Open University Press, 2003).

46. Pollitt and Bouckaert, *Public Management Reform.*

47. Perry, "Antecedents of Public Service Motivation."

48. Pichler and Wallace, "Job Satisfaction across Europe."

49. Annie Hondeghem, "The National Civil Service in Belgium," in *Civil Service Systems in Western Europe*, edited by H. A. G. M. Bekke and F. M. van der Meer (Cheltenham, UK: Elgar, 2000), pp. 120–47.

50. See Vandenabeele, "Development of a Public Service Motivation Scale."

51. Niklas Luhmann and Renate Mayntz, *Personal im öffentlichen Dienst: Eintritt und Karrieren* [Personnel in public service: Entry and careers] (Baden-Baden, Germany: Nomos, 1973); R. Meyer and G. Hammerschmid, "Changing Institutional Logics and Executive Identities. A Managerial Challenge to Public Administration in Austria," *American Behavioral Scientist* 49, no. 7 (2006): 1000–14.

52. Pollitt and Bouckaert, *Public Management Reform.*

53. D. Farinella has contributed to the research; see F. P. Cerase and D. Farinella, "Public Service Motivation: How Does It Relate to Management Reforms and Changes in the Working Situation of Public Organisations—A Case Study of the Italian Revenue Agency," *Public Policy and Administration* 24, no. 3 (2009): 281–308, for a more detailed description of the data collection process.

54. F. P. Cerase, "Italy: The Case of the Revenue Agency," in *Staff Participation and Public Management Reform: Some International Comparisons*, edited by D. Farnham, Annie Hondeghem, and S. Horton (Houndmills, UK: Palgrave, 2005), pp. 184–98.

55. D. Giauque and Y. Emery, *Repenser la guestion publique: bilan et perspectives en Suisse* (Lausanne: Presses Polytechniques et Universitaires Romandes, 2008).

56. A. Ritz, "The Role of Motivation, Commitment, and Leadership in Strengthening Public Sector Performance," *International Review of Administrative Sciences* 75, no. 1 (2009): 53–78.

57. M. A. Hardy, *Regression with Dummy Variables* (Newbury Park, Calif.: Sage, 1993).

58. J. Fox, *Regression Diagnostics* (Newbury Park: Sage, 1991).

59. J. Jaccard, R. Turisi, and C. K. Wan, *Interaction Effects in Multiple Regression* (Newbury Park, Calif.: Sage, 1990); R. M. Baron and D. A. Kenny, "The Moderator-

Mediator Variable Distinction in Social Psychological Research: Conceptual, Strategic and Statistical Considerations," *Journal of Personality and Social Psychology* 51, no. 6 (1986): 1173–82.

60. For an overview, see G. H. McClelland and C. M. Judd, "Statistical Difficulties of Detecting Interactions and Moderator Effects," *Psychological Bulletin* 114, no. 2 (1993): 376–90, and B. P. O'Connor, "Programs for Problems Created by Continuous Variable Distributions in Moderated Multiple Regression," *Organizational Research Methods* 9, no. 4 (2006): 554–67.

61. Jaccard, Turisi, and Wan, *Interaction Effects in Multiple Regression.*

62. O'Conner, "Programs for Problems Created by Continuous Variable Distributions in Moderated Multiple Regression."

63. E. F. Stone-Romero and L. E. Anderson, "Relative Power of Moderated Multiple Regression and the Comparison of Subgroup Correlation Coefficients for Detecting Moderating Effects," *Journal of Applied Psychology* 79, no. 3 (1994): 354–59.

64. Jaccard, Turisi, and Wan, *Interaction Effects in Multiple Regression.*

65. James L. Perry, "Measuring Public Service Motivation: An Assessment of Construct Reliability and Validity," *Journal of Public Administration Research and Theory* 6, no. 1 (1996): 5–23.

66. Vandenabeele, "Development of a Public Service Motivation Scale"; D. Coursey and Sanjay J. Pandey, "Public Service Motivation Measurement: Testing an Abridged Version of Perry's Proposed Measurement Scale," *Administration and Society* 39, no. 5 (2007): 547–68; D. Coursey and others, "Psychometric Verification of Perry's Public Service Motivation Instrument: Results for Volunteer Exemplars," *Review of Public Personnel Administration* 28, no. 1 (2008): 79–90.

67. For the Swiss case, compassion was not included in the set.

68. Perry, "Measuring Public Service Motivation."

69. Pichler and Wallace, "Job Satisfaction across Europe."

70. Jaccard, Turisi, and Wan, *Interaction Effects in Multiple Regression.*

71. Pichler and Wallace, "Job Satisfaction across Europe."

72. H. De Witte and K. Naswall, "'Objective' vs. 'Subjective' Job Insecurity: Consequences of Temporary Work for Job Satisfaction and Organizational Commitment in Four European Countries," *Economic and Industrial Democracy* 24, no. 2 (2000): 149–88; Alfonso Souza-Poza and Andrés Souza-Poza, "Well-Being at Work: A Cross-National Analysis of the Levels and Determinants of Job Satisfaction," *Journal of Socio-Economics* 29 (2003): 517–38.

73. Giauque and Emery, *Repenser la guestion publique.*

74. Pichler and Wallace, "Job Satisfaction across Europe."

NICOLA BELLÉ AND PAOLA CANTARELLI

5 Public Service Motivation: The State of the Art

The concept of public service motivation, or PSM, can be traced back to 1982, when Hal G. Rainey studied middle managers at four public agencies and four private organizations to understand whether they reported any differences in their reward preferences. Results found that "public managers are higher, to a statistically significant degree, on the items concerning public service and work that is helpful to others."[1] Even though he did not use the term PSM, with this statement the author advanced the idea that public and private employees have a different motivational basis. The former are particularly attracted by motives regarding third parties. This does not mean that public sector workers are not self-interested whereas workers in the private sector are. It underlines that desire to help others and work for the common good are stronger motivators in the public rather than the private sector.[2]

In the United States, James Perry and Lois Wise identified the need for dedicated research into PSM for the first time in 1990, given the failure of the ten-year experience of performance-related pay in the American public sector, the long-standing claims of scholars of the existence of a service ethic, and the scant systematic research available. PSM offset the theory of rational choice, which assumes that individuals take decisions to maximize their own utility. PSM, to the contrary, relates to the desire to help others improve their status.[3] The authors based their main arguments on an article by Daniel Katz, "The Motivational Basis of Organizational Behavior," published in 1964. Katz, an expert on psychology, introduced the notion that employee motivation makes the difference in organizations because it affects three fundamental components of organizational behavior: membership, reliable role behavior, and performance.[4]

Many studies have been published since 1982 regarding the definition, measurement, and implications of PSM. However, the construct still has to be fine-tuned and the acquired knowledge needs to be integrated better to enable organizations to implement it and take full advantage of it. In fact, there is still a gap between what is known and what it would be useful to know. Consequently, in this chapter we present a thorough review of existing literature and identify five main streams within it:

1. Defining the concept of PSM
2. Measuring PSM
3. Generalizing the PSM construct
4. Relating PSM to other variables
5. Translating the theory of PSM into practice

The lack of a generally accepted theoretical framework for the PSM construct is clear evidence that additional research is needed. This observation holds true despite the fact that several authors have tried to expand the concept of PSM by drawing on contributions from other disciplines (such as psychological economics, psychology, and political science).

Bruno S. Frey and Felix Oberholzer-Gee were the initiators of the crowding theory after verifying that it is consistent with rational choice principles and so can be integrated into economics. They found that where public spirit prevails, the introduction of monetary incentives for the localization of a facility considered socially desirable but locally unwelcome squeezes out civic duty. Therefore, greater incentives have to be provided to the local population than one would tend to expect when applying standard economic rules. In general, "the use of price incentives needs to be reconsidered in all areas where intrinsic motivation can empirically be shown to be important."[5]

Perry looked at literature on prosocial behavior and institutional theory in order to consider a new paradigm of motivation whereby the boundaries between organizations and society are less defined and the assumptions regarding what motivates people are more heterogeneous. Drawing on this, he called for a theory on motivation that includes society and expresses the differences in motivation between public and private employees. He concluded by suggesting that sociohistorical context, motivational context, individual characteristics, and behavior should all be part of the PSM theory.[6]

Frey and Reto Jegen reviewed all circumstantial evidence studies, laboratory evidence by psychologists and economists, and field evidence achieved by means of econometric studies that showed crowding-in and crowding-out effects. In this way, they corroborated the idea that economic rewards increase extrinsic motivation and decrease intrinsic motivation. Therefore, the effectiveness of the implementation of monetary incentives depends on the relative strengths of the two opposite effects on increased extrinsic motivation and decreased intrinsic motivation.[7]

Bradley E. Wright reinterpreted literature on PSM within the psychological framework of goal theory. Wright shed light on the process by which the values of employees influence their behavior, and he empirically tested the hypothesis that goal theory provides a solid theoretical framework for understanding the effects of task and mission on work motivation and performance. He concluded that "the importance of an organization's mission increases employee work motivation in the public sector by making the job more important, even after controlling for the effect of performance-related extrinsic rewards."[8]

Wouter Vandenabeele considered both the institutional theory and the concept of identity to elaborate a theory that may explain both the causes and the consequences of PSM. He concluded that the more an institution responds to an individual's psychological needs of relatedness, competence, and autonomy, the more likely it is that the individual will independently internalize the institutionalized values of public service. Additionally, a more independent internalization of the values of public service will result in more consistent and intense public service behavior. Intense public service behavior translates into "attraction to government employment, a decreased turnover, an increased performance, increased job satisfaction and ethical behavior e.g. whistle blowing."[9]

In a recent article, Perry, Annie Hondeghem, and Wise called for closer integration of the concept of PSM with other disciplines, further advances in measurement, new methodological research strategies, and tools (such as experiment and field studies), and the translation of theoretical knowledge into human resource management (HRM) practices. Their aim was "reviewing the evolving definitions of PSM, including operational definitions used to measure the construct [as well as] answering the question, what have we learned from PSM research?"[10] They initially recalled existing synergies between PSM, altruism, and prosocial motivation. They then summarized the four different approaches that have been used to measure PSM (single survey item about public service; unidimensional scales; multidimensional scales; and behavioral proxies). They subsequently turned their attention to assessing, on the basis of subsequent research, the validity of the three propositions originally put forward by Perry and Wise in 1990. They hypothesized a relationship between PSM and the other three dimensions of attraction-selection-attrition, performance, and organizational incentive structures.

Methodology

The gap between what we know and what we should know about PSM motivates this chapter, in which we review the literature in order to identify and explain the main streams of research. In contrast to Perry, Hondeghem, and Wise, the current analysis presents the definitions of PSM along with details of the context where they were proposed. By making the contextual factors explicit, we can achieve an understanding of the concerns that each definition was intended to address. Moreover, this work focuses on methodological issues related to the measurement of PSM more extensively than Perry, Hondeghem, and Wise. Different scales are presented that relate to the concerns the author wanted to address rather than the approaches that were used. This chapter also looks at the generalizability of the construct of PSM across sectors and countries outside the United States where the concept was originally introduced. In contrast to Perry, Hondeghem, and Wise, this literature review also aims at grouping articles on PSM based on the type of statistical relationship claimed by the authors. Finally, this analysis adds a closing section recalling the articles and pieces of literature that translate acquired knowledge into HRM practices and policy recommendations.

The literature review was conducted using a snowball technique and considered all works published or presented during the last thirty years.[11] All the articles were categorized using the following dimensions: author, date, title, journal, research question(s), variables, country, sample, institution type, governmental level, sector, research design, methodology, and relevant results. The table was organized with the purpose of keeping track of all the relevant information required to perform an articulate literature review. On the basis of this table, five principal streams of literature were identified related to PSM: definition, measurement scale, generalizability, associations with other variables, and translation from theory into practice.

Defining the Concept of Public Service Motivation

It is vital to define any concept in order to provide a solid framework for further speculation. This is why one branch of literature on PSM has been focusing and continues to focus on defining the concept itself. Despite dealing with different aspects, all definitions of PSM share one fundamental attribute: the orientation toward benefiting others. When the concept was introduced for the first time, the core of the construct was narrower than today. As a matter of fact, the last available definition of PSM tries to integrate contributions from different theories.

The question concerning the role of perception and values as elements of the PSM construct is also strictly related to the issue of defining PSM. Perry, Hondeghem, and Wise considered the same literature concerning the definition of PSM as that presented here, but our discussion offers further details on contextual factors as well as the sample used to test the validity of the definition provided.

Perry and Wise provided the first definition of PSM: "an individual's predisposition to respond to motives grounded primarily or uniquely in public institutions and organizations."[12] They were the first authors to call for dedicated research into the concept of PSM, given the failure of the ten-year experience of performance-related pay in the American public sector, scholars' long-standing claims about the existence of a service ethic, and the scant systematic research available. Two additional contingent factors were predominant in the debate surrounding the U.S. federal government at the time. There was a lasting trend of distrust toward government employees, yet at the same time politicians were adopting policies to regain that trust, on the assumption that public service values could be translated into efficient and effective behavior. However, politicians were implementing these policies with no evidence as to the reliability of this assumption. This was the context within which Perry and Wise proposed their definition, which specifies that PSM comprises rational, norm-based, and affective motives. "Rational motives" are the attitude of maximizing individual utility; "norm-based motives" are the desire to pursue the common good; "affective motives" are the willingness to help others. Building on these ideas, Perry and Wise formulated three propositions:

1. The greater an individual's PSM, the more likely the individual will seek membership in a public organization.
2. In public organizations, PSM is positively related to individual performance.
3. Public organizations that attract members with high levels of PSM are likely to be less dependent on utilitarian incentives to manage individual performance effectively.[13]

With these propositions, they provided an argument against the idea that the public and private sectors could be run in the same way—namely, that employees in government and businesses are more strongly motivated by different factors.

Gene A. Brewer and Sally Coleman Selden suggested another definition of

PSM: strong motives "to perform meaningful public, community, and social service."[14] The starting point for the proposition they presented was the awareness that dealing with the concept in theory was difficult because the term "public service" could have two meanings, referring either to the action of doing something valuable for society or to the public sector workforce itself. The authors also suggested considering PSM to be "prevalent in the public service." Whistleblowers in the U.S. federal government were used as the sample to test the link between PSM and prosocial behavior. The results showed that whistleblowers act consistently with the PSM construct (for instance, they use concern for the common good as grounds to blow the whistle) and assume more PSM-related behavior than less proactive workers.

Hal Rainey and Paula Steinbauer, in their analysis of the literature available at the time, defined PSM as "general altruistic motivation to serve the interests of a community of people, a state, a nation or humankind."[15] Thus, they underlined the link between PSM and altruism in the context of service to the state. They also included PSM among the characteristics that make government agencies effective.

Wouter Vandenabeele in a 2007 article offered the most recent contribution to this initial stream of literature. He focused more attention on values than previous writers had done in his definition, which is based on studies in European countries. He suggested that PSM is "the beliefs, values and attitudes that go beyond self-interest and organizational interest, that concern the interest of a larger political entity and that motivate individuals to act accordingly whenever appropriate."[16] Vandenabeele felt that the proposed definition was capable of overcoming problems in terminology and content in different countries, was broad enough to include many types of value-laden behavioral determinants and to take in interests other than personal and organizational, and was interactive in nature, with its reference to a political body.

As mentioned earlier, the question of the role of perception and value in such a construct is closely related to the issue of defining PSM.

Brewer, Selden, and Rex Facer were interested in understanding how individuals perceived the motives linked to public service. They studied sixty-nine employees and students in the United States and came up with four different kinds of perception of public service motives, which they labeled *samaritans, communitarians, patriots,* and *humanitarians*. The opportunity to help others motivates samaritans. A sense of civic duty motivates *communitarians*. Issues bigger than themselves, such as the common good or advocacy, motivate *patriots*. Sentiments of social justice motivate *humanitarians*. Overall, the authors suggest that although there are different reasons for performing public service, rational, norm-based, and affective motives are always present.[17]

Measuring Public Service Motivation

This stream of literature is focused on methodological issues rather than on the concept of PSM itself. Four separate yet intertwined issues are prevalent when the delineation of a measurement tool for PSM is discussed:

1. Does measuring PSM make any difference?
2. How can PSM be measured? Is the scale internally valid?
3. How can ethics be included in the PSM measurement scale?
4. What strategies should be adopted when PSM is empirically measured?

1. Does Measuring PSM Make Any Difference?

Gerald T. Gabris and Gloria Simo questioned the relevance of studying PSM, also in view of the complexity involved in its measurement: "It could be that PSM exists, but it is virtually impossible to isolate and visualize. . . . Until we can identify and measure it, one can only speculate about its potential effect."[18] Comparing individuals from two public, two private, and two nonprofit organizations, they did not find any difference in the value these employees attached to pay. Therefore, they pointed out, PSM does not really make any difference, stating that "if public sector jobs are made more challenging, monetarily appealing, secure, loaded with responsibility, full of autonomy, and well supervised, then they will . . . produce public servants dedicated to their tasks."[19] But it may well be that the sample they used was too small and not sufficiently representative of the sectors to permit one to draw general conclusions.

2. How Can PSM Be Measured? Is the Scale Internally Valid?

Here we describe in detail the questions and the proposed solutions that emerged in literature about measurement issues. Therefore, the perspective is different from that of Perry, Hondeghem, and Wise, who grouped contributions together according to the fact that studies used (1) single survey items about public service; (2) unidimensional scales; (3) multidimensional scales; or (4) behavioral proxies to measure PSM.

Many measurement scales are now available, but they are all basically more or less a deep modification of the scale introduced by Perry. He suggested that six dimensions—attraction to policymaking (APM), commitment to public interest (CPI), social justice, civic duty, compassion (COM), and self-sacrifice (SS)—could be used to measure PSM. In these six categories were a total of forty subcategories. The empirical pretests and tests on students and public employees suggested that the dimensions of social justice and civic duty should be dropped since respondents did not really perceive any significant difference between them and the dimension of commitment to public interest. All three are actually related to norm-based motives. Conversely, the revised four-dimension scale with twenty-four items showed internal validity, discriminational legitimacy between the dimensions of the four components, and high reliability.[20]

David H. Coursey and Sanjay K. Pandey tested the validity of a tool with three dimensions, obtained by eliminating self-sacrifice, and ten items selected from Perry's measurement scale. When they applied this tool to a sample of U.S. information managers they obtained good support for the shorter measurement tool, thus corroborating the theoretical principles first suggested by Perry and even finding that improvements could be made to the scale.[21]

Perry and others tested the four-dimension and twenty-four-item scale on "a sample of morally-committed individuals who do important service for others but who, for the most past, were not professional public administrators."[22] They found a significant match.

Vandenabeele constructed a theoretical model that he successively tested by means of a confirmatory factor analysis on data from Belgian civil servants. He aimed to compare his model with the model developed by Perry in the United States in 1996. The theoretical model by Vandenabeele suggested that a PSM measurement scale would be composed of the following dimensions: interest in policy and politics, public interest, compassion, self-sacrifice, client orientation, equality, and bureaucratic values. Findings from the test showed that the content of PSM suggested by Perry could be generalized in Belgium, but the empirical nature of the factors differed between the United States and Belgium. The Belgian data led Vandenabeele to infer that democratic governance was also a relevant dimension in determining PSM, so he suggested it should be included in the PSM construct.[23]

Sangmook Kim applied the four-dimension and twenty-four-item measurement tool to Korea and concluded that it was not a good fit for the Korean context. As a result, he modified the scale, keeping the same four dimensions but reducing the number of items to fourteen. The revised measurement tool resulted in a better fit between the measurement tool and Korea, but he obtained an even better fit with a three-dimension scale, after eliminating the APM (attraction to policymaking) dimension. Kim suggested various explanations for this: APM may not be an important dimension for Korean public servants; APM may not be a relevant dimension for PSM at all; items measuring APM may not be accurate enough; the negatively worded items may be a cause of confusion for the respondent and therefore produce unreliable answers.[24] In a later study, Kim focused his attention on the APM dimension, rewording all the negatively worded items in a positive way. He conducted a test on Korean public employers after making this alteration and after the elimination of two other items from the fourteen-item scale. This study ultimately supported the external validity of the four-dimension construct originally proposed by Perry.[25]

Bradley E. Wright and Robert K. Christensen tested the internal validity of four different versions of PSM measurement scale, all of which were mentioned earlier: those of Perry, Coursey and Pandey, Perry and others, and Kim. None of these versions presented consistent evidence of a good model fit across all of the several statistical indices calculated by Wright and Christensen. The best fit between the four versions was achieved with the three-dimension tool used by Coursey and Pandey (omitting the self-sacrifice dimension) with ten items. This version established acceptably strong factor loadings and an adequate fit in five out of seven fit indices.[26]

Finally, Kim and Vandenabeele, publishing in 2010, wanted to broaden the conceptual composition and improve the operational dimensions of the PSM construct in order to make it a globally usable concept that generates cumulative knowledge. To reach their goal they suggested that the dimensions of PSM should be redefined as attraction to public participation, commitment to public values, compassion, and self-sacrifice. The first dimension represents instrumental motives such as participating in activities for social development and advocating for special programs. Such motives are based primarily on altruistic behaviors and are related to the methods of performing meaningful public service. The second dimension represents value-based motives such as responsibility, social justice, and fairness. Such motives concern the terminal public values that individuals want to achieve through their behaviors and actions. The third dimension represents affective motives. It is related to the attitude of identifying oneself with people and groups that individuals want to serve. The fourth dimension represents the altruistic and prosocial origins of PSM, that is, the willingness to sacrifice some private interests and do good for others as a way to satisfy personal needs. Each dimension provides a unique contribution to PSM, which, therefore, is a formative construct.[27]

3. *How Can Ethics be Included in the PSM Measurement Scale?*

Brewer called for the introduction of an ethical dimension in the PSM construct. He noted that both scholars and practitioners consider ethics to be relevant in public administration: "Adding an ethical dimension to the PSM construct, formulating measurement items, and testing the validity of those items" seems reasonable.[28] Do Lim Choi subsequently tested the relationship between ethical sensitivity and the four dimensions of PSM (that is, APM, CPI, COM, SS). He concluded that a statistically significant relationship exists only between ethical sensitivity and compassion; and ethical sensitivity and self-sacrifice.[29]

4. What Strategies Should Be Adopted When PSM Is Empirically Measured?

Wright and Adam M. Grant argued that the research strategies of policy capturing, longitudinal studies, and field experiments would maximize internal validity and what they call the "realism of context." Policy-capturing research designs experimentally manipulate different cues and cue values so that it can be determined how individuals weight, combine, or integrate information when making decisions. Longitudinal studies, by contrast, allow the independent variable of interest to be measured at multiple points in time or prior to observing a change in the dependent variable. Field experiments, then, allow researchers to demonstrate causal relationships between variables while ruling out alternative explanations. All these research designs will, in the end, provide objective data and results for both researchers and practitioners.[30]

Generalizing the Public Service Motivation Construct Internationally

All the studies in this stream aim to verify whether the concept of PSM can be generalized to nations outside the United States. Generalization has been tested across countries, sectors, and roles. In some cases, the same research looks at more than one type of generalization. In this stream the focus is on the concept of PSM rather than on measurement issues.

Studies that apply the measurement scale developed by Perry to foreign nations generally conclude that the model has external validity and therefore holds true in countries outside the United States. Yet all these studies found additional elements to be relevant for the PSM construct in the specific nation studied. Vandenabeele and others compared the United States to the French and Dutch contexts. In addition to the four dimensions of APM, CPI, COM and SS, they found that religion, democratic and bureaucratic values, and the tradition of service delivery by the civil service were also important factors for understanding PSM in France and the Netherlands.[31] Vandenabeele, Scheepers, and Hondeghem subsequently looked at the concept of PSM in the United Kingdom and Germany. The authors confirmed the idea that PSM is a universal concept and holds true in European countries as well. However, they found that the policymaking process, the basis for defining the common good, and the level of government reference differed not only between the United Kingdom and Germany but also between the two European countries and the United States. Moreover, equality, the tradition of service delivery, the skills expected of public servants, and bureaucratic traditions are relevant factors that influence PSM in the United Kingdom and Germany, suggesting that in these two countries, institutions influence behavior.[32]

Donna Lind Infeld and her colleagues compared PSM in the United States and China using responses from students attending a master's degree program in public administration (MPA). In particular, they observed how work values differed. The American students put the highest priority on exciting, stimulating, educational, and challenging work (which are intrinsic motives), whereas the Chinese students considered the same factors to be among the least important. The American students demanded jobs with high self-actualization, altruism, and affluence, whereas Chinese students demanded jobs with a high salary, good benefits, and opportunities for promotion (which are extrinsic motives). Both the American and the Chinese students assigned low importance to the role of leadership for maximizing efficiency, entrepreneurship, and productivity.[33]

Studies to determine whether there is a difference in the level of PSM among public, nonprofit, and private employees all find that PSM is anchored most strongly in public organizations, but both intrinsic and extrinsic motives are present in all sectors. The studies differ in focus and perspective. In 1997 Philip E. Crewson found evidence that private firms are likely to be dominated by economic-oriented employees, while public-service organizations, both public and nonprofit, are likely to be dominated by service-oriented employees. Also, federal workers with a high level of PSM will be more productive and committed to the organization than extrinsically motivated employees.[34] In 2000 David J. Houston argued that PSM does exist and that American public sector employees are more intrinsically motivated than private sector employees, while private sector employees are more extrinsically motivated.[35] Sue A. Frank and Gregory B. Lewis found that sectoral differences in self-reported work effort are primarily a result of the government's offering interesting projects and opportunities to help others and of the older age of public workers.[36] Houston found that public employees are more likely to engage in volunteer work and donate blood than private employees and that nonprofit workers are also more likely to volunteer than for-profit workers, but he found no difference between government employees and private employees with regard to individual philanthropy. He therefore concluded that PSM exists in public service employees, especially those working in government, to a higher degree than in private sector employees.[37]

Mark Buelens and Herman Van den Broeck compared and contrasted employees in the Belgian public and private sectors. They reached the conclusion that the former are less extrinsically motivated than the latter. They also found that position in the organization's hierarchy and job content are more important in determining motivation than sectoral differences.[38] Lotte Bøgh Andersen (2007) looked at Danish dentists and physicians to investigate how professional norms, monetary incentives, and sector influenced behavior. She found that monetary incentives were irrelevant for both public and private practitioners when strong professional norms were in place. Vice versa, monetary incentives influenced behavior when strong professional norms were lacking. With a constant level of economic reward, the sector of employment did not seem to influence behavior significantly. Therefore, monetary incentives and professional norms are more important than sector in order to understand the behavior of health professionals.[39] Andersen, Thomas Pallesen, and Lene Holm Pedersen compared the levels of PSM among private and public physiotherapists in Denmark. The conclusions they reached included that the level of PSM is the same between public and private physiotherapists; private physiotherapists were more highly oriented toward the user and had lower public interest compared to public physiotherapists; and age and gender affected PSM. [40]

Another study of private Danish physiotherapists, by Andersen and Søren Serritzlew, showed that their behavior was affected by public interest and attraction to policymaking but not by compassion. Thus, at least some of the underling principles of PSM can be found in the private sector as well, where they also have an impact on behavior.[41] Stephanie Moulton and Mary K. Feeney: "Why would loan originators offer borrowers public loan programs, particularly when such programs provide no additional (and sometimes reduced) direct financial compensation to the private lenders and potentially increased workloads?" They speculated that "among private loan officers, affinity for government, community ties, and public values are significantly related to the degree of participation in a public serving government program." That is to say that frontline workers have the power to influence public outcomes and the public good through their intrinsic motivation rather than via the institutional structure they belong to. Motivation is boosted by perceptions of government and government programs. "Although government perceptions predict participation in the government program, shared public values predict a substantial increase in the degree of participation in the public program."[42]

Sung Min Park and Jessica Word investigated whether there were differences in motivation between public and nonprofit managers. They found that both types are significantly motivated by intrinsic motives, such as service, reputation, and reduction of red tape. Nonprofit managers are more motivated by the work-family life balance, while public managers are more motivated by promotion, salary, and security.[43]

One study measuring PSM across roles has been published. Bonnie J. Johnson wanted to see whether city planners had a public service ethic. She started with the premise that city planners in the United States have three main roles: technical, facilitator, and political. She found that PSM was only related to the first two roles. She also found that gender (female), age, being a professional, having an entrepreneurial background, personal and family orientation, and the person's level of activism within the community were relevant for the determination of PSM.[44]

Three works made comparisons on the basis of both country and sector. Having compared thirty-eight countries around the world, Vandenabeele and Steven Van de Walle stated: "PSM and its constituting dimensions are only to a certain extent universal. Scores are generally high in Southern European and American countries, and low in Central and Eastern Europe. There is also considerable variation in the dimensions that make up PSM, resulting in different score patterns across regions." They also made a comparison between PSM in the public and private sectors in the thirty-eight countries in their study and concluded: "PSM has a distinct public character. However, . . . not all dimensions under investigation were equally public in character. Although the dimension 'politics and policies' was clearly public, 'compassion' and 'self-sacrifice' were not significantly related to public sector employment."[45]

Houston, too, looked at public and private managers in North America and western Europe to see whether attitudes toward intrinsic and extrinsic motivators were similar and whether the welfare state in the different contexts affected these attitudes. He concluded that public sector employees are more likely to value intrinsic work motivators and devalue extrinsic work motivators. The only unexpected result was that both public and private employees amplified the importance of job security as an extrinsic motive. The author also found some evidence that being a worker serving the government meant different things in different welfare regimes in terms of valuing extrinsic work motives.[46]

A. Chow and colleagues studied the readiness of firefighters in Hong Kong to work or to shirk their duty and compared them to police officers in the United States. In both samples, workers with strong functional (attaching value to the work itself) and solidarity (attaching value to good relations with coworkers) preferences were more likely to work hard. However, solidarity preferences were more important for the Hong Kong firefighters when taking the decision to work hard than they were for the American police officers. It was also found for both firefighters and police officers that interaction with their supervisor and the belief that punishment would be used when necessary were linked significantly to the decision to work hard.[47]

Relating Public Service Motivation to Other Variables

Here, studies are presented according to the statistical analysis performed. Some research looked at causal relationships, defining the antecedents and consequences of PSM, while others verified the correlation between PSM and other organizational and individual variables. The approach is, therefore, different from that of Perry, Hondeghem and Wise, who used the three propositions defined by Perry and Wise in 1990 as their criteria for grouping successively published studies, suggesting a relationship between PSM and the three dimensions of attraction-selection-attrition, individual performance, and organizational incentives system. Also, this chapter reviews a greater number of variables than did Perry, Hondeghem, and Wise.[48]

The most highly debated issue related to this stream of literature is that the majority of the works published are observational, often cross-sectional. Yet, to understand the causal relationships between PSM and other variables it is necessary to perform quasi-experimental research with panel data and, more important, experimental studies.

The Antecedents of Public Service Motivation

A multitude of studies investigate which individual and organizational characteristics determine a higher or lower level of PSM. Individual variables include education, childhood and professional experiences, preferences for different kinds of rewards, perceptions, pride, closeness to God, parental models, political ideology, and age. Organizational variables include the level occupied within the organizational hierarchy, the characteristics of the organization, the amount of bureaucratic red tape, length of membership in the institution, national institutions and politics, and features of the job. Gender is also considered to determine the level of PSM, although findings are mixed with regard to the strength and type of causation.

Perry called for investigation into the factors expected to influence the dimensions of PSM: "Expanding the variables investigated will help to explain larger parts of the variance of PSM and should help to identify interventions to change it."[49] He particularly called for further studies on the role of educational and organizational influences on PSM. In this study he also found that childhood experiences and professional life, in addition to exposure to religion, influence the individual level of PSM in a complex way.

Wright found that just over half of the variance in work motivation among public employees could be explained by job goal specificity, job goal difficulty, and self-efficacy (one's belief in one's capabilities to meet expectations). He also added that work context variables (that is, procedural constraints, organizational goal specificity, and organizational goal conflict) are relevant for understanding work motivation.[50]

Leonard Bright concluded that PSM is strongly linked to gender, educational level, management level, and individuals' financial requirements. Workers with higher levels of PSM were more likely to be female, have more education, be managers, and be satisfied with significantly less economic reward than workers with lower levels of PSM.[51]

Emanuel Camilleri studied government officials in Malta and found that employee perception regarding the organization has an influence on affective and normative organizational commitment, and this in turn has a direct effect on PSM. Also, the status of the family-life cycle directly influences most PSM dimensions but does not influence organizational commitment factors. In a later study, Camilleri confirmed that the work environment, including job characteristics, employee-leader relations, and employee perception of the organization, is the most important factor in predicting PSM among Maltese government employees. Camilleri also discovered that personal attributes, with the exception of age, do not have a major impact on the development of PSM among government workers in Malta. Rather, perception of organizational politics is a positive antecedent of PSM, with remuneration and promotion policies having a positive influence on PSM.[52]

Donald P. Moynihan and Pandey supported the idea that sociohistorical context may shape PSM, referring to education and membership in a professional organization in particular. At the organizational level, red tape and the length of membership in the organization have a negative impact, whereas hierarchical authority and reform efforts have a positive impact, on PSM.[53]

Grant argued that PSM may be enhanced simply by telling and demonstrating to employees how their behavior benefits other people's lives. They undertook a quasi-experiment with undergraduates who were paid to do fundraising. Their findings: "A group of fundraising callers serving a public university [were introduced to] a fellowship student who [had] benefited from the funds raised by the organization. A full month later, these callers increased significantly in the number of pledges and the amount of donation money that they obtained, whereas callers in a control group [who had not met a beneficiary of their efforts] did not change on these measures."[54]

Craig Boardman and Eric Sundquist committed themselves to closing the gap between organizational performance and individual motivation. They proposed the introduction of a new explanatory variable, named perceived public service efficacy, to quantify public servant perception about the benefits that their employing agencies provided to the public. They discovered that an increase in perceived public service efficacy was associated with a decrease in role ambiguity and an increase in job satisfaction and organizational commitment.[55]

Chan Su Jung and Rainey observed that specific goals, clear organizational mission, high commitment to goals, and high perceived goal relevance increased the likelihood that American civil servants consider their duty as public official a motivator.[56]

Jeffrey R. Paine studied U.S. local government and found that closeness to God, parental modeling, professional identification, political ideology, and age are the most important predictors of PSM. Therefore, they were relevant indicators of direction, intensity, and duration of work efforts.[57]

Simon Anderfuhren-Biget and others found that sociorelational factors are good predictors of work motivation, in both the public and other sectors.[58]

Yannis Georgellis and Vurain Tabvuma focused their attention on the level of PSM reported by individuals switching jobs within the same sector or across sectors. They concluded that workers who accepted public sector employment had enhanced satisfaction with their jobs, which Georgellis and Tabvuma took as a proxy for PSM.[59]

Few studies have examined the effect of gender on PSM, and so far these results are mixed. In a 1997 study by Perry, males registered higher scores in the dimensions of commitment to public interest and self-sacrifice; this compared to the genders' equal scores with regard to attraction to policymaking.[60] Leisha DeHart-Davis, Justin Marlowe, and Pandey recorded higher scores for women in the dimensions of attraction to policymaking and compassion, and no difference between genders on commitment to public interest.[61]

The Consequences of Public Service Motivation

Several studies illustrate the organizational consequences of PSM. Specifically, PSM is found to influence variables such as the performance of an individual and an organization, retention, and the appraisal process, in both positive and negative ways.

In Kim's study of Korean civil servants at all government levels, he found that individual factors such as job satisfaction, organizational citizenship behavior, affective organizational commitment, and PSM—rated most to least for shaping the relationship—are important for predicting organizational performance.[62] Camilleri also analyzed the relationship between individual-level factors (personal attributes, perception of organizational politics, and PSM) and the individual performance of public officers in the central government of Malta.[63] Unlike Kim, Camilleri discovered that the impact of PSM on performance is rather low.

Laura Langbein found that for employees of the U.S. federal government, enjoying and appreciating a job are more important than extra money when it comes to their staying with in their jobs. She also found that for a job to be defined good, it must include having discretion on how to do the job, clear individual goals for employees to achieve, a cooperative work environment, and a clear link between individual tasks and organizational mission.[64]

Bright discussed the fact that "PSM is a significant predictor of public employees' desire for personal recognition, task meaningfulness and professional growth, over and above the effects of several confounding variables assessed."[65] The control variables included in the study were management level, racial differences, public sector tenure, age, gender, and education level.[66]

Robert K. Christensen and Steven W. Whiting found that PSM significantly alters the performance appraisal process. They actually observed that "raters with higher levels of PSM placed greater weight on helping behaviors in making their appraisal decisions."[67]

Paine studied local public officials in the United States and reached two main conclusions: PSM is the strongest predictor of the directions of work efforts, and individual and job-related factors are better than PSM for predicting the intensity and duration of work efforts.[68]

Correlation between Public Service Motivation and Other Variables

The studies in this branch correlate PSM to other variables, which can be classed as tangible and intangible. Tangible variables include performance, turnover, different styles of leadership, extra-role behavior, citizen participation, network settings, effort levels, employment-at-will policies, and materials taught in master's degree programs in public administration. Intangible variables include activism levels, social capital, person-organization fit, satisfaction, trust, emotional labor, and culture.

Brewer argued that workers employed in the public sector are much more active in civic affairs and willing to build social capital than any other group of citizens.[69]

The results obtained in a first-stage study led Francesco Paolo Cerase and Domenico Farinella to conclude that Italian Revenue Agency employees showed high levels of PSM, which was also related to work motivation, job satisfaction, and organizational commitment.[70]

Bright observed three public organizations in the United States. In his study, PSM did not have a statistically significant direct influence on job performance when compared to person-organization fit. Incidentally, PSM influences performance indirectly by means of an important contribution toward the person-organization fit.[71] Edmund C. Stazyk reached the same conclusion and added that employees' expectations of rewards do not strongly influence person-organization fit and job satisfaction, but do directly affect employees' turnover intentions.[72]

Perry and others discovered that PSM is significantly related to family socialization, religious activities, and volunteer experiences.[73]

Gabris and Trenton Davis looked at students enrolled in four different master's degree programs in public administration (MPA) in the United States with the aim of understanding whether the students' PSM scores were associated with distinct models of management being taught in different MPA programs. They concluded that the students' PSM was positively related to team management models and negatively related to business agency models, but these relationships were not strong. As a matter of fact, it appeared that students "want to be involved in meaningful problem solving, but they also believe that private sector ideology is an expected skill set which they must develop in their MPA programs."[74] This tradeoff may have caused confusion in the students' set of values, as it is very difficult to simultaneously reconcile the two opposite aspects.

Moynihan, Pandey, and Wright observed that "transformational leadership is associated with higher PSM . . . [and] has both a direct effect on mission valence as well as important indirect effects through its influence on clarifying organizational goals and fostering PSM."[75] In any case, PSM is just one lever, and is not even the strongest, in a set of tools that leaders can use to obtain outcomes related to the mission valence.

Sung Min Park and Rainey studied federal agencies in the United States and concluded that transformation-oriented leaders and public service–oriented motivation are strongly and positively related to job satisfaction, performance, and work quality, and related negatively to turnover intention. They specified that transformation-oriented leaders foster public service–oriented motivation via empowerment.[76]

Jeannette Taylor focused her attention on the public and private sectors in Australia. She observed a strong and direct relationship between PSM and the two work outcomes of job satisfaction and organizational commitment. She also found that intrinsic and extrinsic rewards and work relations with management and coworkers did not influence the relation between PSM and the two work outcomes, despite showing significant and direct effects on them.[77]

Chih-Wei Hsieh and Kaifeng Yang investigated what type of emotional labor relates to PSM. "Emotional labor" refers to employee efforts to actively display socially and organizationally desired emotions as they engage in job-related interactions. Surface acting refers to managing the expression of emotions; deep acting refers to managing actual emotions. Both surface and deep acting are methods for performing emotional labor. They found that the dimension of attraction to policymaking is positively linked with surface acting, and the dimension of compassion is negatively linked to surface acting and positively linked to deep acting. They found no link between emotional labor and commitment to the public interest.[78]

Aleksey Kolpakov tried to relate cultural dimensions to the different motives identified by Perry as components of PSM. He proposed five hypotheses to be tested by future studies.

1. Public servants will score higher in rational motives in collectivistic cultures than in individualistic cultures.
2. Civil and public servants will score higher in rational motives in weak uncertainty-avoidance cultures than in strong uncertainty-avoidance cultures.
3. Civil and public servants will score higher in norm-based motives (commitment to the public interest and loyalty to duty) in collectivistic cultures than in individualistic cultures.
4. Civil and public servants will score higher in norm-based motives (social equity) in feminine cultures than in masculine cultures.
5. Civil and public servants will score higher in affective-based motives in affective cultures than in neutral cultures.[79]

Paul R. Battaglio focused on the common practice of eliminating tenure for civil servants by adopting employment at-will policies (in which either party can break the employment relationship with no liability) as a way to improve public sector efficiency. Using a sample of human resources managers at the state level in the United States, he found that employment-at-will policies are strongly and negatively related to motivation in the workplace. The link was even stronger among minority groups.[80]

In a literature review Laurie E. Paarlberg and Bob Lavigna proposed a new comprehensive framework linking transformational leadership, person-organization fit, socialization, job setting, the goal-setting theory, and the self-determination theory to PSM. They urged organizational leaders to take advantage of the growing body of evidence on relationships involving all these variables when designing HRM programs, considering benefits as well as costs.[81]

Antoinette Weibel and others observed that "pay for performance has a strong, positive effect on performance in the case of non-interesting tasks." The opposite happened with interesting tasks. In the same study, they added that intrinsic motivation boosts work efforts much more than extrinsic motivation. They concluded: "Pay for performance strengthens extrinsic motivation and weakens intrinsic motivation: depending on the relative strengths, pay for performance either hurts or promotes personal efforts. Moreover, hidden costs arise even if the price effect is stronger than the crowding-out effect, as the loss of intrinsically motivated behavior has always to be compensated by external rewards."[82]

From Theory to Practice

From the beginnings of the literature on PSM, some authors have focused on reviewing the contributions available in order to come up with suggestions for HRM practices and policy recommendations. Broadly speaking, these suggestions are intended to improve all steps in the HRM cycle.

Paarlberg, Perry, and Hondeghem provided the most relevant and comprehensive piece of literature related to the issue of translating the acquired knowledge on PSM from theory to practice. Their starting premise was that "although individuals may enter public service with a predisposition to value certain public ideals, values are also influenced by environmental forces. . . . Public service values can be managed in ways that strengthen the relationship between motives and behavior by integrating public service values into the organization's management systems."[83] The authors suggested that there are five levels at which organizations should intervene in order to push employee behavior in the desired direction: individual, job, workplace, organization, and society. The authors made explicit proposals regarding strategies and tactics for applying PSM at the five contextual levels of analysis throughout the HRM cycle, from recruitment to dismissal (see table 5-1). The proposed tactics have mutually reinforcing effects and none used alone will improve performance.[84]

Other articles also deal with the same issue of translating PSM theory into organizational practices. Perry, Debra Mesch, and Paarlberg summed up the discoveries made by social and behavioral sciences with regard to motivating performance in all three sectors. They basically concluded that although pay for performance may result in slight to significant improvements in performance, its effectiveness within the public sector has been low, owing to organizational conditions. Unfortunately, however, group incentives that have generally been effective have not been thoroughly tested in public institutions. But job design emphasizing participation, clear learning goals, and

Table 5-1. *Summary of Strategies and Tactics for Applying PSM*

Unit of analysis	*Strategy*	*Tactics*
Individual	Integrate PSM into human resources management process.	Select based on PSM. Socialize individuals into expectations of behaviors that reflect PSM. Utilize performance appraisals that include observations of behaviors that reflect PSM.
Job	Create and convey meaning and purpose in the job.	Convey social significance of the job. Establish clear goals in line with existing PSM.
Work environment	Create a supportive work environment for PSM.	Create work structure that enhances self-regulation. Encourage cooperative workplace interactions. Create and maintain incentives that align organizational mission and employee PSM. Design compensation systems that emphasize long-term attractiveness to emplyees and do not crowd out intrinsic motivations.
Organization	Integrate public service into organization mission and strategy.	Articulate organization vision and action that reflect commitment to PSM. Promote value-based leadership.
Society	Create societal legitimacy for public service.	Partner with societal institutions to incorporate public service values into curriculum. Advocate for and provide opportunities for pre-service experience. Use media to bring public service to attention of society.

Source: Laurie E. Paarlberg, James L. Perry, and Annie Hondeghem, "From Theory to Practice: Strategies for Applying Public Service Motivation," in *Motivation in Public Management: The Call of Public Service*, edited by James L. Perry and Annie Hondeghem (Oxford Universtiy Press, 2008), p. 286.

rewards has been found to be effective for improving performance and influencing affective outcomes (attitudes toward work).[85] Following the same approach, Perry, Trent A. Engbers, and So Yun Jun reviewed fifty-seven studies published from 1977 to 2008 to sum up what is known about the effectiveness of performance-related pay in government. They listed the factors to be considered for the effective implementation of a pay-for-performance system.

The organizational context, the organizational level, and the type of institution (public or private) may moderate effectiveness. They also suggested avoiding the implementation of a pay-for-performance system simply because everyone else is doing it and suggested that the public service theory and self-determination theory may be better levers for improving performance.[86]

Paarlberg and Lavigna made some suggestions for enhancing the positive influences of PSM on both personal and organizational performance. They suggested using interview tools that enable interviewers to recognize PSM during recruitment; providing opportunities for newcomers to understand the organization's goals and expectations; highlighting how personal behavior makes the difference for the institution and society; setting goals for employees that are clear and challenging; enhancing the self-determination of the workforce by way of participation and shared leadership; and acknowledging and encouraging the creation of transformational leadership.[87]

Jeannette Taylor and Ranald Taylor, using a sample of fifteen countries around the world (Australia, Bulgaria, Canada, Denmark, France, Germany, Great Britain, Israel, Japan, New Zealand, Russia, Slovenia, Spain, Taiwan, United States), observed that all the states considered paid their public workforce slightly above the efficient wages (a wage level higher than the prevailing market rate, which elicits maximum effort), with the exception of the United States, Denmark, France, Bulgaria, and Russia. This may cause a drop in the PSM level. Consequently they argue for the significance of PSM-adjusted wages (the level of wage that ensures high effort without undermining PSM levels). In their view the most cost-effective way to raise effort among government workers is by raising the workers' PSM levels.[88]

Trui Steen and Mark Rutgers critically discussed PSM and the oath of office—the latter being sketched as an explicit demand and portrayal of the former—and urged their readers to view them as values-as-such rather than as management instruments that promote good governance. In their view, PSM and the oath of office are an expression of moral and intrinsic commitment to the general interest instead of instruments to enhance integrity and performance. Also, they warned of the possible negative consequences of PSM and the oath of office: when the values feeding both are only formally but not substantially part of the organization, a sense of frustration may arise and cause dissent and unethical behavior.[89]

Julian Le Grand combined motivational assumptions and the delivery of public service theory. He recognized that any model of public service delivery makes assumptions about the motivation of employees and argued that it is important to make these assumptions about motivation explicit in order to obtain effective and efficient public service delivery and avoid mismatches. He defined four models of motivation and service delivery setting.

1. The trust model. It is effective only if workers are altruistic, public-spirited professionals. In the trust model, no controls are needed for proper service delivery.

2. The mistrust model. It uses rewards and punishments to motivate workers to perform as desired. If the rewards and punishments are perceived to be tools for control, the model fits self-interested employees, but if they are perceived to be reinforcing, the model fits public-spirited workers.

3. The voice model. It is the best fit with nonpaternalistic, public-spirited professionals, but if workers are completely self-interested it has to be combined with the mistrust model or the choice model.

4. The choice model. It is suitable when employees are self-interested or nonpaternalistic, public-spirited professionals.[90]

Josse Delfgaauw and Robert Dur studied self-selection into managerial positions in the public and private sector under a model that assumes the presence of an economy perfectly competitive and people with different levels of ability and PSM. On the basis of this model they argued that "competition between people with different levels of PSM and managerial ability can result in a negative selection of ability into the public sector. . . . Many of the best and brightest agents of the economy reside in the private sector and the least able agents predominantly sort into the public sector. Moreover, agents in the public sector exert lower effort than agents with the same ability in the private sector as the public sector rewards good performance to a lesser extent. . . . [Consequently,] when PSM is sufficiently prevalent in the public sector, agencies should not aim to recruit and retain the best and brightest at all cost, but rather aim at less productive but better motivated people. The benefits of improving the quality of public managers by increasing remuneration to private sector levels are bound to be smaller than the cost."[91]

Conclusion

In this chapter we review the literature on PSM published since 1980 and consider it from several perspectives. Key unanswered questions remain, and these should drive future research. In particular, relevant issues to be investigated include the following:

—What is the relationship between PSM and performance, at the individual and organizational level?

—What is the link between PSM and leadership in public organizations?

—How should HRM practices be designed in light of the different level and degree of PSM shown by employees within the institution?

Notes

1. Hal G. Rainey, "Reward Preferences among Public and Private Managers: In Search of the Service Ethic," *American Review of Public Administration* 16 (December 1982): 288–302 (see 293).

2. Ibid.

3. James L. Perry and Lois Recascino Wise, "The Motivational Bases of Public Service," *Public Administration Review* 50 (May–June 1990): 367–73.

4 . Daniel Katz, "The Motivational Basis of Organizational Behavior," *Behavioral Science* 9 (March–April 1964): 131–46.

5. Bruno S. Frey and Felix Oberholzer-Gee, "The Cost of Price Incentives," *American Economic Review* 87 (September 1997): 746–55 (see 753).

6. James L Perry, "Bringing Society In: Toward a Theory of Public Service Motivation," *Journal of Public Administration Research and Theory* 10 (April 2000): 471–88.

7. Bruno S. Frey and Reto Jegen, "Motivation Crowding Theory," *Journal of Economic Surveys* 15 (December 2001): 589–611.

8. Bradley E. Wright, "Public Service and Motivation: Does Mission Matter?" *Public Administration Review* 67 (January 2007): 54–64 (see 54).

9. Wouter Vandenabeele, "Toward a Public Administration Theory of Public Service Motivation: An Institutional Approach," *Public Management Review* 9 (December 2007): 545–56 (see 553).

10. James L. Perry, Annie Hondeghem, and Lois Recascino Wise, "Revisiting the Motivational Bases of Public Service: Twenty Years of Research and an Agenda for the Future," *Public Administration Review* 70 (September–October 2010): 681–90 (see 681).

11. Leo A. Goodman, "Snowball Sampling," *Annals of Mathematical Statistics* 32 (1): 148–70.

12. Perry and Wise, "Motivational Bases of Public Service," p. 368.

13. Ibid., pp. 370–71.

14 Gene A. Brewer and Sally Coleman Selden, "Whistle Blowers in the Federal Civil Service: New Evidence of the Public Service Ethic," *Journal of Public Administration Research and Theory* 8 (May–June 1998): 413–39 (see 417).

15. Hal G. Rainey and Paula Steinbauer, "Galloping Elephants: Developing Elements of a Theory of Effective Government Organizations," *Journal of Public Administration Research and Theory* 9 (January–February 1999): 1–32 (see 23).

16. Vandenabeele, "Toward a Public Administration Theory of Public Service Motivation," p. 547.

17. Gene A. Brewer, Sally Coleman Selden, and Rex L. Facer II, "Individual Conceptions of Public Service Motivation," *Public Administration Review* 60 (May 2000): 254–64.

18. Gerald T. Gabris and Gloria Simo, "Public Sector Motivation as an Independent Variable Affecting Career Decisions," *Public Personnel Management* 24 (Spring 1995): 33–51 (see 49).

19. Ibid.

20. James L. Perry, "Measuring Public Service Motivation: An Assessment of Construct Reliability and Validity," *Journal of Public Administration Research and Theory* 6 (January 1996): 5–22.

21. David H. Coursey and Sanjay K. Pandey, "Public Service Motivation Measurement: Testing an Abridged Version of Perry's Proposed Scale," *Administration and Society* 39 (September 2007): 547–68.

22. James L. Perry and others, "What Drives Morally Committed Citizens? A Study of the Antecedents of Public Service Motivation," *Public Administration Review* 68 (May 2008): 445–58 (see 454).

23. Wouter Vandenabeele, "Development of a Public Service Motivation Measurement Scale: Corroborating and Extending Perry's Measurement Instrument," *International Public Management Journal* 11, no. 1 (2008): 143–67.

24. Sangmook Kim, "Testing the Structure of Public Service Motivation in Korea: A Research Note," *Journal of Public Administration Research and Theory* 19 (October 2009): 839–51.

25. Sangmook Kim, "Revising Perry's Measurement Scale of Public Service Motivation," *American Review of Public Administration* 39 (April 2009): 149–63.

26. Bradley E. Wright and Robert K. Christensen, "Public Service Motivation: Testing Measures, Antecedents and Consequences," paper presented at the International Public Service Motivation Research Conference, Bloomington, Indiana, June 7–9, 2009. (For online access to all of the conference papers see link at http://www.indiana.edu/~ipsm2009/paper1.pdf.) See also Perry, "Measuring Public Service Motivation"; Coursey and Pandey, "Public Service Motivation Measurement"; Perry and others, "What Drives Morally Committed Citizens?"; Kim, "Revising Perry's Measurement Scale of Public Service Motivation."

27. Sangmook Kim and Wouter Vandenabeele, "A Strategy for Building Public Service Motivation Research Internationally," *Public Administration Review* 70 (September–October 2010): 701–09.

28. Gene A. Brewer, "The Possibility of an Ethical Dimension of Public Service Motivation," paper presented at the International Public Service Motivation Research Conference, Bloomington, Indiana, June 7–9, 2009, p. 2.

29. Do Lim Choi, "Ethical Sensitivity and Public Service Motivation," paper presented at the International Public Service Motivation Research Conference, Bloomington, Indiana, June 7–9, 2009.

30. Bradley E. Wright and Adam M. Grant, "Unanswered Questions about Public Service Motivation: Designing Research to Address Key Issue of Emergence and Effects," *Public Administration Review* 70 (September–October 2010): 691–700 (see 691).

31. Wouter Vandenabeele and others, "Values and Motivation in Public Administration: Public Service Motivation in an International Comparative Perspective," paper presented at the EGPA (European Group for Public Administration) 2004, Ljubljana, Slovenia, September 1–4, 2004.

32. Wouter Vandenabeele, Sarah Scheepers, and Annie Hondeghem, "Public Service Motivation in an International Comparative Perspective: The UK and Germany," *Public Policy and Administration* 21 (Spring 2006): 13–31.

33. Donna Lind Infeld and others, "Work Values and Career Choices of Public Administration and Public Policy Students in the U.S. and China," paper presented at the International Public Service Motivation Research Conference, Bloomington, Indiana, June 7–9, 2009.

34. Philip E. Crewson, "Public-Service Motivation: Building Empirical Evidence of Incidence and Effect," *Journal of Public Administration Research and Theory* 7 (October 1997): 499–518.

35. David J. Houston, "Public-Service Motivation: A Multivariate Test," *Journal of Public Administration Research and Theory* 10 (October 2000): 713–27.

36. Sue A. Frank and Gregory B. Lewis, "Government Employees: Working Hard or Hardly Working?" *American Review of Public Administration* 34 (March 2004): 36–51.

37. David J. Houston, "Walking the Walk of Public Service Motivation: Public Employees and Charitable Gifts of Time, Blood, and Money," *Journal of Public Administration Research and Theory* 16 (January 2006): 67–86.

38. Marc Buelens and Herman Van den Broeck, "An Analysis of Differences in Work Motivation between Public and Private Sector Organizations," *Public Administration Review* 67 (January 2007): 65–74.

39. Lotte Bøgh Andersen, "Professional Norms, Public Service Motivation, and Economic Incentives: What Motivates Public Employees?" paper presented at EGPA (European Group for Public Administration) Study Group 3 (Public Personnel Policies), EGPA 2007, Madrid, September 19–22, 2007 (http://soc.kuleuven.be/io/egpa/HRM/madrid/BoghAndersen2007.pdf).

40. Lotte Bøgh Andersen, Thomas Pallesen, and Lene Holm Pedersen, "Does Employment Sector Matter for Professionals' Public Service Motivation?" paper presented at the International Public Service Motivation Research Conference, Bloomington, Indiana, June 7–9, 2009.

41. Lotte Bøgh Andersen and Søren Serritzlew, "Does Public Service Motivation Affect the Behavior of Professionals?" paper presented at the International Public Service Motivation Research Conference, Bloomington, Indiana, June 7–9, 2009.

42. Stephanie Moulton and Mary K. Feeney, "Public Service in the Private Sector: Private Loan Originator Participation in a Public Mortgage Program," *Journal of Public Administration Research and Theory* 20 (February 2010) (http://jpart.oxfordjournals.org/content/21/3/547.full.pdf?keytype=ref&ijkey=uMZapE9WLkGFEks, pp. 1, 18, 19).

43. Sung Min Park and Jessica Word, "Motivated to Serve: Constructs and Consequences of Work Motivation for Public and Nonprofit Managers," paper presented at the International Public Service Motivation Research Conference, Bloomington, Indiana, June 7–9, 2009.

44. Bonnie J. Johnson, "City Planners, Professional Culture, and Public Service Motivation," paper presented at the International Public Service Motivation Research Conference, Bloomington, Indiana, June 7–9, 2009.

45. Wouter Vandenabeele and Steven Van de Walle, "International Differences in Public Service Motivation: Comparing Regions Across the World," in *Motivation in Public Management: The Call of Public Service*, edited by James L. Perry and Annie Hondeghem (Oxford University Press 2008), pp. 236, 66.

46. David J. Houston, "The Importance of Intrinsic and Extrinsic Motivators: Examining Attitudes of Government Workers in North America and Western Europe," paper presented at the International Public Service Motivation Research Conference, Bloomington, Indiana, June 7–9, 2009.

47. A. Chow and others, "Explaining the Behavior of Civil Servants: The Case of Hong Kong Firemen," paper presented at the International Public Service Motivation Research Conference, Bloomington, Indiana, June 7–9, 2009.

48. See Perry, Hondeghem, and Wise, "Revisiting the Motivational Bases of Public Service"; Perry and Wise, "Motivational Bases of Public Service."

49. James L. Perry, "Antecedents of Public Service Motivation," *Journal of Public Administration Research and Theory* 7 (April 1997): 181–97 (see 193).

50. Bradley E. Wright, "The Role of Work Context in Work Motivation: A Public Sector Application of Goal and Social Cognitive Theories," *Journal of Public Administration Research and Theory* 14 (January 2004): 59–78.

51. Leonard Bright, "Public Employees with High Levels of Public Service Motivation: Who Are They, Where Are They and What Do They Want?" *Review of Public Personnel Administration* 25 (June 2005): 138–55.

52. Emanuel Camilleri, "Toward Developing an Organizational Commitment: Public Service Motivation Model for the Maltese Public Service Employees," *Public Policy and Administration* 21 (Spring 2006): 63–83; Emanuel Camilleri, "Antecedents Affecting Public Service Motivation," *Personnel Review* 36, no. 3 (2007): 356–77; Emanuel Camilleri, "The Relationship between Personal Attributes, Organizational Politics, Public Service Motivation and Public Employee Performance," paper presented at the International Public Service Motivation Research Conference, Bloomington, Indiana, June 7–9, 2009.

53. Donald P. Moynihan and Sanjay K. Pandey, "The Role of Organizations in Fostering Public Service Motivation," *Public Administration Review* 67 (January 2007): 40–53.

54. Adam M. Grant, "Employees without a Cause: The Motivational Effects of Prosocial Impact in Public Service," *International Public Management Journal* 11, no. 1 (2008): 48–66 (see 48).

55. Craig Boardam and Eric Sundquist, "Toward Understanding Work Motivation, Worker Attitudes and the Perception of Effective Public Service," *American Review of Public Administration* 39 (September 2009): 519–35.

56. Chan Su Jung and Hal G. Rainey, "Organizational Goal Characteristics and Public Duty Motivation in U.S. Federal Agencies," paper presented at the International Public Service Motivation Research Conference, Bloomington, Indiana, June 7–9, 2009.

57. Jeffrey R. Paine, "Motivation to Serve the Public: Testing the Measures and Exploring the Antecedents in Local Government," paper presented at the International Public Service Motivation Research Conference, Bloomington, Indiana, June 7–9, 2009.

58. Simon Anderfuhren-Biget and others, "Motivating Employees of the Public Sector: Does Public Service Motivation Matter?" *International Public Management Journal* 13, no. 3 (2010): 213–46.

59. Yannis Georgellis and Vurain Tabvuma, "Does Public Service Motivation Adapt?" *Kyklos* 63 (May 2010): 176–91.

60. Perry, "Antecedents of Public Service Motivation."

61. Leisha DeHart-Davis, Justin Marlowe, and Sanjay K. Pandey, "Gender Dimensions of Public Service Motivation," *Public Administration Review* 66 (November–December 2006): 873–87.

62. Sangmook Kim, "Individual-Level Factors and Organizational Performance in Government Organizations," *Journal of Public Administration Research and Theory* 15 (April 2005): 245–61.

63. Camilleri, "Relationship between Personal Attributes, Organizational Politics, Public Service Motivation and Public Employee Performance."

64. Laura Langbein, "The Impact of Love and Money on Quitting in the Federal Government: Implications for Pay for Performance," paper presented at the International Public Service Motivation Research Conference, Bloomington, Indiana, June 7–9, 2009.

65. Leonard Bright, "Why Do Public Employees Desire Intrinsic Workplace Opportunities?" *Public Personnel Management* 38 (Fall 2009): 15–37 (see 30).

66. Ibid.

67. Robert K. Christensen and Steven W. Whiting, "The Role of Task Performance and Organizational Citizenship Behavior in Performance Appraisals across Sectors: Exploring the Role of Public Service Motivation," paper presented at the International Public Service Motivation Research Conference, Bloomington, Indiana, June 7–9, 2009, p. 13.

68. Jeffrey R. Paine, "Relating Public Service Motivation to Behavioral Outcomes among Local Elected Administrators," paper presented at the International Public Service Motivation Research Conference, Bloomington, Indiana, June 7–9, 2009.

69. Gene A. Brewer, "Building Social Capital: Civic Attitudes and Behavior of Public Servants," *Journal of Public Administration Research and Theory* 13 (January 2003): 5–26.

70. Francesco Paolo Cerase and Domenico Farinella, "Explorations in Public Service Motivation. The Case of the Italian Revenue Agency," paper presented at EGPA (European Group for Public Administration) 2006, Milan, September 6–9, 2006.

71. Leonard Bright, "Does Person–Organization Fit Mediate the Relationship between Public Service Motivation and the Job Performance of Public Employees?" *Review of Public Personnel Administration* 27 (December 2007): 361–79.

72. Edmund Stazyk, "Striking a Balance: The Role of Person-Organization Fit in Shaping Employee Job Satisfaction and Turnover Intentions in Local Government Employees," paper presented at the International Public Service Motivation Research Conference, Bloomington, Indiana, June 7–9, 2009.

73. Perry and others, "What Drives Morally Committed Citizens?"

74. Gerald T. Gabris and Trenton J. Davis, "Measuring Public Service Motivation in MPA Students: Does the Construct Influence Student Perceptions toward the Application of Management Techniques and Role Behavior in the Public Sector?" paper presented at the International Public Service Motivation Research Conference, Bloomington, Indiana, June 7–9, 2009, p. 2.

75. Donald P. Moynihan, Sanjay K. Pandey, and Bradley E. Wright, "Pulling the Levers: Leadership, Public Service Motivation and Mission Valence," paper presented at the International Public Service Motivation Research Conference, Bloomington, Indiana, June 7–9, 2009, p. 1.

76. Sung Min Park and Hal G. Rainey, "Leadership and Public Service Motivation in U.S. Federal Agencies," *International Public Management Journal* 11, no. 1 (2008): 109–42.

77. Jeannette Taylor, "Organizational Influences, Public Service Motivation and Work Outcomes: An Australian Study," *International Public Management Journal* 11, no. 1 (2008): 67–88.

78. Chih-Wei Hsieh and Kaifeng Yang, "Linking Public Service Motivation with Emotional Labor in Government: An Empirical Assessment," paper presented at the International Public Service Motivation Research Conference, Bloomington, Indiana, June 7–9, 2009.

79. Aleksey Kolpakov, "Developing a Cross-Cultural Framework for Public Service Motivation," paper presented at the International Public Service Motivation Research Conference, Bloomington, Indiana, June 7–9, 2009.

80. Paul R. Battaglio Jr., "Public Service Reform and Motivation: Evidence from an Employment At-Will Environment," *Review of Public Personnel Administration* 30 (September 2010): 341–63.

81. Laurie E. Paarlberg and Bob Lavigna, "Transformational Leadership and Public Service Motivation: Driving Individual and Organizational Performance," *Public Administration Review* 70 (September–October 2010): 710–18.

82. Antoinette Weibel, Katja Rost, and Margit Osterloh, "Pay for Performance in the Public Sector: Benefits and (Hidden) Costs," *Journal of Public Administration Research and Theory* 20 (April 2010): 387–412 (see 404).

83. Laurie E. Paarlberg, James L. Perry, and Annie Hondeghem, "From Theory to Practice: Strategies for Applying Public Service Motivation," in *Motivation in Public Management: The Call of Public Service*, edited by James L. Perry and Annie Hondeghem (Oxford University Press, 2008) pp. 268–93 (see 268).

84. Ibid.

85. James L. Perry, Debra Mesch, and Laurie E. Paarlberg, "Motivating Employees in a New Governance Era: The Performance Paradigm Revisited," *Public Administration Review* 66 (July–August 2006): 505–14.

86. James L. Perry, Trent A. Engbers, and So Yun Jun, "Back to the Future? Performance-Related Pay, Empirical Research, and the Perils of Persistence," *Public Administration Review* 69 (January–February 2009): 39–51.

87. Laurie E. Paarlberg and Bob Lavigna, "Using Research on Altruism, Prosocial Behavior and Public Service Behavior to Change How We Manage in Public Organizations," paper presented at the International Public Service Motivation Research Conference, Bloomington, Indiana, June 7–9, 2009.

88. Jeannette Taylor and Ranald Taylor, "Do Governments Pay Efficiency Wages? Evidence from a Selection of Countries," paper presented at the International Public Service Motivation Research Conference, Bloomington, Indiana, June 7–9, 2009.

89. Trui Steen and Mark Rutgers, "There Are Always Two Sides to the Coin: The Upshot of an Instrumental Approach towards Public Service Motivation and the Oath of Office," paper presented at the International Public Service Motivation Research Conference, Bloomington, Indiana, June 7–9, 2009.

90. Julian Le Grand, "Knights and Knaves Return: Public Service Motivation and the Delivery of Public Service," *International Public Management Journal* 13, no. 1 (2010): 56–71.

91. Josse Delfgaauw and Robert Dur, "Managerial Talent, Motivation, and Self-Selection into Public Management," *Journal of Public Economics* 94 (October 2010): 654–60 (see 658).

PART III

Leadership and Public Sector Reforms

CHRISTOPHER POLLITT

6 What Can We Learn from Thirty Years of Public Management Reform?

A fundamental point is that there are always at least three kinds of learning—and especially so in the case of public management reform. The first kind is simply (or not so simply) learning *what has happened*. The second is *unlearning*—that is, learning what errors there were in some of the views that one held oneself, or influential others held, in the past. We could call this correcting false impressions. The third kind of learning is *finding explanations*: identifying reasons and processes that help us understand *why* things happened as they did.

Public management reform is a difficult area for all three kinds of learning. It is not a scientific laboratory. It is a marketplace in which several powerful groups compete to tell their stories and sell their programs. Politicians are obviously one group—they want us (or the electorate) to believe that they can make things better, and that they have the right answers. In some ways contemporary politics in western Europe and North America has become "technical politics": less and less about launching ambitious new policies and more and more about presenting one's own party as better able to manage current problems than the opposition. Top civil servants are another group. They often have reform ideas of their own, and in any case they will be the ones required to lead the change, so they certainly have strong interests in getting their voices heard. Consultants are a third important group—much more important in some countries than in others, but a growing force in many.[1] In the early 2000s the U.K. government spent more on management consultants than did the private sector.[2] For consultancies, reforms mean more business and higher profits—they have a vested interest in ongoing change and the constant invention or reinvention of new reform "products." Academics (like me) are a fourth group—in most cases much less influential than the three groups just mentioned, but nevertheless having some importance in certain countries, such as the Netherlands and Sweden. Some academics act as advisers and some act as critics, both nationally and internationally, but either way they are one of the groups trying to establish their own interpretations and stories as the best ones.

Given such a crowded and competitive marketplace it is inevitable that some tall stories will be told. Some oversimplifications will be made. A good deal of special pleading is likely to occur. For example, students need to learn that most government reports on organizational reforms are not the unvarnished truth—rather they are often highly selective and optimistic versions of reality. Consequently, we—like our students—have a considerable task in front of us if we want to sort out what has really happened from what some self-interested party *says* has happened, or is about to happen.

Ten Key Observations

As space is limited I will now move straight to ten key observations about the character of public management reform (PMR) as we have experienced it since 1980:

1. *PMR has gone from being a dusty, technical backroom activity fifty years ago to being akin to a fashion accessory.* In some countries every political party now has to have a program for public service reform. "Better management" is seen as the answer to a much wider range of problems than used to be the case—it has become a policy in its own right. But we should not assume that PMR will remain an object of such political and media attention. What goes up can go down again, and in some countries there are signs of "reform fatigue."

2. *Alongside this shift has come a huge growth in the "reform industry."* There is now a considerable community that makes its living from promoting and advising on further reforms—especially the international management consultancies, but also academics, ex–public servants, and political advisers.[3] This creates something of a self-serving international community of "continuous reformers," focused partly on the now ubiquitous national reform units, aided and abetted by the World Bank, the Organization for Economic Cooperation and Development, the UN, and other international organizations. They are part of the competitive marketplace of ideas—an increasingly international marketplace—referred to in earlier.

3. *There also are more media than there were fifty years ago, and they are more aggressive and less respectful of governments than they were then.* Short-term

media and popular pressures on politicians to "do something" are even more acute than previously.[4] In the short term a reorganization may be the only thing, or at any rate the least difficult thing, that a minister can do, especially in the United Kingdom, where there are relatively few constraints on undertaking reorganization initiatives.[5] In some countries the media have actually become significant reform advocates themselves, calling for particular types of solutions and fiercely attacking types of reform they do not approve of.[6] In the United States, virulent attacks on anything that could be construed as strengthening the federal government have become almost routine among powerful right-wing media. In the United Kingdom, commentators in high-circulation newspapers and other media outlets have attacked the healthcare reforms proposed by the coalition government of David Cameron. Earlier, in 1991, various media outlets made merciless fun of Prime Minister John Major's Citizen's Charter.

4. *There is a semireligious quality to much reform thinking*, as has been pointed out by Christopher Hood, among others.[7] The amount of hard, attributable evidence we have that reforms are working—and *how* things work in particular contexts—is small in comparison to the claims that are frequently made. Reforms are often built more on faith and reputation than on proven past good works.[8] The field is prone to waves of fashion, as new theologies are spawned by individuals and groups anxious to make their reputations. One unfortunate consequence of this is that implementing a reform can become as much about getting a theologically correct interpretation as about solving the original problems the reform was meant to deal with.

5. *Often the central ideas of a new reform technique are good, but in the selling they become overblown and oversold.* Take, for example, Business Process Reengineering (BPR): the essential insight that processes are a useful unit of analysis was a powerful one, but look at the apocalyptic claims then made in the best-selling *Re-engineering the Corporation.*[9] This book envisaged BPR as *the* vital move in strengthening American corporations against foreign competition, and as something that would simply sweep away past ways of doing things, which were said to be of no interest to the re-engineer. It also claimed—with scant supporting analysis—that BPR was as necessary for government as for private companies. Another example: Total Quality Management (TQM) was the important idea that quality should ultimately be decided by consumers rather than producers, but in some hands it became a doctrine that everything in the organization had to be uprooted and changed. "Total"became, in effect, "Totalitarian."[10]

6. *Contextual factors are still regularly and seriously underestimated (especially culture, time, place, and task).* Too many politicians, consultants, and

even academics are looking for the "next big thing," instead of looking for particular solutions to particular, well-researched problems in specific contexts. So we have had "partnerships," "network approaches," "lean," "benchmarking," "performance contracting," "relational contracting," "collaborative management," and a host of other techniques and approaches, each of which may work under certain circumstances but not under others.

7. *There are huge differences between countries and even between sectors.* These differences are not all problems to be eliminated—they represent different histories, different choices, different priorities. The idea that everyone will or should converge on one particular model of "good governance" or one set of "best practices" is both wrong and dangerous.[11] The story that all public sectors used to be large traditional bureaucracies, then they were all swept by the wave of New Public Management, and now they are all shifting to regimes of New Public Governance, is actually a fairy tale.[12] It was never like that.[13]

8. *There is an unfortunate tendency to believe that ideas for reform will be found outside, not inside, one's organization.* Too many people believe that the answer is to bring in experts and "best practice" from somewhere "out there." But what is "enlightened practice" for another organization may well not be "best practice" for one's own.[14] Indeed, the best-practice approach itself "can seldom claim to produce the consummate causal understandings necessary to justify its application in other settings, particularly where variables omitted from the research may be influential."[15] It stands to reason that often the people who know best how to improve an organization are already in that organization. They are the ones who need to be identified and listened to.

9. *Exporting and importing management reforms between countries requires a subtle and complex process of translation.* One is not taking some standardized device and simply plugging it into another socket. Devices (the "plugs") are not standardized. Fierce debates rage over just what TQM or benchmarking or "evidence-based policymaking" *is*. Reforms are never just neutral technical instruments. Neither are the contexts ("sockets") standard. So what may have worked well in one country (or even sector) may work badly or not at all in another.[16] So we need to look closely at the context: What is the local organizational culture? Has this organization had any experience with this kind of reform before? Who are the opinion makers in this organization? What is the current state of morale? Who are the key external stakeholders? What has been the recent history?

10. *The explanation for why things happened (or didn't happen) is usually complex, and is likely to evolve over time.* We need to dig into the particulars to find out why a particular program or technique worked in this place and

time, but not in that one.[17] Indeed, time itself is often an important factor—reforms are frequently changed or dropped before enough time has passed to get a clear and stable view of the reforms' longer-term benefits and limitations. The hectic pace of modern politics, fueled by the short attention span of the mass media, tends to amplify this volatility. Often ideas go round in circles, with the same basic idea coming back a few years or even decades later, now being presented under a new, fashionable name.[18] Often the proponents don't even realize that it has been tried before—organizational memories have in some ways been getting shorter. For example, we could ask how far governments currently engaged in large reductions in public spending have learned from previous exercises in making big spending cuts.[19] All this is regrettable, because some reforms take three, five, or even ten years to reach their full potential, and the past is full of interesting insights about what may happen if one does X or Y.[20]

So What Can We Learn?

What can be learned as we look back on thirty years or more of PMR in the developed countries? Seven main lessons are proposed:

1. Distrust anyone who claims to have the answer before there has been a detailed diagnosis of the particular problems of the particular organization. In particular, distrust those who argue that X must be implemented because "everyone else" is doing X. Actually, there are no universal solutions because there are no universal problems. Evidence-based problem solving means just that—you cannot solve your problems until you have gathered your evidence, evidence that should be specific to your organization and its problems, or to broadly similar organizations or problems.

2. If a reform is thrust upon you from above, try hard to adapt it to fit the particular history, culture, and task of your organization.

3. Maximize your use of the knowledge and wisdom, both formal and tacit, that already exist within your organization. Do this even if it is held by people who appear to be resistors or opponents.

4. If you use external consultants, ensure that they serve your purposes and do not begin to act like Gods (or, worse still, managers!). Remember, you will soon have to do without them.

5. Work as hard as you can to secure a realistic time frame for reform. Try to avoid having a change process jammed into a few weeks or months, so that everyone is rushed and under pressure. Ensure continuous monitoring but try to avoid premature evaluation.

6. Seize opportunities, "windows," chances, whenever they present themselves. Many successful reforms, big and small, exist only because reform leaders have jumped through "windows of opportunity."

7. Expect some failures. Bounce back from the small ones and take the big ones as indications that either your original diagnosis or your prescription was faulty.

Notes

1. Denis Saint Martin, "Management Consultancy," in *The Oxford Handbook of Public Management,* edited by Ewan Ferlie, Laurence E. Lynn Jr., and Christopher Pollitt (Oxford University Press, 2005), pp. 671–94.

2. National Audit Office, *Central Government's Use of Consultants*, reported by the Comptroller and Auditor General, HC 128, Session 2006–2007, December 15, 2006 (London: Her Majesty's Stationery Office).

3. Kerstin Sahlin-Andersson and Lars Engwall, *The Expansion of Management Knowledge: Carriers, Flows and Sources* (Stanford, Calif.: Stanford Business Books, 2002); Saint Martin, "Management Consultancy."

4. Donald F. Kettl, Christopher Pollitt, and James H. Svara, "Towards a Danish Concept of Public Governance: An International Perspective," Report to the Danish Forum for Top Executive Management (Copenhagen: Forum for Public Service, 2004).

5. Christopher Pollitt, "New Labour's Re-disorganization: Hyper-Modernism and the Costs of Reform—A Cautionary Tale," *Public Management Review* 9 (December 2007): 529–43.

6. B. Jacobsson and Göran Sundström, "Between Autonomy and Control: Transformation of the Swedish Administrative Model," in *Change and Continuity in Public Sector Organizations*, edited by Paul G. Roness and Harald Saetren (Bergen, Norway: Fagbokforlaget, 2009), pp. 103–26.

7. Christopher Hood, "Public Management: The Word, the Movement, the Science," in *The Oxford Handbook of Public Management*, edited by Ewan Ferlie, Laurence E. Lynn Jr., and Christopher Pollitt (Oxford University Press, 2005), pp. 7–26.

8. Christopher Pollitt, "Justification by Works or by Faith? Evaluating the New Public Management," *Evaluation* 1 (July 1995): 133–54.

9. Michael Hammer and James Champy, *Reengineering the Corporation: A Manifesto for a Business Revolution*, rev. ed. (New York: Harper Business Essentials, 1995).

10. Robert P. McGowan, "Total Quality Management: Lessons from Business and Government," *Public Productivity and Management Review* 18 (Summer 1995): 321–31; Mark J. Zbaracki, "The Rhetoric and Reality of Total Quality Management," *Administrative Science Quarterly* 43 (September 1998): 602–36.

11. Matt Andrews, "Good Government Means Different Things in Different Countries," *Governance* 23 (January 2010): 7–35; Annie Bartoli, "The Study of Public Management in France: la spécificité du modèle français d'administration," in *The Study*

of Public Management in Europe and the US: A Comparative Analysis of National Distinctiveness, edited by Walter Kickert (London and New York: Routledge, 2008), pp. 14–41; Martin Painter and B. Guy Peters, *Tradition and Public Administration* (Basingstoke, UK: Palgrave Macmillan, 2010); Christopher Pollitt, "Simply the Best? The International Benchmarking of Reform and Good Governance," in *Comparative Administrative Change and Reform: Lessons Learned* (festschrift for Guy B. Peters), edited by Jon Pierre and Patricia W. Ingraham (McGill-Queens University Press, 2010), pp. 91–113.

12. Stephen P. Osborne, *The New Public Governance: Emerging Perspectives on The Theory and Practice of Public Governance* (London and New York: Routledge, 2010).

13. Walter Kickert, ed., *The Study of Public Management in Europe and the US: A Comparative Analysis of National Distinctiveness* (London and New York: Routledge, 2008); Laurence E. Lynn Jr., *Public Management: Old and New* (New York and London: Routledge, 2006); Edoardo Ongaro, *Public Management Reform and Modernization: Trajectories of Administrative Change in Italy, France, Greece, Portugal and Spain* (Cheltenham, UK, and Northampton, Mass.: Edward Elgar, 2009); Christopher Pollitt, Sandra Van Thiel, and Vincent Homburg, *New Public Management in Europe: Adaptations and Alternatives* (Basingstoke, UK: Palgrave Macmillan, 2007); Christopher Pollitt and Geert Bouckaert, *Public Management Reform: A Comparative Analysis—NPM, Governance and the Neo-Weberian State*, 3rd ed. (Oxford University Press, 2011).

14. Laurence E. Lynn Jr., Carolyn J. Heinrich, and Carolyn J. Hill, *Improving Governance: A New Logic for Empirical Research* (Georgetown University Press, 2001).

15. Ibid., p. 156.

16. Christopher Pollitt and Geert Bouckaert, *Continuity and Change in Public Policy and Management* (Cheltenham, UK: Edward Elgar, 2009); Pollitt and Bouckaert, *Public Management Reform*; Lourdes Torres and Vincente Pina, "Reshaping Public Administration: The Spanish Experience Compared to the UK," *Public Administration* 82, no. 2 (2004): 445–64.

17. Ray Pawson and Nick Tilley, *Realistic Evaluation* (London: Sage, 1997).

18. Paul C. Light, *The Tides of Reform: Making Government Work, 1945–1995* (Yale University Press, 1997); Christopher Pollitt, *Time, Policy, Management: Governing with the Past* (Oxford University Press, 2008).

19. Christopher Pollitt, "Cuts and Reforms: Public Services as We Move into a New Era," *Society and Economy: Journal of the Corvinus University of Budapest* 32, no. 1 (2010): 17–31.

20. Ibid., pp. 16, 18.

MONTGOMERY VAN WART

7 *Leadership Competencies and Their Relevance to Italian Government Reform*

Which leadership competencies are related to government reform? Since there are different types of reform, what are the specific competencies related to those distinct reform types? [1] What types of reform are currently being instituted in Italy, through both the historic Legislative Decree 150/2009 and related legislative enactments, and how do they relate to the practical competencies needed by Italian administrators?

There are literally hundreds of theories that explain leadership.[2] Some theories are meant to have universal applicability while others are intended to explain leadership in a vast array of special circumstances. Theories generally try to use as few concepts as possible to explain as much of a phenomenon as possible. This elegance is useful for teaching and scientific purposes but has made transference to the organizational world problematic.[3] Even though the organizational world has found these theoretical perspectives useful, it has nonetheless largely insisted on focusing on *competency-based approaches* to leadership.[4] Competencies are the concrete traits, skills, and behaviors that are the building blocks of effective management and leadership.[5] Examples include energy, communication, delegation, motivation, and environmental scanning. Competency-based approaches make sure that leadership approaches can be translated into concrete strategic purposes through systems design (position descriptions, performance evaluations, and so forth), training, and system evaluation.[6]

One useful and well-supported leadership theory regarding change is called the Full Range Leadership Theory, developed by Bernard Bass.[7] Like many theories, it strives for elegance by proposing as few elements as possible. Sadly, many of the global concepts in the Full Range Leadership Theory, such as management by exception and contingent reward, have little meaning to frontline leaders. Like many macro-level theories, it needs to be translated into specific terms that, first, are meaningful and, second, can be applied by operational leaders.

In this chapter I will first briefly describe a competency framework consistent with the worldwide literature on leadership. The framework provides a relatively comprehensive and cohesively organized set of micro-level concepts to be used in the wide variety of situations with which managers and leaders must cope and grapple. The framework can be used to translate different *theories* into universally understood concepts. However, as an overall *framework* it does not propose how leaders should act in specific situations or prescribe which competencies to emphasize on a daily, weekly, or yearly cycle of activities. Next, the chapter will introduce Bernard Bass's theory of transformational change. This well-regarded theory is strong in providing an abstract notion of the global elements necessary for transformational change but is weak in providing the related competency requirements for success. The chapter then identifies the relevant competencies necessary in order to effectively provide the leadership styles recommended by Bass. Finally, the chapter ends with a brief discussion of the types of reform legislatively enacted by the Italian government recently, specifically through Legislative Decree 150/2009 but also some of the implications of related administrative initiatives that are both complementary to 150/2009 because they are largely aimed at internal efficiency and overall effectiveness, as well as some that are possibly countervailing because they are aimed at cost cutting regardless of performance issues. It divides the reform initiatives into four fundamental types, using the analysis of Paul Light. The chapter concludes with a discussion of these types of leadership and their related competencies that should be emphasized in order to achieve the different types of reform proposed.

For simplicity, leadership will generally be treated as if it were the primary province of the formal leader with executive or managerial responsibilities. However, leadership is as much a process and community activity as an executive or heroic activity, and with more space, such additional levels of analysis could complement the discussion.[8] Also, although the elements of leadership in various domains such as political, social movement, and organizational leadership have common elements, they differ markedly in the types of situations where they can effectively be applied. The focus here is on organizational settings, in particular on those administrative settings in government agencies.[9]

A Comprehensive Leadership Framework: The Leadership Action Cycle

Leadership involves, among other things, an array of assessment skills, a series of characteristics (traits and skills) that the leader brings to a leadership setting, and a wide variety of behavioral competencies.[10] As study after study has indicated, standard management in which systems changes are minimal still requires a tremendous repertoire of skills, typically ranging from ingrained personal attributes to behaviors that contribute to the effectiveness of task, people, and organizational functions.[11] Managing change dramatically compounds these requirements.[12] Furthermore, all managers tend to be bombarded with interruptions, problems, and conflicting demands.[13] For our discussion we can define leaders as managers who must also assist their organization—internally and externally—to adapt to the environment, adjust the organizational culture, and refine and institutionalize the appropriate changes. This sets up a daunting task for leaders because of the variety of challenges that leaders face over relatively short periods of time. Thus, although leaders do not need all significant competencies all of the time, it is amazing how many they do need on occasion, and how important even rarely used competencies can be in specific situations. The study of major leadership competencies, then, provides not only a useful tool in translating different situational needs but also acts as a developmental tool, given the inevitable need for nearly all competencies over time.

The model reviewed here has five major functional areas. The first is leader assessment. Leaders must be able to assess the dynamics occurring in the organization, the external environment, and the constraints that they face in carrying out routine functions and nonroutine changes. How well do followers understand their roles? Do they have all the necessary skills, and are they motivated to work hard? Are organizational processes supportive of productivity, teamwork, and morale? Is the organization creative and innovative enough to stay abreast of contemporary practice? Does the organization have an eye to the opportunities and threats occurring outside its boundaries, and is it able to adapt quickly and flexibly? In addition, leaders must know their constraints: those stemming from the law, from their position, from lack of resources, and from their own leadership limitations. They must also know how to push these bounds back (with the exception of law, in the public sector), when necessary over time, in order to meet the challenges that leaders face. Finally, in conducting this ongoing assessment, leaders must be able to set goals and priorities for themselves and for their organizations.

Leaders come to various situations in different stages of readiness. Leader characteristics are a large part of that readiness. Although no absolute predetermined set of characteristics is necessary in all leadership situations, certain traits and skills tend to be significantly more important than others. Traits are characteristics that are primarily inherent and become a part of one's personality, whereas skills are characteristics that are primarily learned. This is not to say that traits cannot be enhanced, especially through training or indoctrination; nor is it to say that some people do not have a natural gift for some skills. For example, some leaders tend to be perceived as self-confident and this tends to be an innate personality characteristic; nonetheless, those with excellent technical training and substantial experience become far more self-confident than they would otherwise be. The traits that are commonly held to be most useful to leaders in a variety of situations include self-confidence, decisiveness, resilience, energy, need for achievement, willingness to assume responsibility, flexibility, service motivation, personal integrity, and emotional maturity. Skills that researchers have found are of the highest utility for leaders are communication skills, social skills, influence and negotiation skills, analytical skills, technical skills, and the skill of continual learning.

Leaders also bring a set of leadership "styles" to situations. A style can be thought of as the dominant pattern of behavior for a leader in a particular position. Rather than referring to all aspects of leadership, style normally refers to a pattern of behaviors to deal with followers and the external environment in different situations. Like leadership characteristics, styles are antecedent to leadership in that they are prior aspects of the leader's repertoire and to some degree are an explicit method of accomplishing specific goals. Yet styles, like leadership characteristics, are expressed through specific actions that leaders take in doing their jobs. Some leaders have only a few styles in their repertoire, while others have many that they can use in various situations. Of course, just because a leader uses a particular style does not mean that he or she uses the style effectively or in the correct situations. Common midlevel style patterns identified by researchers include laissez-faire, directive, supportive, participative, delegative, achievement-oriented, inspirational, strategic, collaborative, and combinations of these styles executed simultaneously. (Note that Bass's theory proposes two macro-level style types, which will be discussed later.)

Leaders act. These actions or behaviors can be thought of as occurring in three domains. First, leaders have tasks to accomplish. Their organization, division, or unit has work that it must produce, no matter whether it is an actual physical product or a relatively nebulous service. Some of the standard tasks of leaders include monitoring and assessing work, operations planning, clarifying roles, informing, delegating, problem solving, and managing innovation. Second, leaders have followers, and it is the followers who actually accomplish the mission of the organization. Thus, good leaders never lose sight of the fact that they accomplish their goals through and—just as important— with others. Common people-oriented behaviors include consulting, organizing personnel, developing staff, motivating, managing teams and team building, managing personnel conflicts, and managing personnel change. Finally, leaders are expected to know more than how to design and coordinate work processes; they are expected to know how the product of these efforts will integrate and compare with those of other organizations and external entities. If production and people constitute the mission of leadership, then organizational alignment and adaptability constitute the vision of leadership. Today more than ever, good leaders must not only be competent in their profession and skillful with people, they must also have well-articulated visions that are compelling to a wide variety of constituencies. Commonly accepted organizational behaviors include scanning the environment, strategic planning, articulating the mission and vision, networking, performing general management functions, decisionmaking, and managing organizational change.

Finally, leaders must be able to evaluate how they have done. This is an ongoing and complex activity. It requires balancing numerous competing interests. It also requires adjusting plans and priorities as new operational problems occur, some problems are resolved, and, less frequently but very critically, new opportunities and threats materialize suddenly. It requires examination of one's own performance as well as the performance of the organization. Figure 7-1 identifies the general causal relationship of these elements. Putting aside unusual situations, such as unexpected crises, the model essentially recommends: think about your organization in its environment first (along with your own constraints) in order to set goals, know your traits and skills well enough so that you capitalize on your strengths and improve or mitigate your critical weaknesses, know your style preference but be as flexible as possible, balance your actions across domains of responsibility according to your assessment, and evaluate what you and your organization have done.

Having surveyed the competencies generally found to be the most universal for organizational leaders in a variety of situations, we will now turn to a particular model of transformational leadership. It is a model of particular usefulness in times of change and reform, such as is currently confronting the Italian government.

An Overview of Bass's Theory of Transformational Leadership

Bass provides a solid theoretical framework with his Full Range Leadership Theory. Bass conceives leadership as a single continuum progressing from nonleadership to transactional leadership to transformational leadership.[14] Nonleadership provides haphazard results at best; transactional leadership provides conventional results; but transformational leadership can provide, as his book title indicates, "performance beyond expectations." He theorizes leadership as having an additive nature in general. However, it is important to keep in mind that Bass only uses a positive notion of transformational leadership, so his theory explains the phenomenon when leaders are successful. Here we will focus on this positive supposition, while bearing in mind, however, that it is simplistic because some technically "successful" transformational leaders are nonetheless destructive in terms of the diminished legacy that they bequeath to their organizations.

Bass asserts that transformational leadership is a widespread phenomenon across levels of management, types of organizations, and around the world. It is therefore a universal theory without contingency factors. Like other transformational theories, it does assume that both the quality of the transformational factors executed and the number of styles and factors used will have a moderating effect on the performance. That is, there is a substantial additive effect of the styles.

The laissez-faire approach, starting with an essentially nonleadership style, takes a hands-off approach to leadership. Laissez-faire leaders are largely uninvolved in operations, are sloppy about details, resistant to participation in problem solving, lax in decision making, negligent in providing feedback, and indifferent to subordinates' needs. This is the negative aspect of laissez-faire leadership, but it should be noted that postponing treatment of issues can be strategic and therefore positive also, depending on the situation.[15] Management-by-exception is a style that uses mistakes or deviations from standards as corrective opportunities and that emphasizes the importance of negative feedback. In the more lax or passive form of management-by-exception, the manager intervenes or takes corrective action only after a mistake has been made or a problem has become obvious. A manager with an active management-by-exception style simply indicates that he or she is monitoring more closely and intervening before problems can go outside the unit. Neither of these styles is necessarily bad in and of itself. However, Bass holds that it is generally an inferior style that should be used sparingly. Extensive use of this style creates fear and intimidation and discourages initiative and creativity.

Figure 7-1. *The Leadership Action Cycle*

LEADER ASSESSMENT

Organization and environment
1. Task skills
2. Role clarity
3. Innovation and creativity
4. Resources and support services
5. Subordinate effort
6. Cohesiveness and cooperation
7. Organization of work and performance strategies
8. External coordination and adaptability

Constraints
1. Legal and contractual constraints
2. Limitations of position power
3. Availability of resources
4. Limits of leadership abilities

Leader priorities
1. Technical performance
2. Follower development
3. Organizational alignment
4. Service and ethical focus
5. Balance and integration of foci

LEADER CHARACTERISTICS

Traits
1. Self-confidence
2. Decisiveness
3. Resilience
4. Energy
5. Need for achievement
6. Willingness to assume responsibility
7. Flexibility
8. Service motivation
9. Personal integrity
10. Emotional maturity

Skills
1. Communication
2. Social skills
3. Influencing and negotiating
4. Analytic skills
5. Technical skills
6. Continual learning

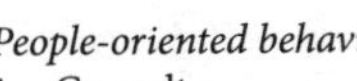
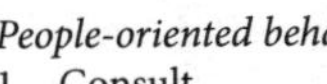

LEADER STYLES

1. Laissez-faire
3. Supportive
4. Participative
5. Delegative
6. Achievement-oriented
7. Inspirational
8. Strategic
9. Collaborative
10. Combined

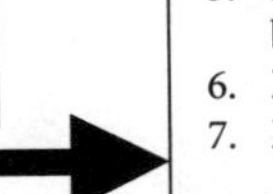

LEADER BEHAVIORS

Task-oriented behaviors
1. Monitor and assess work
2. Operations planning
3. Clarify roles
4. Inform
5. Delegate
6. Problem solving
7. Manage innovation and creativity

People-oriented behaviors
1. Consult
2. Plan and organize personnel
3. Develop staff
4. Motivate
5. Manage teams and team building
6. Manage personnel conflict
7. Manage personnel change

Organizational behaviors
1. Scan the environment
2. Strategic planning
3. Articulate the mission and vision
4. Network and partner
5. Perform general manage-ment functions
6. Decisionmaking
7. Manage organizational change

LEADER EVALUATION AND DEVELOPMENT

Development
1. Self-study
2. Experience
3. Education

Evaluation
1. Technical performance
2. Follower performance
3. Organizational alignment
4. Service mentality and ethical focus

Source: Author.

The more progressive and positive portion of transactional leadership is contingent reward. Managers using contingent reward find out what employees value and vary the incentives that they offer accordingly. An employee willing to take on one assignment may be released from another. A high-performance employee may get a large raise or a promotion. Generally such leadership is at its best when the work and incentives are negotiated and mutually agreed upon in advance. Although contingent reward is a fundamental part of most organizational systems and represents a practical reality—we expect rewards for hard work—it does have its weaknesses. First, used exclusively, contingent reward systems can easily lead to extensive tit-for-tat systems where only what is specifically rewarded gets done. Second, contingent rewards are generally set up as individual reward systems and therefore do not directly account for group achievements. Transformations are inevitably team, organization, or systems achievements. Furthermore, an exclusive reliance on contingent rewards may leave many, perhaps most, managers and executives with few leadership options when resources are extremely scarce or diminishing but the organizational needs are critical or increasing.

One of the four factors designated as transformational by Bass and others in the transformational school is called "individualized consideration." It is very similar to the supportive roles proposed in transactional theories. It refers to coaching, professional and personal support, individualized treatment based on specific needs, increased delegation as employees mature professionally, and so forth. In short, it can be summarized as being based on respect and empathy.

Bass calls the next factor or style "idealized influence," which is very similar to the concept of charisma. Those who exhibit idealized influence function as powerful role models for their followers. Followers identify with leader goals and emulate leaders' actions. This requires a perception by followers of a high level of integrity and wisdom.

"Intellectual stimulation" is the factor of leadership that encourages people to create new opportunities, to solve problems in new ways, and to envision a different future. Not only does it foster intellectual flexibility in followers, it also requires the ability to reexamine competing values. This style emphasizes techniques such as information sharing, brainstorming, vision articulation, and employee development targeted at effectuating specific organizational improvements. These types of leaders are often thought of as idea people or visionaries.

The final factor in Bass's taxonomy is "inspirational motivation"—in a sense, the most critical element of a transformational style. When leaders successfully use inspirational motivation, their followers are able to transcend their self-interests long enough to become passionate about organizational pride, group goals, and group achievements. Through enhanced "team spirit," leaders are able to motivate followers to pursue higher standards or to make sacrifices, without reliance on extrinsic incentives. Although the greater good is expected to redound to followers at some point in the future, there is generally not an exact commitment or transaction contract because of the uncertainty or abstractness of the goals.

All four transformational elements are generally present in concert during successful change initiatives, but that is not to say that the leader must supply all of them. Colleagues may supply their own consideration; low-key trust may successfully substitute for bold charisma; young, highly motivated professionals in the group may provide the intellectual stimulation; and inspirational motivation may be largely the result of a rich and proud tradition as well as a professional indoctrination instilling strong ethical values. The major elements of the two macro-level styles, transactional and transformational leadership, are summarized in figure 7-2.

Of all the transformational theories, Bass's is the most highly researched, and it has been given a good deal of positive support.[16] His additive approach is intuitively appealing as well as relatively elegant, considering the large number of styles that it incorporates. Further, one senses that Bass's approach builds on earlier transactional theory, even though the earlier theory and concepts are somewhat minimized. In terms of weaknesses, one of the most obvious is its universality, which implies that transformational leadership is better in all leadership levels and situations. This would seem to be contradictory to the reality experienced by many leaders, especially those working at ground-level operational levels. Second, the overlap and lack of clarity of the transformational concepts are problematic. Part of the problem is structural, however, because higher-level human motivations are abstract and are related in extraordinarily complex ways. Additionally, the nomenclature of the concepts is not always easy to understand and remember. Even though his transformational factors have the mnemonic of all starting with *i*, differences between concepts such as those between individualized consideration and idealized influence have to be explained and memorized.

Articulating Bass's Theory in Competency Terms

Bass's theory, understandably, emphasizes transformational elements at the expense of transactional elements. Although studies indicate that employees consider transactional styles only slightly less important than transformational styles in general, Bass's theory provides relatively little specificity at a concrete

Figure 7-2. *Bernard Bass's Full-Range Leadership Theory*

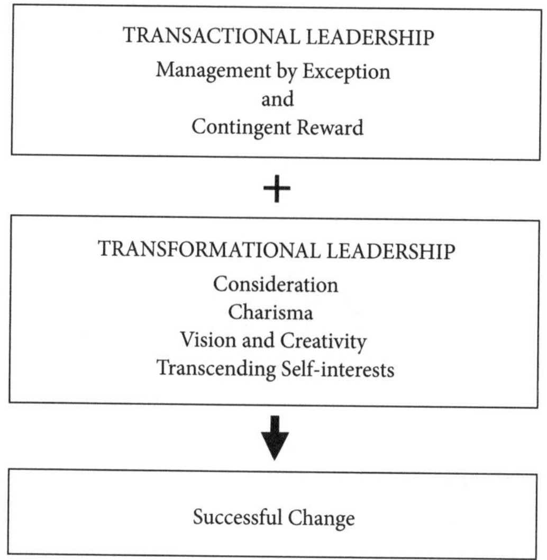

Source: Author.

competency level[17] For the purpose of this study, we will combine management by exception and management by contingent reward into a single style. What types of traits and skills do transactional leaders need? Some of the more obvious traits and skills include being communicative, analytic, and technical. The behaviors emphasized would primarily be found in the task domain: monitoring and assessing work, operations planning, delegation, performing general management functions, and clarifying roles. The styles most commonly used would be laissez-faire, directive, delegative, and achievement-oriented.

The Full Range Leadership Theory details the macro-level elements for successful transformation much more fully than the transaction elements, and indeed, the research supports the idea that change is exceedingly difficult to design, execute, and institutionalize.

The first element in Bass's model is (individualized) consideration. Followers will be distrustful and unmotivated if they feel that their leader does not care about their well-being. In terms of our competency taxonomy, the trait that lends itself to feeling and showing consideration is a service motivation toward employees and clients. The types of behaviors that exhibit consideration are informing, consulting, planning and organizing personnel, and developing staff. The predominant leader style is a supportive one focused on listening, helping, and empowering followers.

The second element is transcending self-interests ("inspirational motivation"). Leadership must get individuals and groups to let go of their short-term personal priorities and selfish preferences in order to achieve long-term group success that ultimately cascades opportunities back to the individuals involved. Personal integrity and emotional maturity are key traits if the requisite trust is to be developed. Behaviors that facilitate the group to transcend its self-interests include motivation, team building, managing personnel conflict, managing personnel change, and networking and partnering. Participative and collaborative leadership styles are necessary.

The third element in Bass's transformational leadership style is vision and creativity ("intellectual stimulation"). Leaders need to know in what direction the organization needs to go, and how to get there. Vision is not just created by the leader, but is the combined effort of the leader and followers in a synergetic relationship. The traits and skills that reflect vision and creativity include flexibility and continual learning. The behaviors include problem solving, managing innovation and creativity, scanning the environment, strategic planning, decisionmaking, and managing organizational change. The predominant leadership style is strategic.

The fourth element in Bass's transformational leadership style is charisma ("individualized influence"). At a minimum, leaders need to be likable and able to interact competently with followers and external stakeholders. Ideally, of course, leaders are inspiring and praiseworthy and have superb social graces. The types of traits and skills commonly associated with this element are self-confidence, decisiveness, resilience, energy, need for achievement, willingness to assume responsibility, social skills, and influencing and negotiating skills. The behavior most associated with charisma is articulating the mission and vision. The specific leadership style most connected to charisma is an inspirational style. Figure 7-3 relates these competencies to Bass's model.

Dissecting Italian Reform According to Light's Types of Reform

We have already discussed the fact that leaders must assess the situation they must deal with and act accordingly, using the appropriate traits, skills, and behaviors to execute appropriate leadership styles. We have examined the competencies emphasized in a change-oriented style. Is it possible to define the type of change in the Italian administrative context, and in this way define the major elements and concrete competencies even more specifically? To look at this question, we will first use Paul Light's well-known analysis of reform by types to better understand how narrow or broad the Italian reform effort is. Next, we will superimpose the legislative mandates of Legislative

Figure 7-3. *Bernard Bass's Full-Range Leadership Theory with Competencies*

TRANSACTIONAL LEADERSHIP

Management by Exception and Contingent Reward

Traits and skills: Communication, technical skills, analytic skills

Behaviors: Monitor and assess work, operations planning, clarify roles, delegate, perform general management functions

TRANSFORMATIONAL LEADERSHIP

Consideration

Traits and skills: Service motivation

Behaviors: Inform, consult, plan and organize personnel, develop staff

Charisma

Traits and skills: Self-confidence, decisiveness, resilience, energy, need for achievement, willingness to assume responsibility, social skills, influencing and negotiating

Behaviors: Articulate the mission and vision

Vision and Creativity

Traits and skills: Flexibility, continual learning

Behaviors: Problem solving, manage innovation and creativity, scan the environment, strategic planning, decisionmaking, manage organizational change

Transcending Self-interests

Traits and skills: Personal integrity, emotional maturity

Behaviors: Motivate, manage teams and team building, manage personnel conflict, manage personnel change, network and partner

Successful Change

Source: Bernard M. Bass, *The Bass Handbook of Leadership: Theory, Research, and Managerial Applications* (New York: Free Press, 2008).

Decree 150, of March 4, 2009, onto that analysis. Finally, we will make some general observations about the status of Italian reform in the two years since Legislative Decree 150/2009.

Light points out that reform can accomplish four very different purposes. First, some reform is intended to make organizational processes as *efficient* as possible.[18] For example, a personnel-intensive process might be reengineered to involve fewer steps and take advantage of new technology. Second, some reform is intended to make organizational structures, functions, and responsibilities as *economical* yet as functionally complete as possible. Examples of such reforms are when two agencies are merged to reduce overhead, when a mandate is removed from an agency, or when regulatory reductions allow for more timely responses, and as a result consume less resources. Some examples of economical reform mean providing a missing service that is critical to the success of the agency's mission. A third type of reform is that whose aim is to enhance *accountability*, what Light calls the "watchful eye." Are appropriate checks and balances in place, is due process followed, and is the organization's mission protected from individual and group distortions or manipulations? All of these three types of reforms rely heavily on transactional leadership in terms of technical skills, analyzing accomplishing needed tasks, planning operations, directing the changes, and communicating expectations and changes. Achievement-oriented leaders must pursue the goals of efficiency, economy, and accountability.

To the degree that the reforms involve change, transformational leadership, though significantly less emphasized, nevertheless is critical for high levels of success. It does not matter whether the type of change is process change, attitude change, or change in organizational missions and culture. A mere transactional leadership style is unlikely to be successful for a number of reasons. To begin with, followers must feel that they are important and have been considered, even when they are being required to do more, are being required to do new things, and are being held more accountable. Also, because change generally requires giving up comfortable habits and often involves considerable sacrifice, the transcendence of self-interests turns change from being a burden and hardship to being an adventure and privilege. Change rarely can succeed by means of cookie-cutter solutions; rather, change requires flexibility, continual learning, problem solving, strategic planning, and environmental scanning, which involve the vision and creativity subset of transformational change. Finally, change is nerve-wracking, exhausting, and confusing. Successful change efforts need leaders who are self-confident, resilient, and energetic, and who have the social and influence skills to articulate appealing visions and inspire others to follow.

The fourth type of reform that Paul Light discusses consists of providing management with the flexibility to *manage creatively* and to incentivize the organization to be excellent in service and forward-thinking in vision. Light echoes Tom Peters in calling this liberation management.[19] Liberation management involves employee empowerment, managerial innovation, and appropriate experimentation and risk taking. Liberation management reverses

Figure 7-4. *Paul Light's Four Types of Reform*

1. Efficiency (scientific management): Focuses on expertise and technical improvements
2. Economy (war on waste): Focuses on doing the right thing and making sure that the right thing is done through inspections and audits
3. Accountability (watchful eye): Ensures due process is in place for employees and the public
4. Liberation Management (higher performance): Focuses on outcomes, new ways of doing things, and managerial flexibility

Source: Paul C. Light, *The Tides of Reform: Making Government Work, 1945–1995* (Yale University Press, 1997).

the emphases of transactional and transformational leadership. Transformational leadership skills are most important for liberated managers. Liberating managers encourages radical change rather than minor improvement, inspiration over compliance, internal evolution to meet external forces rather than external forces mandating internal change. Yet, as Bass's theory suggests, liberated managers had better avoid totally neglecting transactional leadership. Technical competence, good analysis, careful monitoring, solid operations planning, and basic general management functions can never be completely overlooked. Light's four types of reform are summarized in figure 7-4.

Narrower reform agendas can involve just one of these types of reform. Larger reform efforts can address several or even all of these reform types. Some reform types go together relatively easily such as efficiency and economy. When changing an organizational structure, why not simultaneously streamline some outdated processes? Some reform types produce greater tensions as a result of trying to achieve competing goals. Both providing greater accountability in terms of more checks and balances and liberating management from constraints to be more creative can potentially be inconsistent. Of course, well-structured liberation management should change the emphasis on the types of accountability so that accountability is not reduced, but simply restructured.

Earlier reforms such as those implemented in 1993 and 1998 established a framework of managing civil servants through collective bargaining, but analysts agree that the reform generally led to higher costs without any improvement of services.[20] The managerial controls provided to tackle the out-of-control collective bargaining process in Legislative Decree 286/1999 were never even implemented. Although some exceptions in improvements in regional governments and policy frameworks can be noted, the overall picture in terms of administrative efficiency, economy, accountability, and innovation was very poor. With the Great Recession of 2008, a policy window opened to push for a more robust and comprehensive set of reforms through Legislative Decree 150/2009.

How do the three pillars of Italian reform—modernization of public administration, innovation and digitization within public administration and the country, and better relationships between public administration and citizens and business—in Legislative Decree 150/2009 match up against Light's analysis? On the surface it might seem that modernization would strengthen efficiency, innovation and digitization would strengthen efficiency and economy, and enhancing the relation to citizens would focus on liberation management. Closer analysis indicates that all three pillars have a variety of reform types embedded in the initiatives.

The pillar of reform called *modernization of public administration* involves the following:

—Transparency and integrity
—Performance evaluation
—Meritocracy and rewards
—Managerial responsibility
—Disciplinary sanctions
—Collective bargaining

The transparency and integrity initiatives that have led to disclosure of salary information and to the creation of a new Anticorruption and Transparency Service emphasize accountability. The scope of performance evaluation initiative is not only to help services work better (efficiency), but also to emphasize accountability when performance measurement schemes enable better tracking of the quantity and quality of results. The meritocracy and rewards initiative emphasizes excellence and managerial enterprise, and strongly supports liberation management. The managerial responsibility initiative gives more flexibility to senior managers (liberation management), and also proposes to make them more accountable for results. Disciplinary sanction for false medical certificates, refusal to transfer, and persistent poor performance is clearly focused on increasing accountability. The purpose of collective bargaining initiatives is to bring more regularity to the process, and thus more economy; nonetheless, the regulatory change clearly seeks to enhance union accountability on the one hand and to provide more opportunities to reward entrepreneurial managers in light of liberation management on the other.

The pillar of reform called *innovation and digitization of public administration* (which is also known as e-Gov 2012) involves both large doses of efficiency in terms of doing things faster and more cheaply, and economy in terms of actually providing new services. In education, health, and justice, digitization will allow opportunities to provide service at a distance, more quickly, and with more basic information being accessible for self-service. This enhances efficiency. It will also bring about new services: citizens' ability to use and access information directly and to customize their requests, and, with the mass scale of outreach, reductions in the cost of public administration.

To be successful and overcome the inevitable barriers to successful implementation, these new initiatives will require substantial doses of liberation management.

The pillar of reform that focuses on *improving the relationship between public administration and the citizen-business community* has five subinitiatives. The certified e-mail initiative is an e-mail address that ensures the sender of the actual delivery of the message to the designated address and provides the same legal value as a letter sent by registered mail. The friendly networks initiative emphasizes expanding access points for citizens, as well as a liberation management perspective in making a cultural change to embrace a more open and welcoming approach to the public. The "friendly line" initiative seeks to be the first access point for citizens and would be a new service, and the "smart inclusion" initiative provides Italy's first distance learning, entertainment, and clinical data management for hospitalized children. These fall within the definition of economy. However, the "show your face" initiative gauges customer satisfaction, and aiding feedback and efficiency also provides accountability in the short term. The implementation of new services is a policy directive to enhance efficiency, and the enhancement of customer services also requires liberation management in order to be successful.

What, then, can be said of the blend of transactional and transformational skills necessary to achieve the greatest level of success in the Italian reforms? Certainly, many aspects of the reforms, narrowly conceived, require a more transactional leadership skill set. Setting up performance measurement systems, reducing fraud, waste, and abuse, requiring professional discipline of individuals and organizations, cutting unnecessary services, and adding new services that are clearly understood and for which resources are readily available are examples of types of reform that are more transactional in nature. On the other hand, some of the narrow reforms call for more transformational skills such as emphasizing managerial discretion and employee merit, introducing entirely new services whose implementation is vague, and changing the culture of public administration itself to be less self-absorbed and more customer-friendly. The entire scope of change also emphasizes transformational skills because the number of transactional adjustments are meant to add up to a paradigm change in administrative culture and productivity. Therefore, strong transactional skills may be sufficient for leaders in many of the narrow areas of technical reform. Some policy leaders, relatively insulated from the details of internal organizational functioning, may need to be primarily transformational leaders, rallying the troops to keep moving despite resistance and obstacles. However, in general, the range and scope of Italian reform is so ambitious that most aspects of the reform will require leaders with both transactional and transformational skills, as Bass recommends. Leaders will need to inspire while clamping down on abuse, and leaders will need to pay close attention to the technical aspects of legal strictures and organizational realities while advocating change. Transformational leaders do not need to personally possess the full range of competencies identified, but they do need to ensure that those competencies are well represented in the leadership team. This is a tall order, but is clearly required if the ambitious Italian reform effort is to be as successful as hoped.

It is generally agreed that major cultural transformation of institutions takes five to ten years,[21] but the first phase (which is all that can be informally reported here) is a necessary, but not sufficient, foundation for long-term success. The modernization initiatives have been well launched.[22] The official reform website has been well developed and kept up-to-date. Recently the performance evaluation has been expanded legislatively (104/2010). Merit standards have been strengthened and the opportunities for gain sharing have been enacted into regulation (but not implemented to date). Disciplinary actions have been much strengthened: the requirement for doctors' certificates and the publication of absentee reports has reduced absenteeism by over one-third since the implementation of the reforms. Collective bargaining has yielded significant concessions in the tight economy, such as the increased ability to transfer employees, curbed use of state-owned cars (and, often, staff drivers), and reduced retirement benefits. The e-government initiatives to increase the use of the Internet in the public sector, especially in health and education, have met with significant progress. Dramatic improvement in citizen outreach has been achieved. Citizens can now routinely send certified documents electronically, there are actively used citizen complaint mechanisms, and citizen evaluation of public administration services is now relatively routine. Recognition of the need to train public administrators is recognized, but the scope seems limited to date. The robustness of these reforms has been supported not only by additional legislation to complement

150/2009, but also by legislation to cut costs (78/2010 and 98/2010) and reduce the number of government employees by 300,000.

But government-reported success may not provide the complete picture, which has yet to be independently corroborated, nor does it ensure long-term success.[23] At least three issues will need further research. First, what are the ramifications of the first-phase activities to date? To what degree are they in fact changing the culture in positive directions? Is productivity up or has there simply been a work displacement? Although the wealth of data provided by the government is encouraging, further research and corroboration are necessary for a more nuanced understanding. Second, the bulk of the success to date has been policy-driven, stemming from the law. To what degree will management innovation become a major driver of change and innovation? Can Italy, as it attempts to modernize, at least to some degree escape the worst of the bureaucratic shackles that are holdovers from its administrative law tradition? The limited training, cuts in large numbers of personnel, and the continuance of a statutory thrust in reform do not seem to bode well for liberation management. Third, will the reforms of 150/2009, named after the minister of public administration and innovation, Renato Brunetta, be adopted and continued in the new government and under the new minister, Philip Griffi Patrons (as of November 29, 2011)? In the past Italian reforms have been famously repudiated by successive governments for ideological advantage. For example, the name of the ministry changed from "public administration and innovation" to "public administration and simplification." However, the fiscal and political environment would seem to encourage continuation of the reform policy, and the affiliation of the current minister with the former minister would seem to indicate a likelihood of continuation.

Conclusion

Transactional leadership, with its managerial and achievement-oriented focus, requires a substantial number of competencies to maximize efficiency, economy, and accountability.[24] Transformational leadership, with its change orientation, thrives on additional competency clusters such as consideration, transcending self-interests, vision and creativity, and charisma. Italian reform under the 150/2009 legislation and related legislative reform decrees includes a number of reforms that when narrowly conceived are largely transactional. Some of them, such as moving to a more merit-based system with greater managerial flexibility and a culture of innovation, are clearly transformational. Furthermore, taken together the overall scope of the long-term reform effort is largely transformational.

The need for such sweeping reforms indicates that internal transformation was not forthcoming in the past, even after the reform legislation of the 1990s and 2001, either because it was not successfully implemented or because it was subverted.[25] Transactional skills are likely to be much stronger than transformational skills but require less discipline than the new Italian public law calls for. The new and critical transformational skills are likely to be largely deficient because of a lack of opportunity and practice. Changes in the law and executive mandates will provide the rationale and initial impetus for change. Yet ultimately the overhaul of Italian public administration cannot be achieved solely by legislative and executive orders. It will need internal champions, role models located throughout the public service, and guidance and support to reinvigorate public administration and change its very culture.[26] This means that transformational skills will need to be encouraged and supported at all levels of Italian government, through extensive training programs, widespread investments in new education, and role modeling.[27] This challenge will provide exciting opportunities to both those designing the change and those experiencing it. At the conclusion of the first two-year phase (2009–11), the reforms seem to be off to a good start, but the challenges presented by administrative subversion, cultural integration, and transitions in leadership will require time and further investigation before the degree of long-term success can be accurately assessed.

Notes

1. Paul C. Light, *The Tides of Reform: Making Government Work, 1945–1995* (Yale University Press, 1997).

2. Joseph C. Rost, *Leadership for the Twenty-First Century* (New York: Praeger, 1991); Bernard M. Bass, *The Bass Handbook of Leadership: Theory, Research, & Managerial Applications* (New York: Free Press, 2008).

3. Montgomery Van Wart, "Public Sector Leadership Theory: An Assessment," *Public Administration Review* 63 (March–April 2003): 214–28; Montgomery Van Wart, *Leadership in Public Organizations: An Introduction*, 2nd ed. (Armonk, N.Y.: M. E. Sharpe, 2011); Montgomery Van Wart and Kevin O'Farrell, "Organizational Leadership and the Challenges in Teaching It," *Journal of Public Affairs Education* 13 (Spring–Summer 2007): 427–38.

4. George P. Hollenbeck, Morgan W. McCall, and Robert F. Silzer, "Leadership Competency Models," *Leadership Quarterly* 17 (August 2006): 398–413.

5. David G. Winter, *Navy Leadership and Management Competencies: Convergence among Tests, Interviews and Performance Ratings* (Boston: McBer, 1979); Robert E.

Quinn and others, *Becoming a Master Manager: A Competency Framework* (New York: Wiley, 1996); Belle Rose Ragins, Bickley Townsend, and Mary Mattis, "Perceptions of Mentoring Roles in Cross-Gender Mentoring Relationships," *Journal of Vocational Behavior* 37 (December 1990): 321–39; Montgomery Van Wart, *Dynamics of Leadership: Theory and Practice*, 2nd ed. (Armonk, N.Y.: M. E. Sharpe, 2011).

6. L. D. Eyde and others, "High Performance Leaders: A Competency Model," report no. PRDC-99-02, prepared for the U.S. Office of Personnel Management (Washington: Employment Service, Personnel Resources and Development Center, 1999).

7. Bernard M. Bass, *Leadership and Performance beyond Expectations* (New York: Free Press, 1985).

8. Mary Uhl-Bien, "Relational Leadership Theory: Exploring the Social Processes of Leadership and Organizing," *Leadership Quarterly* 17 (December 2006): 654–76; Mary Uhl-Bien, Russ Marion, and Bill McKelvey, "Complexity Leadership Theory: Shifting Leadership from the Industrial Age to the Knowledge Era," *Leadership Quarterly* 18 (August 2007): 298–318.

9. James Macgregor Burns, *Leadership* (New York: Harper & Row, 1978); Barbara Kellerman, "What Every Leader Needs to Know about Followers," *Harvard Business Review* 85 (December 2007): 84–91; Barbara Kellerman, *Followership: How Followers Are Creating Change and Changing Leaders* (Boston: Harvard Business Press, 2008).

10. Montgomery Van Wart, "A Comprehensive Model of Organizational Leadership: The Leadership Action Cycle," *International Journal of Organization Theory and Behavior* 6, no. 4 (2004): 173–208.

11. Robert L. Katz, "Skills of an Effective Administrator," *Harvard Business Review* 33 (January–February 1955): 33–42; Bass, *Bass Handbook of Leadership*.

12. Rosabeth Moss Kanter, *The Change Masters* (New York: Simon & Schuster, 1983); Rosabeth Moss Kanter, Barry A. Stein, and Todd D. Jick, *The Challenges of Organizational Change: How Companies Experience It and Leaders Guide It* (New York: Free Press, 1992); Montgomery Van Wart and Evan Berman, "Contemporary Public Sector Productivity Values: Narrower Scope, Tougher Standards, and New Rules of the Game," *Public Productivity & Management Review* 22 (March 1999): 326–47.

13. Henry Mintzberg, *The Nature of Managerial Work* (New York: Harper & Row, 1973).

14. Bass, *Bass Handbook of Leadership*, 2008.

15. Van Wart, *Dynamics of Leadership*, pp. 54–55.

16. Francis J. Yammarino and Fred Dansereau, "Multi-Level Nature of and Multi-Level Approaches to Leadership," *Leadership Quarterly* 19 (April 2008): 135–41; Francis J. Yammarino and others, "Leadership and Levels of Analysis: A State-of-the-Art Review," *Leadership Quarterly* 16 (December 2005): 879–919.

17. Tracey Trottier, Montgomery Van Wart, and Xiao Hu Wang, "Examining the Nature and Significance of Leadership in Government Organizations," *Public Administration Review* 68 (March 2008): 319–33.

18. Light, *Tides of Reform*.

19. Tom Peters, *Liberation Management: Necessary Disorganization for the Nanosecond Nineties* (New York: Fawcett Columbine, 1992).

20. Organization for Economic Cooperation and Development, *Modernising the Public Administration: A Study on Italy* (Paris: OECD, 2010); Edoardo Ongaro and Giovanni Valotti, "Public Management Reform in Italy: Explaining the Implementation Gap," *International Journal of Public Sector Management* 21, no. 2 (2008): 174–204.

21. Kanter, *Change Masters.*

22. Renato Brunetta, "Relazione al Parlamento sullo stato della pubblica amministrazione, 2010–2011" [Report to parliament on the state of public administration, 2010–2011], 3 vols. (Rome: Ministry of Public Administration and Innovation, November 2011).

23. For a related set of questions and critiques, see Calogero Marino, "The Evaluation of Public Managers' Performances in the Light of Italian Public Administration Reform," SSRN Working Paper Series (N.p. : Social Science Research Network, 2011).

24. Gary Yukl, *Leadership in Organizations,* 5th ed. (Englewood Cliffs, N.J.: Prentice Hall, 2002).

25. Giorgio Pastori, "Recent Trends in Italian Public Administration," *Italian Journal of Public Law* 1, no. 1 (2009): 1–27.

26. Michael Barzelay, *Breaking Through Bureaucracy: A New Vision for Managing in Government* (University of California Press, 1992).

27. Montgomery Van Wart, "The First Step in the Reinvention Process: Assessment," *Public Administration Review* 55 (September–October 1995): 429–38; Montgomery Van Wart, *Changing Public Sector Values* (New York: Garland, 1998); Montgomery Van Wart, N. Joseph Cayer, and Steve Cook, *Handbook of Training and Development in the Public Sector* (San Francisco: Jossey-Bass, 1993).

MARIANNUNZIATA LIGUORI, MARIAFRANCESCA SICILIA, AND ILEANA STECCOLINI

8 Politicians and Administrators: Two Characters in Search of a Role

Our title is a play on the title of a celebrated Italian work first performed in 1921, *Sei personaggi in cerca di autore* [Six characters in search of an author], by Luigi Pirandello. Pirandello won the Nobel Prize for literature in 1934, "for his bold and ingenious revival of dramatic and scenic art." Contemporary politicians and administrators are indeed players on a public stage, seeking their appropriate contemporary roles.

Introduction

The relationships and roles of politicians and administrators have long been a well-debated issue in the literature on public administration.[1] In the traditional model of public administration, administrators are viewed as bureaucrats, professionals, and mere executors of the political mandate. According to this model, politicians provide guidance whereas administrators provide neutral skills for the benefit of the policy process and for translating decisions into concrete results.[2]

Waves of "modernization" in the public sector have meant that administrators are increasingly being asked to wear the hat of managers.[3] Once again, however, politicians and administrators are seen as actors with separate functions: the former are supposed to play a strategic role, deciding on broad policies and setting targets for managers, and the latter are expected to reach these targets in an efficient and effective manner.[4]

This standard "dichotomic" outlook has been challenged by more empirical approaches, which tend to view the boundaries between the political and the managerial spheres as being more blurred.[5] According to these approaches, the two roles are complementary and overlapping instead of separate. Furthermore, their actual features are far from being fixed and may depend on contextual, organizational, and individual factors.[6]

In order to contribute to this debate, in this chapter we investigate the emerging roles of politicians and administrators by achieving a better understanding of their overlapping components and combinations. Our study was conducted by taking a survey of Italian politicians and administrators at the level of local governments (LGs) of political units with more than 80,000 inhabitants. The findings suggest that three broader factors (in terms of roles and behaviors) exist—which we call managerial, professional, and political—and that the two roles are blurred in some cases and even swapped in others.

In the following section we review the relevant literature; in the third section we describe our analytical methodology; in the next section we present and discuss results; and in the final section we draw some conclusions and suggest ways forward for research.

Developments and Unresolved Issues in the Relationship and Roles of Politicians and Administrators

Developments in the roles of politicians and administrators and the unfolding of their relationship are characteristic of the public sector. According to traditional theory, there is a strict separation between politicians and administrators, based on the idea that the former define policies and the latter implement them.[7] This image of a clear division of labor exalts the authority of politicians, who dominate administrators. The latter are seen as bureaucrats, experts with professional know-how and skills who are responsible for the efficient implementation of policies; they are considered neutral and lacking authority and discretion to make their own decisions.[8] The two actors have been seen to have different decision-making criteria: administrators tend to rely on technically defined and feasible solutions, whereas politicians make decisions with a view to political advantage and consensus.[9]

The traditional model of public administration, based on the primacy of politicians and the neutrality and professionalism of administrators, is reversed in the model suggested by New Public Management (NPM).[10] NPM backs the drive to transform bureaucrats into managers, who are seen as central actors in the process of change because their focus on efficiency, effectiveness, and results embodies economic rationality.[11] The role of administrators as managers is supposed to be less concerned with the neutral use of professional expertise than with defining and reaching goals, as well as with quality management of financial and human resources. The normative division of roles between politicians and managers is resumed in this new model, but the primacy of politics gives way to the primacy of management. The managerial sphere is granted greater autonomy from the political one, under the manifesto of "letting the managers manage."[12]

An increasing number of authors have pointed out that there is no clear-cut division between politicians and administrators and that the normative models tend to be rather simplistic. In particular, these studies show that both politicians and administrators may discharge their roles with a mix of activities, ranging from management and administration to policy and mission definition.[13] In some cases, the idea of complementarity has been put forward in the place of dichotomy to illustrate their complex relationship, characterized by distinction and overlap, interdependency and reciprocal influence.[14] Politicians and administrators operate together in the common pursuit of sound governance.[15] This not only makes their roles complementary, it also makes them interdependent. Both politicians and administrators contribute to public activities and interests on the basis of their distinctive perspectives, competencies, and roles.[16]

Some authors have tried to describe and classify the types of roles performed by the two categories of actors. Joel D. Aberbach, Robert D. Putnam, and Bert A. Rockman have identified nine types of roles—technician, advocate, broker, facilitator, partisan, policymaker, trustee, legalist, and ombudsman—and posit that the combination of these roles generates different relationships between the two actors.[17] The authors acknowledge the unlikely occurrence of a pure dichotomic situation and suggest that multiple in-between roles are possible. In particular, using a sample from seven countries—the United States, Sweden, Germany, Britain, the Netherlands, France, and Italy—they investigated the roles of politicians and administrators and the expected traits and capabilities at the level of the national state. Their results show that politicians' profiles are more oriented to the partisan, advocate, facilitator, and ombudsman profiles, whereas administrators are more strongly oriented toward the technician and broker roles. Three main factors statistically emerge from a factor analysis of the aforementioned roles: politics/technics, combining the roles of technician, advocate, partisan, and ombudsman; authority/responsiveness, combining broker, trustee, and policymaker, and umpire/player (trustee and legalist). It should be noted that each of these factors comprises both the political and administrative dimensions, in other words, all factors can be referred back to the roles of both politicians and administrators. More recently, Joel Aberbach and Bert Rockman proposed a view of politicians as energizers and administrators as equilibrators.[18]

Building on the study of Aberbach, Putnam, and Rockman, Miro Hacek reports on the findings of a survey on the central state government of Slovenia, showing that Slovenian politicians and administrators are quite unanimous in identifying desirable attributes for civil servants.[19] By investigating the role played by the two actors during policymaking and adopting the classification of Aberbach, Putnam, and Rockman, he finds that politicians appear to lean more toward the roles of advocate, broker, facilitator, partisan, and policymaker.[20] Civil servants see themselves in the role of advocates fighting for or representing the interests of a broad social group, as technicians solving technical problems, as trustees representing the state, and as legalists focusing on the legal processes and definitions of one's responsibility or activity. Both actors believe that brokering, mediating, and conciliating skills are more desirable in politicians, whereas the desirable attributes for civil servants are organizational, managerial, and intellectual skills, in addition to the mandatory neutrality in the implementation of the law. Thus, in Slovenia the two groups of actors appear more distinct than what is highlighted by Aberbach, Putnam, and Rockman.

James Svara adopts an alternative approach and depicts four different types of activities that can be performed by politicians and administrators: mission, policy, administration, and management.[21] Although he delineates fewer, more broadly defined activities rather than specific roles, he is one of the few authors who compare the results of surveys conducted at the local level with studies of U.S. municipalities conducted in 1985 and 1996. He shows that the roles of politicians and administrators become increasingly blurred over time.[22] Indeed, politicians are increasingly involved in administration rather than in achieving the organization's mission while, simultaneously, administrators are becoming more involved in achieving the mission. Poul Erik Mouritzen and James Svara also point out the blurring of roles.[23] More recently, Tansu Demir takes a different view, distinguishing between political skills (policymaking and goal setting) and managerial skills (personnel management and organizational coordination). The authors propose that such skills are complementary rather than separate.[24]

Building on previous literature and extending the study of Aberbach, Putnam, and Rockman, our aim is to investigate the emerging roles of administrators and politicians at the LG level.[25]

Purpose and Methods

In order to carry out our research we conducted a survey of all sixty-five Italian municipalities with at least 80,000 inhabitants. (We did not count the three municipalities where the elected political bodies are temporarily replaced by a central government delegate.)

Previous studies have focused mainly on higher levels of government. However, LG represents an interesting setting for investigating the roles and capabilities of politicians and administrators, whose dynamics are more accessible and visible at this level, as Svara points out.[26] In each municipality we selected three departments for study, taking the variety of their activities into consideration: environment, public infrastructure, and culture. The selection criterion draws on Trevor Brown and Mark Potoski's classification of output measurability of the service provided. [27] Undeniably, different types of activities may impact the perception of roles by civil servants and politicians. According to Brown and Potoski, public infrastructure departments have the highest output measurability followed by environment and culture departments.

A questionnaire was prepared and submitted to the top managers of the departments and the related elected politicians of the cabinet (the aldermen directly responsible for the service). The final response rate was 23 percent, with administrators representing 54 percent and politicians 46 percent.

In order to assess the perception of the actors' own role, we drew on the questionnaires of Aberbach, Putnam, and Rockman and Hacek, where different statements identified the various roles. Following Hacek, we initially referred to the nine role categories of Aberbach, Putnam, and Rockman. In particular, the role of *technician* focuses on solving technical policy problems and applying specialized knowledge; the *advocate* fights for the interests of a broad social group, class, or cause; the *broker* mediates and resolves conflicts of interest and political conflicts; the *facilitator* protects the interests of specific clientele groups or constituents; the *partisan* focuses on party politics; the *policymaker* formulates policy; the *trustee* focuses on his or her role as representative of the state and government; the *legalist* focuses on legal processes or legalistic definitions of responsibilities; and the *ombudsman* undertakes casework to protect and defend the interests of individual constituents and clients.[28]

Respondents were asked to express their view on a five-point Likert scale showing the level of agreement with the statement describing their performed role, where 1 was "completely disagree" and 5 was "completely agree."[29] An open-ended option, "other," was also given. A pretest performed on an initial sample of twenty respondents showed that the trustee role was highly correlated to the partisan and legalist roles and the ombudsman role to the policymaker role (all cases showing Pearson's correlation greater than 80 percent). Consequently, only the remaining seven categories were used in the analysis. As a further validity check, we ran an ANOVA (analysis of variance) on the final sample of respondents to assess the impact of certain contingent factors such as geographical position, department, and actual role (administrator or politician) on the perception of the investigated roles. According to the ANOVA, perceived roles are not statistically influenced by these variables. This strengthened the results of our analysis. We were then able to focus on the dichotomy between administrators and politicians.

Adopting the categories and methodology of Aberbach, Putnam, and Rockman, we ran an exploratory factor analysis using the role items as components to evaluate possible emerging latent role factors at the LG level.[30] We then extended their procedure and performed a t-test (for unequal variance on the managerial and the political factors, for equal variance on the professional one) of the difference in means comparing the three emerging role factors and the actual role (that is, politician or administrator) performed by the respondents.[31] For each of the three factors, the new score was computed as the average of the components identified through the factor analysis. All statistical analyses were carried out using STATA 11.

Administrators versus Politicians: Emerging Roles in LGs

In their study on central governments, Aberbach, Putnam, and Rockman support the Weberian idea of separation between the political and bureaucratic worlds, where the former is mainly focused on advocacy and mediation of interests, and the latter leans more toward the application of specialized and legalistic competence.[32] The authors also confirm these results in the Italian context. With reference to the Slovenian state, Hacek builds on this idea, showing that politicians are more oriented to the roles of advocate, broker, facilitator, partisan, and policymaker, while civil servants prefer to fill the roles of advocates, technicians, trustees, and legalists.[33]

Following the procedure of Aberbach, Putnam, and Rockman, we ran a factor analysis to assess whether the roles of politicians and administrators also revolve around the three factors previously identified (that is, political/technical, authority/responsiveness, and umpire/player) at the LG level.[34] Our analysis immediately highlights the existence of three latent factors (see table 8-1), although the aggregate role components differ from those in previous studies. Our first factor comprises broker, advocate, and facilitator roles, which may reflect a more managerial perspective in carrying out activities. The second factor scores highly on legalist and technician roles, mirroring a professional and bureaucratic profile stronger than what traditional literature would tend to identify. The third factor includes partisan and policymaker roles, and so can be interpreted as the politics-oriented factor.

Table 8-1. *Principal-Factor Analysis of the Perceived Roles of Politicians and Administrators*[a]

	Factor 1 = Managerial role	*Factor 2 = Professional role*	*Factor 3 = Political role*
Broker	.800	–.254	.023
Advocate	.792	.121	.273
Facilitator	.709	.254	.266
Legalist	–.061	.860	.025
Technician	.104	.782	–.050
Partisan	.099	.058	.850
Policymaker	.296	–.111	.743

Source: Authors' calculations.

a. Extraction Method: principal component analysis; Rotation Method: varimax with Kaiser normalization; rotation converged in four iterations.

Whereas each factor comprises both political and administrative roles for central government in Aberbach, Putnam, and Rockman, our factor analysis separates role contents more sharply.[35] In fact, it aggregates political, managerial, and professional/bureaucratic activities as separate factors. Such differences might be explained by the different levels of analysis taken into consideration—LGs as well as the consequences of the "managerialist" wave—which have not resulted in a "separation" of the roles of politicians and managers but in a separation of three theoretically clear roles instead, which are also those traditionally conceptualized in public management literature.[36] These results suggest the importance of moving away from the theoretical conceptualization of "politicians," "managers," and "professionals" as three neatly distinguished extremes and favor the analysis of the variety of their combinations, as is found in reality.

As a second step, we compared the three emerging factors with the actual roles, politician versus administrator, performed by the actors in their organizations. The t-test for the managerial and political factors displays a significant difference in means, where politicians possess the highest level of both (see tables 8-2 and 8-3).

The same analysis for the professional factor shows that the two actors do not differ in their combination of legal and technical roles (table 8-4). For politicians this is also the factor with the lowest overall score reported.

The managerial factor is the most important for both politicians and administrators: although significantly different, it also has the highest average score both overall and for each actor. The political factor has the lowest combined average score and also has the least consensus among administrators.

Table 8-2. *T-Test between the Managerial Factor and the Actual Performed Role*
Two-sample t-test with unequal variances

Group[a]	*Observations*	*Mean*	*Standard error*	*Standard deviation*	*[95 percent confidence interval]*	
0	45	4.444444	.1032578	.6926745	4.236342	4.652547
1	58	3.965517	.1228949	.9359397	3.719424	4.21161
Combined	103	4.174757	.0855294	.8680289	4.00511	4.344405
Diff		.4789272	.1605158		.1604995	.7973549

Diff = mean(0) – mean(1) t = 2.9837
Ho: diff = 0 Satterthwaite's degrees of freedom = 100.805

Ha: diff < 0	Ha: diff ! = 0	Ha: diff > 0
Pr(T < t) = 0.9982	Pr(|T| > |t|) = 0.0036	Pr(T > t) = 0.0018

Source: Authors' calculations.
a. 0 = politicians; 1 = managers.

These results support the idea that it is difficult to identify largely different and separate portfolios of activities for the two actors. Their roles are somewhat overlapping and profoundly interrelated. In line with suggestions in previous literature, we find politicians to be (statistically) keen on performing political roles (partisan and policymaker; see table 8-3). Policymaking and policy design appear to occupy the political realm more than the administrative realm. In an increasingly heterogeneous society, the diversity of interests at stake requires both partisan negotiation and conflict resolution.[37] Surprisingly, however, politicians perform a significant managerial role, too.

Table 8-3. *T-Test between the Political Factor and the Actual Performed Role*
Two-sample t-test with unequal variances

Group[a]	*Observations*	*Mean*	*Standard error*	*Standard deviation*	*[95 percent confidence interval]*	
0	45	3.866667	.1407053	.9438798	3.583094	4.15024
1	58	3.034483	.1368683	1.042358	2.760409	3.308557
Combined	103	3.398058	.1062844	1.078668	3.187244	3.608873
Diff		.8321839	.1962929		.4426742	1.221694

Diff = mean(0) – mean(1) t = 4.2395
Ho: diff = 0 Satterthwaite's degrees of freedom = 98.5502

Ha: diff < 0	Ha: diff ! = 0	Ha: diff > 0
Pr(T < t) = 1.0000	Pr(|T| > |t|) = 0.0001	Pr(T > t) = 0.0000

Source: Authors' calculations.
a. 0 = politicians; 1 = managers.

Table 8-4. *T-test between the Professional Factor and the Actual Performed Role*
Two-sample t-test with unequal variances

Group[a]	*Observations*	*Mean*	*Standard error*	*Standard deviation*	*[95 percent confidence interval]*	
0	45	3.266667	.1399856	.9390517	2.984544	3.548789
1	58	3.534483	.1352006	1.029657	3.263748	3.805217
Combined	103	3.417476	.0980723	.9953251	3.22295	3.612002
Diff		−.2678161	.1969071		−.6584269	.1227947

Diff = mean(0) – mean(1) t = −1.3601
Ho: diff = 0 Satterthwaite's degrees of freedom = 101

Ha: diff < 0	Ha: diff ! = 0	Ha: diff > 0
Pr(T < t) = 0.0884	Pr(|T| > |t|) = 0.1768	Pr(T > t) = 0.9116

Source: Authors' calculations.
a. 0 = politicians; 1 = managers.

This might reflect the need to obtain consensus, especially at the local level, deeply influenced by the actual capacity to satisfy the needs of the electorate rather than by ideological positions and declarations. Thus, politicians would also seem to play a role in the phase of policy implementation. It is worth noticing that they are generally perceived to play a managerial role more than managers themselves, whereas the opposite is not true: managers are not seen to play a more political role than politicians (see tables 8-2 and 8-3).

Both actors are equally involved in technical and legalistic roles (see table 8-4). This finding might have a double explanation. On the one hand, such skills are considered necessary in order to carry out political and administrative duties. Public service provision is by nature strongly influenced by legal, technical, and professional constraints, which limits choices and narrows the spectrum of activities of actors.[38] This reflects the awareness of both actors that they are working to further the interests of society at large, which demands the correct handling of legal and formal issues, especially in a country of civil law such as Italy. Such issues permeate their activity, representing a fundamental condition to safeguard the achievement of their institutional mission. This also reflects a typical bureaucratic approach, which still seems to be predominant.[39]

On the other hand, technical and legal aspects can be viewed as the background that is taken for granted for all public officials, so the professional factor might not be perceived as specifically qualifying either politicians or administrators. This interpretation is supported by the data, which, for these aspects, show the lowest average score when compared with the other two factors (that is, the political and the managerial ones). The relevance of technical skills, traditionally seen as the core feature of the bureaucrat, has been supplanted by other activities of a more managerial nature, also thanks to the recent processes of modernization.[40]

Conclusions

In this chapter we aimed to investigate the emerging roles of administrators and politicians at the LG level. For this purpose we adopted and extended the methodology of Aberbach, Putnam, and Rockman that was previously used for a similar study on central government.[41] Our results confirm that interdependence also exists in LGs rather than dichotomy between the two investigated actors. A factor analysis highlights the existence of three latent role factors, which can be named managerial (broker, advocate, and facilitator), professional (legalist and technician) and political (partisan and policymaker). These differ from the factors previously identified by Aberbach, Putnam, and Rockman and tend to be combined in both politicians and administrators, rather than being clearly split between them.[42]

From a joint interpretation of the factor analysis and the t-tests we infer that the managerial factor is most highly valued by both politicians and administrators, followed by the professional and the political one. Interestingly, politicians tend to score significantly more than administrators in both the political and managerial factors, whereas the two actors appear to be aligned as regards the professional factor.

This evidence highlights the existence of a "gray area" of activities in which both politicians and administrators aim to contribute, acting like "two characters in search of a role." The managerial factor and its related role components represent the main character who plays on the LG stage, and consequently both actors try to gain center stage. The political factor represents the "supporting character." Laws, technical knowledge, and professional rules set the scene for the actors to perform.

The policy implications of our study unquestionably concern the implementation of future reforms. Indeed, policymakers should acknowledge the existence of not two but three dimensions—political, managerial, and professional—within LGs and try to keep these balanced. Emphasizing only one of the three, as often happens during processes of modernization, may foster organizational tension that may ultimately hamper the success of both the LG and the reform process itself. "There is no such thing as a small part" rings as true in government as it does in the theater.

This study also suggests further avenues of research in order to look into the variables affecting the perception of roles and their changes over time. It would also be interesting to replicate the present study in different countries and settings.

Notes

1. Joel D. Aberbach, Robert D. Putnam, and Bert A. Rockman, *Bureaucrats and Politicians in Western Democracies* (Harvard University Press, 1981); Tansu Demir and Ronald C. Nyhan, "The Politics-Administration Dichotomy: An Empirical Search for Correspondence between Theory and Practice," *Public Administration Review* 68 (January–February 2008): 81–96; H. George Frederickson and Kevin B. Smith, *The Public Administration Theory Primer* (Boulder, Colo.: Westview Press, 2003); Miro Hacek, "The Relationship Between Civil Servants and Politicians in a Post-Communist Country: A Case of Slovenia," *Public Administration* 84 (March 2006): 165–84; Patrick Overeem and Mark R. Rutgers, "Three Roads to Politics and Administration: Ideational Foundations of the Politics-Administration Dichotomy," in *Retracing Public Administration*, edited by Mark R. Rutgers (Amsterdam: JAI/Elsevier International, 2003), pp. 153–60; James H. Svara, "The Politics-Administration Dichotomy as Aberration," *Public Administration Review* 58 (January 1998): 51–58; James H. Svara, "The Shifting Boundary between Elective Officials and City Managers in Large Council-Manager Cities," *Public Administration Review* 59 (January 1999): 44–53; James H. Svara, "Complementarity of Politics and Administration as a Legitimate Alternative to the Dichotomy Model," *Administration & Society* 30 (January 1999): 676–705; James H. Svara, "The Myth of the Dichotomy: Complementarity of Politics and Administration in the Past and Future of Public Administration," *Public Administration Review* 61 (March–April 2001): 176–83; James H. Svara and James R. Brunet, "Finding and Refining Complementarity in Recent Conceptual Models of Politics and Administration," in *Retracing Public Administration,* edited by Rutgers, pp. 161–84; James H. Svara, "The Search for Meaning in Political-Administrative Relations in Local Government," *International Journal of Public Administration* 29 (December 2006): 1065–90; Woodrow Wilson, "The Study of Administration," *Political Science Quarterly* 2 (June 1887): 197–222.

2. Wilson, "Study of Administration," 201.

3. David Osborne and Ted Gaebler, *Reinventing Government* (New York: Plume, 1992); Christopher Pollitt and Geert Bouckaert, *Public Management Reform: A Comparative Analysis* (Oxford University Press, 2000).

4. Audit Commission, *We Can't Go On Meeting like This: The Changing Role of Local Authority Members* (London: Her Majesty's Stationery Office, 1990).

5. Frederickson and Smith, *Public Administration Theory Primer;* Svara, "Politics-Administration Dichotomy as Aberration"; Svara, "Shifting Boundary between Elective Officials and City Managers in Large Council-Manager Cities"; Svara,

"Complementarity of Politics and Administration as a Legitimate Alternative to the Dichotomy Model"; Svara, "Myth of the Dichotomy"; Svara and Brunet, "Finding and Refining Complementarity in Recent Conceptual Models of Politics and Administration"; Svara, "Search for Meaning in Political-Administrative Relations in Local Government."

6. Joel D. Aberbach and Bert A. Rockman, "The Past and Future of Political-Administrative Relations: Research from 'Bureaucrats and Politicians' to 'In the Web of Politics'—and Beyond," *International Journal of Public Administration* 29 (December 2006): 977–95; B. Guy Peters, *The Politics of Bureaucracy* (London: Routledge, 2001); Poul Erik Mouritzen and James H. Svara, *Leadership at the Apex: Politicians and Administrators in Western Local Governments* (University of Pittsburgh Press, 2002); Dag I. Jacobsen, "The Relationship between Politics and Administration: The Importance of Contingency Factors, Formal Structure, Demography, and Time," *Governance* 19 (April 2006): 303–23.

7. Aberbach, Putnam, and Rockman, *Bureaucrats and Politicians in Western Democracies;* B. Guy Peters, *Comparing Public Bureaucracies: Problems of Theory and Method* (University of Alabama Press, 1988); Max Weber, "Bureaucracy," in *Classics of Public Administration*, edited by Jay M. Shafritz and Albert C. Hyde (Orlando: Harcourt Brace College Publishers, 1922); Wilson, "Study of Administration."

8. Aberbach, Putnam, and Rockman, *Bureaucrats and Politicians in Western Democracies*; Tansu Demir and Ronald C. Nyhan, "The Politics-Administration Dichotomy: An Empirical Search for Correspondence between Theory and Practice," *Public Administration Review* 68 (January–February 2008): 81–96; Ferrel Heady, *Public Administration: A Comparative Perspective* (New York: Dekker, 1984).

9. Aberbach, Putnam, and Rockman, *Bureaucrats and Politicians in Western Democracies*; Weber, "Bureaucracy."

10. Christopher Hood, "A Public Management for All Seasons," *Public Administration* 69 (Spring 1991): 3–19; Christopher Hood, "The New Public Management in the 1980s: Variations on a Theme," *Accounting, Organizations and Society* 20 (February–April 1995): 93–109; G. Jan Van Helden, "A Review of the Policy and Management Instruments Project for Municipalities in the Netherlands," *Financial Accountability and Management* 14 (May 1998): 85–94; Christopher Humphrey, Peter Miller, and Robert W. Scapens, "Accountability and Accountable Management in the UK Public Sector," *Accounting, Auditing and Accountability Journal* 6 (1993), no. 3: 7–29; Olov Olson, James Guthrie, and Christopher Humphrey, "International Experiences with "New" Public Financial Management (NPFM) Reforms: New World? Small World? Better World?" in *Global Warning: Debating International Developments in New Public Financial Management,* edited by Olov Olson, Christopher Humphrey, and James Guthrie (Oslo: Cappelen Akademisk Forlag, 1998), pp. 17–48.

11. Kuno Schedler, ". . . and Politics? Public Management Developments in the Light of Two Rationalities," *Public Management Review* 5, no. 4 (2003): 533–50.

12. Osborne and Gaebler, *Reinventing Government.*

13. Aberbach, Putnam, and Rockman, *Bureaucrats and Politicians in Western Democracies;* Svara, "Politics-Administration Dichotomy as Aberration"; Svara, "Shifting Boundary between Elective Officials and City Managers in Large Council-Manager Cities"; Svara, "Complementarity of Politics and Administration," 676–705; Svara, "Myth of the Dichotomy"; Svara and Brunet "Finding and Refining Complementarity"; Svara "Search for Meaning in Political-Administrative Relations in Local Government"; Kasper M. Hansen and Niels Ejersbo, "The Relationship between Politicians and Administrators: A Logic of Disharmony," *Public Administration* 80 (December 2002): 733–50.

14. Tansu Demir, "The Complementarity View: Exploring a Continuum in Political—Administrative Relations," *Public Administration Review* 69 (September/October 2009): 876–88.

15. Svara, "Myth of the Dichotomy."

16. Poul Erik Mouritzen and James H. Svara, *Leadership at the Apex: Politicians and Administrators in Western Local Governments* (University of Pittsburgh Press, 2002).

17. Aberbach, Putnam, and Rockman, *Bureaucrats and Politicians in Western Democracies.*

18. Aberbach and Rockman "Past and Future of Political-Administrative Relations."

19. Miro Hacek, "The Relationship between Civil Servants and Politicians in a Post-Communist Country: A Case of Slovenia," *Public Administration* 84 (March 2006): 165–84.

20. Aberbach, Putnam, and Rockman, *Bureaucrats and Politicians in Western Democracies*, pp. 86–87.

21. Svara, "Politics-Administration Dichotomy as Aberration"; Svara, "Shifting Boundary between Elective Officials and City Managers in Large Council-Manager Cities"; Svara, "Complementarity of Politics and Administration as a Legitimate Alternative to the Dichotomy Model"; Svara, "Search for Meaning in Political-Administrative Relations in Local Government."

22. Svara, "Search for Meaning in Political-Administrative Relations in Local Government."

23. Mouritzen and Svara, *Leadership at the Apex.*

24. Demir, "Complementarity View."

25. Aberbach, Putnam, and Rockman, *Bureaucrats and Politicians in Western Democracies.*

26. Svara, "Search for Meaning in Political-Administrative Relations in Local Government."

27. Trevor L. Brown and Mark Potoski, "Transaction Costs and Institutional Explanations for Government Service Production Decisions," *Journal of Public Administration Research and Theory* 13 (October 2003): 441–68.

28. See Aberbach, Putnam, and Rockman, *Bureaucrats and Politicians in Western Democracies*; Hacek, "Relationship between Civil Servants and Politicians in a Post-Communist Country."

29. Previous studies show that intrinsically ordinal variables with more than four categories can be treated as continuous. See Paul M. Bentler and Chih-Ping Chou, "Practical Issues in Structural Modeling," *Sociological Methods & Research* 16 (August 1987): 78–117; Henk Ter Bogt, "Politicians in Search of Performance Information," *Financial Accountability & Management* 20 (August 2004): 221–52.

30. Aberbach, Putnam, and Rockman, *Bureaucrats and Politicians in Western Democracies.*

31. The original study—Aberbach, Putnam, Rockman, *Bureaucrats and Politicians in Western Democracies*—did not consider this additional test.

32. Aberbach, Putnam, and Rockman, *Bureaucrats and Politicians in Western Democracies.*

33. Hacek, "Relationship between Civil Servants and Politicians in a Post-Communist Country."

34. Aberbach, Putnam, and Rockman, *Bureaucrats and Politicians in Western Democracies.*

35. Ibid.

36. Pollitt and Bouckaert, *Public Management Reform.*

37. Elio Borgonovi, *Principi e sistemi aziendali per le amministrazioni pubbliche* [Managerial principles and systems for public administration] (Milan: Egea, 1996).

38. Eugenio Anessi Pessina, *Principles of Public Management* (Milan: Egea, 2002).

39. Borgonovi, *Principi e sistemi aziendali per le amministrazioni pubbliche*; Ewan Ferlie and others, *The New Public Management in Action* (Oxford University Press, 1996); Norman Flynn, *Public Sector Management* (London: Financial Times, 2002); Fabrizio Panozzo, "Management by Decree: Paradoxes in the Reform of the Italian Public Sector," *Scandinavian Journal of Management* 16 (December 2000): 357–73; Pollitt and Bouckaert, *Public Management Reform.*

40. Pollitt and Bouckaert, *Public Management Reform;* Osborne and Gaebler, *Reinventing Government.*

41. Aberbach, Putnam, and Rockman, *Bureaucrats and Politicians in Western Democracies.*

42. Ibid.

PART IV

Measuring Public Sector Performance: Managing Governments by Numbers

GEERT BOUCKAERT

9 Public Sector Performance: Managing Governments by the Numbers

"Minister," said Humphrey in his most injured tones, "you said you wanted the administration figures reduced, didn't you?"

"Yes," I agreed.

"So we reduced them."

Dimly I began to perceive what he was saying. "But . . . you only reduced the *figures*, not the actual number of administrators!"

Sir Humphrey furrowed his brow. "Of course."

"Well," I explained patiently, "that is not what I meant."

Sir Humphrey was pained. "Well really, Minister, we are not mind-readers. You said reduce the figures, so we reduced the figures."

—JONATHAN LYNN AND ANTONY JAY
The Complete "Yes Prime Minister"

To better understand how governments manage by numbers it is necessary first to look at the logic of numbers, and then at the logic of management. The logic of numbers includes a logic of consequences and appropriateness that is applied to performance. The logic of public management has increasingly included performance measures to manage internal and external relationships. This results in four types of managing by numbers in the public sector: performance administration, managements of performances, performance management, and performance governance.

These logics and models need to be qualified in reality. First, managing numbers as done by governments is a topic where politics and internal audit may be in tension. Second, it is necessary to have a cost-benefit analysis (CBA) of managing by numbers (of which managing numbers is a part), since costs and benefits are sometimes out of balance. This has also to do with a mismatch of supply and demand of numbers, or with an unbalanced use and non-use of numbers (benchmarks). Obviously the availability of numbers remains an issue, also within the OECD, even if consolidation and deconsolidation is possible. It is not easy to know how much governments are managing by numbers, but there is evidence in five trajectories to improve the input-output ratio.

Logics of Numbers

Numbers may be connected to different logics. A performance logic of numbers "works" in a different way depending on whether it is linked to a logic of consequences or to a logic of *appropriateness.*

Logic of Consequences and Logic of Appropriateness

"It's the economy, stupid," said President Clinton when socioeconomic outcomes were below expectations. It means that whatever we have been doing, there has been no impact for responsibility, nor can blame be taken. This is opposite to a logic of consequences where the right resources guarantee the right activities that provide the right outputs, which then result in the right effects. Right could also be wrong resources, activities, outputs, and outcomes, depending on circumstances and intermediate variables.

This logic of consequences is crucial for institutions and their policies and management.[1] The profession of policy experts and of managers is to know these logics of consequences and to make these chains of consequences happen. A chain of consequences immediately implies also responsibility and accountability mechanisms. This logic becomes a driver for activities. It is possible to describe the causal mechanisms of the performance chain, and to "measure" the consequences.

To manage government activities, this logic of consequences is necessary but not sufficient.[2] There is also a need for a logic of appropriateness. This logic of appropriateness becomes a driver for activities in the public sector. Issues of integrity, values, state of law, privacy, openness, and transparency are all elements that frame the logic of appropriateness for the public sector. This logic can also be described in its mechanisms and measured in its degree of appropriateness.

Managing governments is about following these two logics, even if combining the "logic of expected consequences" and the "logic of appropriateness" "is less obvious than James G. March and Johan P. Olson's readers may be led to think."[3]

Logics of Performance Numbers

The purpose of having performance information available is to be informed and to use this information. However, numbers are the result of the activity of measuring. It is therefore necessary to develop a measurement practice that consists of a series of activities that include detection, collection, storage, processing, comparison, communication, integration. Like all activities, the activity of generating performance numbers and of measurement are not necessarily neutral and without an impact on behavior. There are three models for describing measurement as an activity.[4]

First, the thermometer model implies that measuring as an activity has no effect on the status and the behavior of the object or subject measured (even if there is technically a temperature flux from the thermometer to the "body," which is infinitesimally small compared to the flux from the "body" to the thermometer, which tells us the temperature of that body). A hidden speeding camera measures exactly the speed of the cars and does not affect the behavior of the drivers.

A second category assumes that measurement has an impact on behavior. This may be a functional impact, meaning that measurement contributes to the objectives of the organization, or a dysfunctional impact, meaning that measurement does not push the organization in the direction of its objectives. A functional speeding camera system is one that is immediately visible to drivers in the area that it covers. This becomes a dysfunctional system just outside the camera's reach, since most drivers, upon exiting the area covered by the camera, will speed up once out of the view of the camera. A solution to the problem of speeding is, therefore, to measure the average speed of a trajectory.

The third model, a special type of measurement, is the placebo model of a measuring activity. It is an "empty" measurement tool, but has the equivalent impact of a functioning measuring tool. There is a pretended measurement, and as a consequence, behavior is affected as if behavior had been measured. A visible speeding camera that is not actually connected, or the announcement of speeding cameras even when they are not put in place, will affect behavior as intended. Such a placebo measurement will be functional.

It is obvious that governments want thermometer and functional logics of numbers. Governments do not want dysfunctional logics, and ultimately they also do not want placebos, either, since this is not a sustainable model and undermines trust in functional measurement models.

Figure 9-1. *Three Dimensions for a Sustainable Performance Measurement System*

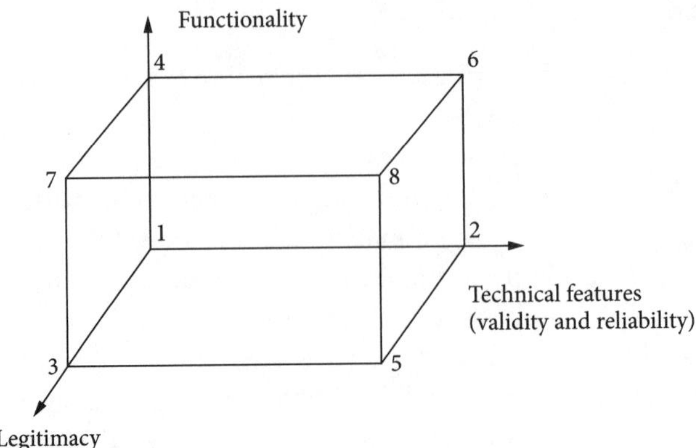

Source: Geert Bouckaert and John Halligan, *Managing Performance: International Comparisons* (London: Routledge, 2008), p. 107.

Numbers work inside governments according to the logic of these numbers. Three dimensions are crucial (see figure 9-1). First, indicators need to be valid and reliable. This technical dimension contributes to an objective treatment of information, even if performance information is qualitative or perception-based.

A second dimension is that the indicators need to be accepted by those whom they concern. When indicators are not "owned," they loose their legitimate status and all kinds of distorting behaviors will be generated. Third, indicators need to be functional and contribute to getting closer to realizing the objectives of the organization. These logics of numbers in the public sector are crucial to the consideration of managing government by numbers.

Logics of Public Management

In managing governments by numbers, it is necessary to clarify the logic of public management. There are different ways to approach this question, such as taking into account the shift from administration to management, the difference between private and public management, or the differences between management functions of personnel, finance, organization, and so on.

In all definitions of management there are elements of a shared focus in an organization on a common objective that implies that responsibility is taken for the performance of a system.

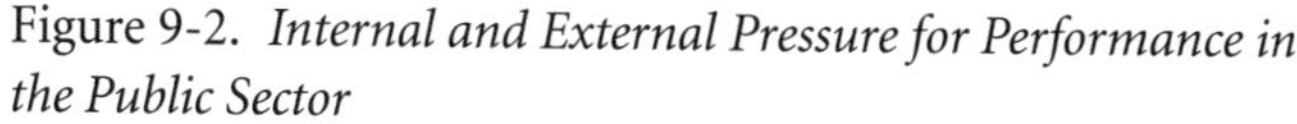

Figure 9-2. *Internal and External Pressure for Performance in the Public Sector*

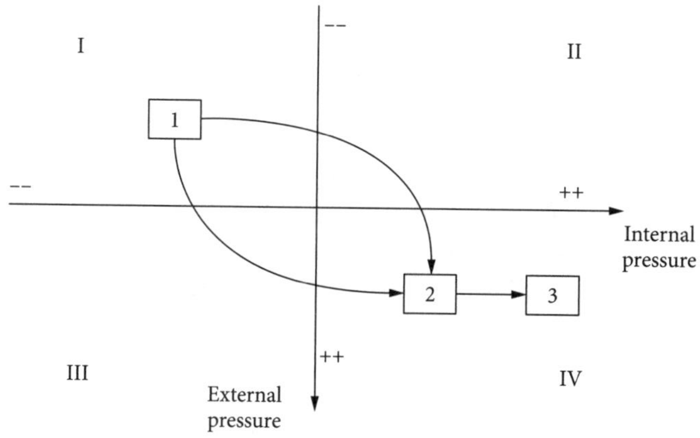

Source: Geert Bouckaert and John Halligan, *Managing Performance: International Comparisons* (London: Routledge, 2008), p. 55.

For the purpose of demonstrating the shift from not managing governments by numbers toward doing so, it is useful to look at how different management functions have changed and have taken performance information into account. Performance indicators play a key role—thus becoming key performance indicators, or KPIs—in organizing pressure to get better performance. By constantly emphasizing the importance of measuring, making performance numbers available for comparison, and creating a culture of performance, pressure for performance pushes toward performance.

This pressure has shifted (see figure 9-2) from low internal and low external pressure (quadrant I) to high internal and high external (quadrant IV), and probably is still continuing to increase in many countries in continental Europe.

Managing governments by numbers implies that logics of consequences and of appropriateness are constantly combined with logics of numbers to focus upon and to pressure for performance of the public sector.

This needs to happen for all relationships that are relevant to an organization. Figure 9-3 shows the internal and the external relationships that need to be taken into account to guarantee that governments increasingly are managed by numbers (numbers cited in this discussion refer to figure 9-3). Internal relationships, in the broad meaning of the phrase, imply not just the "black box" of the administration but also the link of the administration with the

Figure 9-3. *Internal and External Relationships for Managing Governments by Numbers*

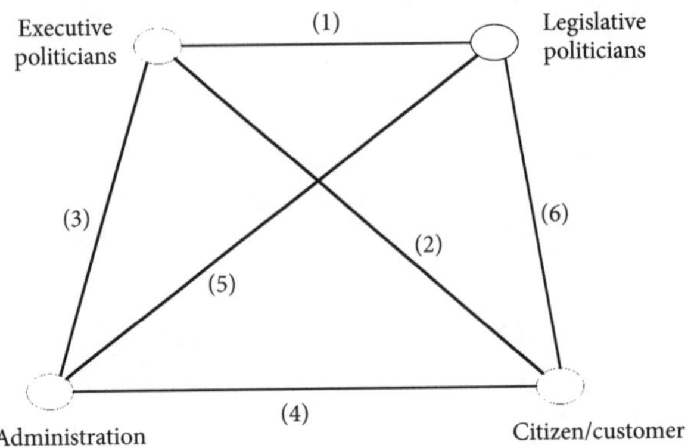

Source: Geert Bouckaert and John Halligan, *Managing Performance: International Comparisons* (London: Routledge, 2008), p. 201.

executive (3) and the legislative (5). Also the link between the executive and the legislative belongs to the relationships under internal scrutiny.

External relationships are those between the legislative (6), the executive (2), and the administration (4) and citizens qua citizen, customer, business, or NGO.

Public sector reform has put many new methods and techniques into position, internally and externally, to incorporate performance information in public sector management.

From an external point of view, the relationship between the administration and its customers (citizens, business, NGOs, other levels of government) has been "upgraded" by vouchers, benchmarks, specific charters, and satisfaction surveys. Administrations, in delivering services, have been affected by external pressures for better performance by CCT (compulsory competitive tendering), PPP (public-private partnership), market testing, and SLAs (service-level agreements). The link between the legislative branch and citizens now also has an ombudsperson service. The executive-citizens connection has been redefined in certain countries by general citizen charters.

Internally between government and parliament, performance-based budgets and performance audits have significantly allowed for a change in institutional checks and balances. The administration and its link with the legislative branch has been amended by adding hearings about contracts and their implementation. Contracts have ruled the relationship between the executive and the administration. Within the administration, all kinds of monitoring systems have been installed (ISO; Balanced Score Card, or BSO; Common

Assessment Framework, or CAF; European Foundation of Quality Management, ERQM; Management Accountability Framework, MAF) in order to follow up in a systematic way. Personnel management has been upgraded with performance information for intake, contracts, promotion, pay, and exit. Internal contract management is cascading down the performance-based contracts between the executive and the administration. Financial management has its operational budgets as derived from the performance-based budgets or contracts, cost accounting, and performance reporting. Finally, strategic management clearly focuses on KPIs in a multi-annual perspective.

This combined internal and external pressure for performance by importing numbers in all management functions and in all relationships has been organized and institutionalized to define responsibilities and accountabilities in general, and to manage all relationships in particular. Hence, a system of managing governments by numbers was designed and in many countries was also installed, even if the degree of applying indicators to activities and the coherence of looking at the connection of input/activity/output/outcome did not always match initial ambitions.[5]

Managing Governments by Numbers

International comparative and diachronic research shows four models (table 9-1) and logics of managing government performance, which implies measurement, incorporation, and the use of performance information.[6]

The analysis of managing governments by numbers results in four ideal types, or pure models: performance administration; managements of performances (double plural) as a siloed system; performance management as a comprehensive and integrated system; and performance governance as an open system. Obviously, reality is more complex than ideal types.

The starting position is termed *traditional/pre-performance* and it essentially recognizes that "performance" objectives in a generic sense can be found in most systems of public administration, but that many of them might be regarded as premodern management. In these cases, the expectation is that "performance" will be generalized and diffuse, with goals not defined in terms of performance. Input-driven and tax-collecting organizations, within law-based systems focusing on procedures and due process, may have a very implicit interest in performance. Data will be scarcely available, may not have an information value, will not be integrated, and will be hardly usable. A pre-Weberian bureaucracy covers this model quite well. There is an intuitive and subjective idea of performance, but ultimately there is an unawareness of what is functional because performance is not on the agenda.

Table 9-1. *Four Ideal Types of Managing Performance*

	Traditional/ pre-performance	*Performance administration*	*Managements of performances*	*Performance management*	*Performance governance*
1. Measuring	Intuitive, subjective	Administrative data registration, objective, mostly input and process	Specialized performance measurement systems	Hierarchical performance measurement systems	Consolidated performance measurement system
2. Incorporating	None	Some	Within different systems for specific management functions	Systemically internal integration	Systemically internal and external integration
3. Using	None	Limited: reporting, internal, single loop	Disconnected	Coherent, comprehensive, consistent	Societal use
4. Limitations	Functional	Ad hoc, selective, rule based	Incoherence	Complex, perhaps not sustainable as a stable system	Uncontrollable, unmanageable unawareness

Source: Author, based on Geert Bouckaert and John Halligan, *Managing Performance: International Comparisons* (London: Routledge, 2008), pp. 221–22.

With the first Ideal Type, *performance administration*, a commitment to measurement and performance is expected, but the relationship may not be explicit or well developed, and the application is often ad hoc. The performance administration ideal type's focus on measurement is inclined to be technically oriented, but its level of coherence may depend on which generation of measurement system is under discussion. This type is therefore relevant both to early experiments with measurement and performance and to successive phases of greater sophistication, including focused applications in recent times. There is an intuitive and generalized concern for performance that is registered and administered. Measurement becomes another administrative procedure that may be part of an administrative and legal setting, not a managerial or policy context. Information generated from these administrative procedures is disconnected from performance improvement strategies. Sophisticated rules for registering and administering performance are not developed to generate information to affect either managerial functions or elements of a policy cycle, but to improve registration of resources used and the way procedures have been implemented. This information is used for internal reporting purposes. Its only ambition is to reach the standards of the operating procedures. Therefore, single-loop learning is of the essence. A classical rule-based Weberian bureaucracy fits this type.

The second ideal type, *managements of performances,* is more complex. This category is intermediate between performance administration and performance management and arises where management and performance have been linked but the connections between them are underdeveloped because concurrent systems are operating. Managing several different performances includes performance measurement but goes beyond its administration. Managements of performances implies different types of performances according to different and unconnected systems. It results in the need to manage silos. This results in a diverse range of managements of different performances of organizations and programs. A diverging set of performance measurement systems feeds information into a disconnected set of management systems, resulting in different performances for different purposes, which are not necessarily linked in a hierarchical and logical way. Asymmetrical development of these function-based measurement systems makes them not very consistent, coherent, comprehensive, or integrated between these functions. However, within some functions there may be a high level of sophistication and development, even up to driving an improvement and reform process in other functions.

Performance management has distinctive features: coherence, integration, consistency, convergence, and comprehensiveness. It includes a solid performance measurement system beyond administration and proliferation. It includes an integration of performance information, which goes beyond ad hoc connectedness, for the purpose of using it in a coherent management improvement strategy. Performance management is conceived as a framework with system properties. It may also comprise several management and policy systems (management and policy information systems, and management and policy control systems). A framework may require different performance measurement systems for different purposes, but they must be hierarchically connected to satisfy the criteria of performance management as an ideal type. The performance management type also requires an explicit policy on measurement for managing the different functions and their performances. A crucial question is to what extent this complex ideal type is sustainable, especially in a dynamic and unstable environment.

It is possible to extrapolate toward a fourth ideal type, *performance governance*, which covers the broadest and deepest span and depth of performance. It also requires a matching set of instruments to cover this span and depth of control. Obviously, this refers to government-wide and broad societal coverage within a regional international arena.

One further question concerns the relationship between performance and management. What differentiates more developed from less developed systems of "managing government by numbers" are the level of incorporation and the use of incorporated performance information, that is, the application of management. Figure 9-4 gives the full picture of the scope of the "numbers," and the full and consistent management and policy cycle. Obviously, reality diverges from these four ideal models.

The implication for "managing government by numbers" is to develop a policy on the scope of performance. This could be a minimal scope (economy and efficiency), a broader scope (plus effectiveness and cost effectiveness), or a maximal scope (plus trust). It is notable that the Organization for Economic Cooperation and Development (OECD) with its "Government at a Glance" initiative takes a maximal scope.[7]

In conclusion, measurement is necessary but not sufficient; incorporation in documents and procedures is needed. And incorporation is necessary but not sufficient; use is also needed.

Related Topics and Conditions

These logics and models need to be qualified in reality. Managing numbers by governments is the first area where politics and internal audit may be in tension. Second, it is necessary to have a CBA of managing by numbers since costs and benefits are sometimes out of balance. This has also to do with a mismatch of supply and demand of numbers, or with an unbalanced use and non-use of numbers (benchmarks). Obviously, the availability of numbers remains an issue, also within the OECD, even if consolidation and deconsolidation is possible. It is not easy to know the status of how much governments are managed by numbers, but there is evidence of five trajectories to improve the input-output ratio in the public sector.

Managing Numbers by Governments

Controlling nonfinancial information becomes an important element in politics today. This implies that an independent authority with the capacity to validate data is crucial. As a consequence, internal audit but also statistical institutions have gained power and authority in an evidence-based policy context. Increasingly, performance measurement policies become political since the choice of certain measures is not neutral and becomes part of agenda setting and of making problems visible or not. To the extent that quality standards for numbers are different depending on the use of accounting standards or statistical standards, managing numbers by governments becomes a political issue.

A Cost-Benefit Analysis (CBA) of Managing by Numbers

A perception of an imbalance between benefits and costs puts pressure on keeping a full span of performance management. Costs of numbers are certain, unconditional, undisputable, clearly connected to organizations, and immediate. However, benefits of numbers are not always certain, are conditional and disputable, spread more widely over a system, and are oriented more toward the future. This means that costs and benefits have different natures, where benefits are less firm and tangible than costs for performance information.

A perception of excessive cost compared to benefits caused the Netherlands to generate the principle of "comply or explain": comply with the regulations to provide performance information, or else "explain" why you are not complying.

In addition to this observation, the supply of and demand for numbers do not always match. Two zones of frustration emerge in managing governments by numbers: one where numbers are expected but not provided, and one where numbers are provided though not expected nor requested, let alone used. Obviously, the challenge is to improve the supply-demand interaction by moving to a more matching position as shown in box D of figure 9-5. This implies that supply and demand need to be organized, and their matching as well, to avoid these zones of frustration and these mismatches. For that purpose there is a

Figure 9-4. *An Ideal Model for Managing Governments by Numbers*

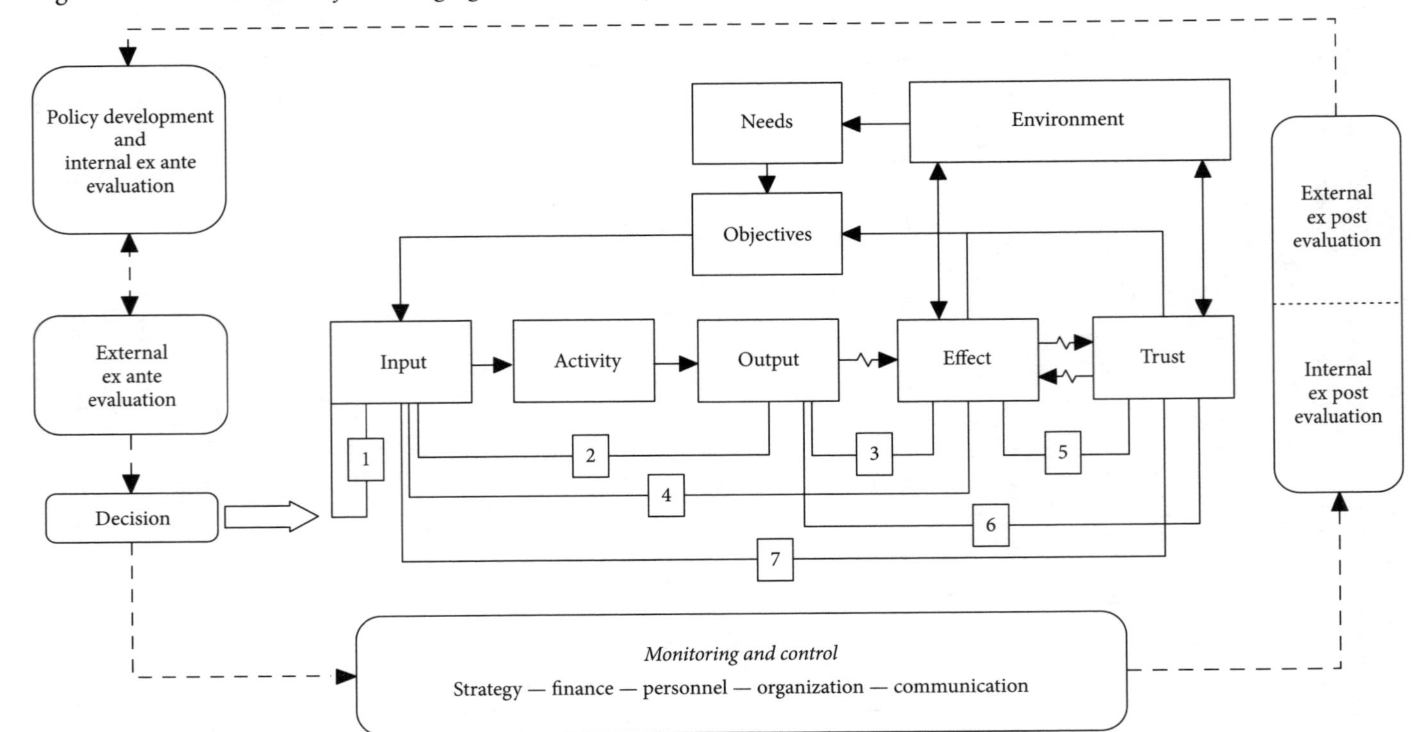

Source: Geert Bouckaert and John Halligan, *Managing Performance: International Comparisons* (London: Routledge, 2008), p. 121.

Figure 9-5. *Matching Supply of and Demand for Numbers in Managing Governments*

			DEMAND	
		NO DEMAND	WEAK	STRONG
NO OFFER		A	B1	B2
OFFER	WEAK	C1	D1	D2
	STRONG	C2	D3	D4

Source: Geert Bouckaert and John Halligan, *Managing Performance: International Comparisons* (London: Routledge, 2008), p. 113.

need to shift from supply (availability of data) to demand (need for managing). It is very tempting only to use data that are available rather than data that are necessary to manage and therefore need to be collected. Therefore a demand-driven supply will increase the changes of effective use, and of a balanced cost-benefit analysis. This demand-generating supply should be driven and triggered by relevant problems such as, for example, savings, capacity, quality, legitimacy, flexibility, or mobility. In conclusion, benefits may be enhanced by organizing a demand that drives supply.

Once demand is driving the supply of numbers, effective incorporation and use of numbers will probably also be more obvious, and non-incorporation and non-use will be more avoidable.

There may be many reasons for non-use of performance data.[8] Poor quality or perceived insufficient quality may be a technical reason. Psychological barriers may be another, since "satisficing" and bounded rationality define limits. There may be cultural barriers as a result of different professional cultures (for example, engineers versus social workers), or an entrepreneurial versus a bureaucratic culture. There also may be an institutional reason. A balance of power between finance and line departments, or a balance of professions (auditors and managers versus content professionals). In any case, there are significant consequences of non-use, such as, for example, exaggerated claims for "best practices," weak institutional memories, or reduced accountability. At the same time there are significant functional behavioral effects of using performance information such as, for example, learning and innovation,

Figure 9-6. *Managing Different Levels of Governments by Numbers*

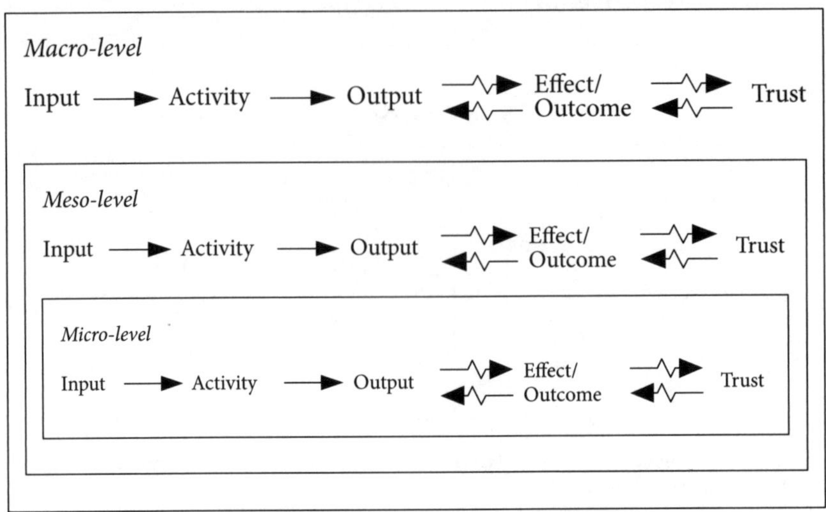

Source Geert Bouckaert and John Halligan, "Managing Performance across Levels of Government: Lessons Learned or Reproducing Disconnections?" in *Policy, Performance and Management in Governance and Intergovernmental Relations: Transatlantic Perspectives*, edited by Edoardo Ongaro and others (Cheltenham, UK: Edgar Elgar, 2011), p. 249.

grounded steering and control, and substantial responsibility and accountability mechanisms.

Managing by Numbers, but at Which Level of Government?

Since the public sector consists of different levels of government, with a micro-level (organizations), policy fields (with clusters of organizations at different levels), and the macro or whole-of-government level, there is a depth of performance and hence an implication for consolidating and deconsolidating numbers to manage government (see figure 9-6).

Micro-level performance is about inputs (quantity and quality), which are processed into activities (quantity and quality), which result in outputs (quantity and quality). These outputs, services, or products leave the black box and enter society. This is the micro- and organizational level with a direct transfer of an output to a user-customer-citizen. These outputs are sometimes directly consumable (permit, subsidy, information). In many cases outputs just concern the degree of availability (for example, using a resurfaced highway), sometimes even for the next generation (for example, water purified), or they are indivisible public goods (for example, a legal framework). The quantitative aspect may be expressed in financial or in physical terms, number of full-time equivalents or budgets approved, number of inspections or transactions processed, and number of services delivered.[9]

Resources and activities also have a qualitative dimension (for example, skills and competencies of civil servants, or internal waiting time, or internal error rates). The focus on output quality has gained momentum as part of a citizen- and customer-focused performance definition. Increasingly, quality is linked to organizations' use of managerial models—both generic models such as International Standard Organization, Balanced Score Card, the European Foundation for Quality Management model, or the European Common Assessment Framework and other quality models that are country-specific such as the Management Accountability Framework in Canada. The latter became a guarantee, safeguard, and proof of qualitative output.[10] One could assume a direct, almost linear, relationship between resources as inputs, activities as throughputs resulting in products, and services as outputs. However, government is not a mechanistic, routine-based machine.[11]

Increasingly, control systems monitor quantity and quality as output features, but this is not sufficient. Citizens as customers receive and perceive these outputs with levels of expectations. In reality, both expectation and perception levels vary. In reality, there is a clustering of different perceptions (for example, waiting time, error rates, timeliness of service delivery) within levels of expectation. Obviously, one could also have a clustering of different expectations within levels of perception. The encounter of output quantity and quality with individual perception levels and expectation levels results in levels of satisfaction. This positive or negative satisfaction also influences perceptions and expectations positively or negatively, hence the reverse mechanism. There is a particular level of satisfaction because of an effect or outcome: a letter has arrived on time, the bus transported a citizen to the right place in due time, the municipal sports center was fit for use, the garbage collection team collected all the garbage, the roads were repaired quickly and competently, and so forth. There is an effect or outcome that needs to be measured, for example, the level of street cleanliness or crime levels in city districts, which could be as "objective" as possible. In addition, there is a subjective interpretation, influenced by perceptions and expectations (for example, a feeling of cleanliness or of security), that results in satisfaction. Research has shown that there is not always a good correlation between the "objective" and the "subjective" types of effects and outcomes or between a producer-defined increase in quality of a service and a change in satisfaction level.[12]

THE MICRO-LEVEL: ORGANIZATIONS. A crucial final aspect of the micro-model is the level trust in the individual service-delivering organization (including staff that members of the public encounter "at the window"). Trust levels have an impact on satisfaction and are in many cases crucial to the proper functioning of service delivery.[13] The degree of trust in public sector organizations felt by citizens (and vice versa, the level of trust felt by public sector employees in citizens and customers) is a crucial societal mechanism to construct control systems. Lacking or decreasing trust levels of the public sector in its own citizens leads to the need for additional inspections or monitoring-based control systems. Adequate and increasing trust levels represent social capital that can be used to increase support for service delivery upgrades, contributing to the effectiveness and outcome of outputs.

Trust levels may also have an impact on effects or outcomes. Teaching in schools, hospital therapies, or police security may be more effective when parents and children trust their teachers, patients trust their doctors, and citizens trust their security services. In the field of coproduction (for example, public-private partnerships, or citizens as customers who contribute to public service delivery), trust is crucial to upgrade constant output quantity and quality to higher levels of effectiveness. According to Kaifeng Yang and Marc Holzer, "The ambiguity of the performance-trust link does not suggest that performance is unimportant; rather, it implies there is much more to be learned about the business of government."[14]

Within public sector and public management reform, New Public Management has put too much emphasis on single organizations' performance. The ideologically driven assumption that autonomous agencies that are connected and coordinated through market-type mechanisms has not only ignored the primacy of politics, but also the importance of government as a system of organizations that establishes performance. New Public Management has put too much emphasis on audits of single-organizational performance. Of course, there is a need to connect perception, expectations, satisfaction, and trust, as elements in performance level. And obviously, benchmarks of single organizations and of clusters of comparable organizations have made variations in performance visible and have allowed the establishment of bench learning. Nevertheless, the micro-level, though necessary, is not sufficient to manage governments by numbers.

THE MESO-LEVEL: POLICY FIELDS. Since effects or outcomes are realized by a range, a chain, or a network of organizations, public sector performance measurement systems should not just be organized at the individual organizational (micro) level but also at the level of a policy field (for example, education, health, environment, security), or a product or service chain such as the food or security chain. This is the meso-level. Outcomes and effects may be objective or subjective. Also outcomes and effects are affected by the changing policy environment. This results in the construction of "logic models" that represent a sequence (beyond the organizational clusters in a black box) of outputs, intermediate outcomes and effects, and ultimate and final outcomes and effects, or impacts.[15] These logic models are in many cases designed by sectoral policy specialists.

These models and sequences are not linear and continuous. There are disconnections. This results in a "first Grand Canyon" in the public sector measurement system, between outputs and a disrupted and distant, almost unreachable but visible sequence of intermediate and ultimate effects and outcomes—for example, police outputs do not necessarily lead to increased security.

Absent market mechanisms in the public sector—even if quasi-markets are being established—the politically based value assessment of effect priorities, the changing perceptions and expectations of the citizenry and civil society, and environmental contingencies result in a disrupted link between outputs on the one hand and intermediate outcomes and objective and subjective effects on the other.

A "second Grand Canyon" emerges between the end outcomes and effects to the ultimate level (meso-level) of trust. Effective school, health, and security policies and systems could lead to a level of trust in these policies and systems, and this trust could facilitate their effectiveness, but this connection is very conditional and cannot be taken for granted. There is also a reverse influence: particular levels of trust may affect levels of effects or outcomes. Comparable levels of output quantity and quality, with similar levels of intermediate outcomes, may result in higher levels of ultimate outcomes because of higher trust levels. School outcomes may be higher if students and parents trust their schools and teachers. Hospital outcomes may be higher if patients trust their doctors and hospitals. Police outcomes may result in higher levels of safety if citizens trust their police. It is useful, possible, and necessary to understand performance at this meso-level. It invites questions regarding the links among inputs, outputs, effects and outcomes, and trust.

This need to improve the correspondence of outputs and outcomes has three implications at this meso-level. First, new coordination mechanisms are needed among projects of major policy programs, among organizations in a policy field, and among stages of a service chain, especially after the disastrous organizational fragmentation driven by the New Public Management ideology.[16] Recognition of this state of affairs has led to efforts to reintegrate organizational strategic plans and develop cross-organizational policy designs. There is more integrated implementation using a holding company concept through consolidated budgets, or an integration of organizational performance audits and policy evaluations, also called "landscape reviews." These options should improve the focus on ultimate outcomes. This also implies that managing governments by numbers implies managing and monitoring coordination.

Second, from a practical point of view there is a need to integrate managerial and policy-related professional communities—for example, auditors and evaluators—to connect different levels of performance.

Third, there is a need to manage how micro is connected to meso, and how meso is realized through micro.

THE MACRO-LEVEL: WHOLE OF GOVERNMENT. The macro-level entity is government or governance-wide within an international regional cross-border arena.[17] Increasingly, synthetic indicators at a country level and whole-of-government level, such as World Competitiveness Yearbook and Growth Competitiveness Index, include public sector performance as an indicator of government efficiency. The World Competitiveness Yearbook estimates government efficiency along five dimensions: public finance; fiscal policy; institutional framework, including survey data on government decisions, political parties, transparency, public service, bureaucracy, and bribing and corruption; business legislation; and societal framework, including survey data on justice, risk of political instability, social cohesion, discrimination, and gender issues.

It could be said that in the public sector even societal outcomes and effects are not ends in themselves. The ultimate ambition is to guarantee a functional level of trust by the citizens of a region in all its institutions and organizations, and especially in its *public* institutions and organizations. Linking effects or outcomes to trust is like trying to bridge the "second Grand Canyon" in the public sector. The assumption that effects and outcomes may positively influence trust is weak and has not been corroborated by either theories or empirical studies.[18] However, public sector reform has always, implicitly or explicitly, referred to the ambition to bridge this major chasm.

A whole-of-government approach carries three levels of implications for this macro-level performance model. First, the use of government-wide indicators is increasing; an example is the societal indicators used throughout the Canadian government. The need to show the value added by the public sector to a country's competitiveness results in international benchmarks of quality-of-life indicators. It is therefore important to link the macro-level to the meso- and micro-levels, but also to consolidate the micro- and meso-levels into a macro-level. This consolidation-deconsolidation exercise is not just a technical and statistical matter, but a crucial matter of assigning responsibilities and organizing mechanisms for accountability, as part of managing government by numbers.

Second, management science and policy science need to be connected and further linked to political science because of the priority setting between policy fields. Third, from a practical point of view there is a need to share performance information among the public sector, executive politicians, legislative politicians, and civil society. This is the aim of the governance performance perspective.

Managing Government by Numbers: Five Trajectories to Improve the Input-Output Numbers

Finally, numbers allow for management and reform-minded policymakers to make choices that are based on much more then just numbers. This is part of the logic of appropriateness. Issues of equity, of the rule of law, of protecting civil rights, of enforcing principles of transparency and openness may be in tension with a logic of consequences. For example, according to a pure efficiency rationality it may be acceptable to drop charges for traffic violations if the procedure to prosecute is too expensive compared to the penalty. By analogy, according to a pure efficiency rationality it may be acceptable to stop service delivery in remote areas since the cost is too high. These cases prove that the next five trajectories should be qualified.

Five possible trajectories emerge in managing governments by numbers (see figure 9-7). They involve doing . . .

. . . more with less. This is a common slogan, but is seldom implemented.

. . . more with the same. This is a more comfortable position for the administration and for the customer.

. . . the same with less. This is a recognizable pattern, especially for services that cannot be reduced, such as security, health, or education.

. . . less with much less. This is an atrophying level of service.

. . . much more with more. This is an investment strategy, which could be combined with an e-government approach.

Conclusion

Increasingly, governments are managed by numbers. This solves certain problems, but not all, and also creates new problems. This shift from managing without to management by numbers also helps to make legally defined responsibilities substantial and tangible and substantiates accountability beyond a formal level.

From this point of view it is important to combine the logic of numbers with the logic of governmental systems based on consequences and appro-

Figure 9-7. *Five Trajectories to Manage Governments by Numbers*

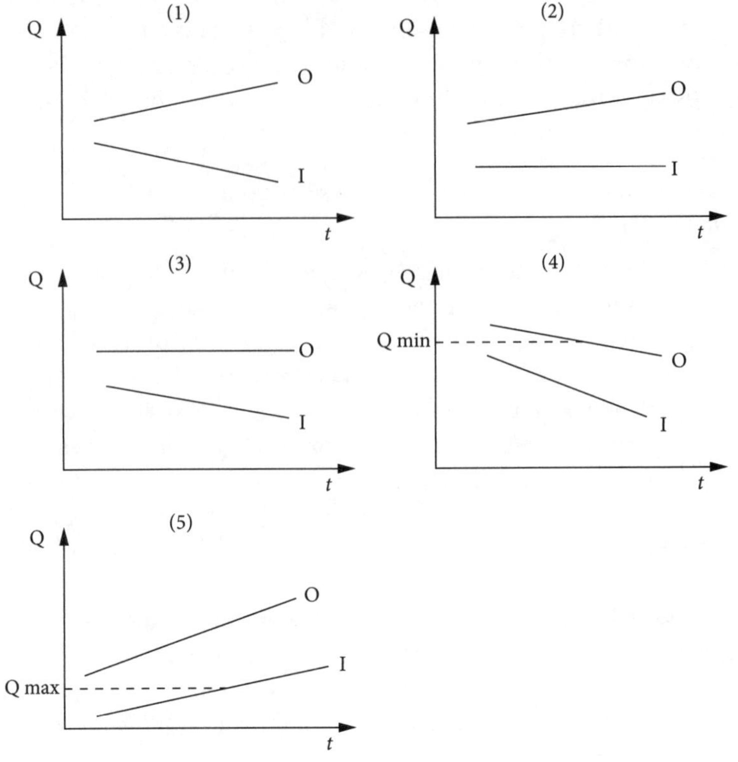

Source: Author.

priateness into the logic of public management. To do this it is important to look at the management of numbers—the cost-benefit analysis of managing by numbers—to guarantee a sufficiently large scope and depth of performance, to match the supply of numbers to the demand for them, and to choose trajectories by using numbers in a broader context.

Notes

1. James G. March and Johan P. Olson, *Rediscovering Institutions* (New York: Free Press, 1989).

2. Organization for Economic Cooperation and Development, *Measuring Government Activity*, edited by Christopher Pollitt, Geert Bouckaert, and Wouter Van Dooren (Paris: OECD, 2009), p. 130.

3. Kjell Goldmann, "Appropriateness and Consequences: The Logic of Neo-Institutionalism," *Governance* 18 (January 2005): 35–52 (see 35).

4. Geert Bouckaert and John Halligan, *Managing Performance: International Comparisons* (London: Routledge, 2008), p. 440.

5. Christopher Pollitt and Geert Bouckaert, *Public Management Reform: A Comparative Analysis—NPM, Governance and the Neo-Weberian State,* 3rd ed. (Oxford University Press, 2011), p. 367.

6. Bouckaert and Halligan, *Managing Performance*, p. 440.

7. Organization for Economic Cooperation and Development, *Government at a Glance* (Paris: OECD, 2010)

8. Wouter Van Dooren, Geert Bouckaert, and John Halligan, *Performance Management in the Public Sector* (London: Routledge, 2010), p. 208.

9. Harry Hatry, *Performance Measurement: Getting Results* (Washington: Urban Institute Press, 1999).

10. Organization for Economic Cooperation and Development, *Measuring Government Activity* (Paris: OECD, 2009), p. 130.

11. Geert Bouckaert and Arie Halachmi, "The Range of Performance Indicators in the Public Sector: Theory vs. Practice," in *Re-engineering and Performance Measurement in Criminal Justice and Social Programmes*, edited by Arie Halachmi and David Grant (Brussels and Perth, West Australia: International Institute of Administrative Sciences/Ministry of Justice, 1996), pp. 91–106.

12. Bouckaert and Halligan, *Managing Performance*, p. 440.

13 Steven Van de Walle and Geert Bouckaert, "Public Service Performance and Trust in Government: The Problem of Causality," *International Journal of Public Administration* 26 (August 2003): 891–913.

14. Kaifeng Yang and Marc Holzer, "The Performance-Trust Link: Implications for Performance Measurement," *Public Management Review* 66, no. 1 (January–February 2006): 114–26 (see 123).

15. Harry Hatry, *Performance Measurement: Getting Results* (Washington D.C.: Urban Institute Press, 1999).

16. Geert Bouckaert, B. Guy Peters, and Koen Verhoest, *The Coordination of Public Sector Organisations* (Basingstoke, UK: Palgrave Macmillan, 2010), p. 311.

17. Andreas Obser, "Multilateral Organisations' Performance Assessment: Opportunities and Limitations for Harmonisation among Development Agencies," discussion paper 19 (Bonn: German Development Institute, 2007).

18. See Steven Van de Walle, Steven Van Roosbroek, and Geert Bouckaert, "Annex: Data on Trust in the Public Sector," prepared for the Organization for Economic Cooperation and Development (Paris: OECD, 2005) (www.oecd.org/dataoecd/25/52/41951220.pdf).

DENITA CEPIKU, ANDREA BONOMI SAVIGNON, AND LUIGI CORVO

10 *Strategic Management in Italian Ministries: An Empirical Assessment of Gains from and Gaps in Reforms*

In the two decades since 1990, governments have been facing very important challenges: the global financial and economic crisis, climate change, and demographic ageing are just the most recent of known issues that need to be addressed. Citizens are turning to the state, seeking immediate solutions to complex problems and demanding high-quality public services. While society's expectations of government are increasing, the resources available to meet these needs are becoming increasingly limited. As the current global crisis has shown, one of the imperatives is to find a balance between providing short-term solutions to the most immediate problems and ensuring intergenerational equity in a long-term perspective. Public sector reforms since 1990 have been driven by the belief that there is a performance deficit and have emphasized the need for agencies to define and measure strategic goals, targets, and achievements.[1] In this setting, strategic management becomes a key notion in support of evidence-based policymaking.

Literature Review

Strategic planning, lately also called "strategic thinking" and "strategic management," has been singled out as one of the critical areas of public management research as well as a still-relevant approach in the new post-Weberian organization.[2] It has been defined as a disciplined effort to produce fundamental decisions and actions that shape and guide what an organization is, what it does, and why it does it, within legal bounds.[3] Empirical evidence has indicated that strategic planning is associated with higher performance.[4] A consistent part of this empirical literature draws on the Miles and Snow model in recognizing a taxonomy of "ideal types" for organizational strategy adopters in relation to structure.[5]

The process varies from context to context. The conventional approach to strategic management includes the following steps:

1. Development of an initial agreement concerning the strategic planning effort
2. Identification and clarification of mandates
3. Development and clarification of mission and values
4. Assessment of the external environment
5. Assessment of the internal environment
6. Identification of the key strategic issues
7. Development of strategy
8. Description of the organization in the future

Implementation of each step requires the use of specific instruments.[6]

The strategic management process not only is a disciplined path toward goal achievement but also represents a genuinely innovative cultural approach for public organizations.[7] It is an opportunity to promote a confrontation moment for decisionmaking between policymakers and managers, to increase engagement through staff participation, and to revisit what is truly important for the organization.

The literature has highlighted the following issues:

1. The specificities of strategic management in the public sector, namely, the relevance of democracy and politics, activities regulated by law, and funding based on taxes
2. The preconditions of the political and administrative context that enable effective strategic management
3. The aims and benefits of strategic management in a post–New Public Management (NPM) era
4. The different approaches: rational planning and political decisionmaking models, logical incrementalism, and strategy absence
5. The different stages of strategy formulation, implementation, and control[8]

More recently, the literature has emphasized a concern with issues of cross-cutting (the need to coordinate with other ministries), the need to integrate strategic planning with other processes, and the advent of new instruments such as scenario planning.[9]

The theory of strategic management belongs to the rational approaches to public sector decisionmaking and thus is a response to the objections raised in public administration toward bounded rationality.[10]

We acknowledge a gap when it comes to linking the quality of management to the performances achieved, which is especially true for research carried on outside the United States and United Kingdom that focuses on the central level of government—that is, on one of the extremes in Barry Bozeman's publicness continuum.[11] However, in this chapter our aim is neither to demonstrate that strategic management matters nor to link organizational characteristics to the choice—and effectiveness—of strategic stances; rather, our objective is to analyze whether other aspects, such as policy and context, also influence the take-up of strategic planning processes in the public sector.[12] In other words, in this chapter we make an effort to connect policy design and policy management.[13]

To do this we view "snapshots" of the state of art of strategic management in Italian ministries between, first, the mid-nineties' reforms and the provisions introduced in 2006, and, second, the recent reform of strategic planning introduced in 2009. We aim to present an overview and understanding of the way strategic management has been adopted and implemented in ministries, also as a result of the process of central policy design and implementation. We conclude by identifying some relevant policy implications.

Research Methods

The object of our research, strategic management in central government, is at an intermediate state of development.[14] Our research draws on two bodies of literature: a reasonably mature theory and an unexplored setting, namely, central government in non-Anglo-Saxon countries.[15]

For our study we analyzed the main official documents of the ministries and the central guidance documents—issued by the Committee for Strategic Planning and, later on, the Commission for Evaluation, Transparency, and Integrity—and undertook valuable nonparticipant observation, made possible by our taking part in the activities of the Committee for Strategic Planning (at the Office of the President of the Council of Ministers) from 2006 to 2008.

The relevant variables were determined via document analysis and observation with the aim of identifying groups of trend-sharing ministries, using cluster analysis techniques and including a longitudinal comparison of the years 2007, 2008, and 2009.

Research Objectives

This chapter has a *descriptive* aim—exploring strategic management patterns in Italian ministries in 2007, 2008, and 2009—and a *normative* aim—assessing the effectiveness of the laws and central guidelines provided since 2006 and the feasibility of the new reform introduced in 2009, with the aim of identifying policy and operational implications.

Rich, detailed, and evocative data are produced on the strategic management process in all Italian ministries. Exploring whether and to what extent strategic management occurs in Italian ministries includes an exploration of the inescapable steps that precede strategy formulation (such as environmental analysis, stakeholder mapping and engagement, risk management, and so on) as well as other methodological aspects of strategy formulation in terms of key features of goals and indicators, interaction between the different actors (central government, policymakers, and senior civil servants), linkage between the strategic planning process and the budgeting, performance measurement, and communication systems.

Information was gathered on the approach adopted by Italian ministries in introducing strategic management and on the results achieved; on the main actors of the strategic management process; on how the strategies were developed and implemented; and on the instruments used (SWOT analysis, scenario planning, portfolio analysis, stakeholder mapping and engagement, risk mapping and management, mission, vision, goals and indicators, and performance and target agreements, among others). Additional investigated areas included the interaction of strategic management with other management systems, especially performance budgeting and human resources management.

The second aim—in alignment with the normative nature of the theory of strategic management—relates to the issue of how to make public organizations more likely to engage in strategic management, despite all factors that lead to "myopia, slack and bureau autonomy."[16] Attempts were made to identify cluster groups of ministries with similar features and to discriminate between sets of strategy adopters, in order to provide conclusions on how both strategic management in ministries and central guidance can be improved. We identify both supply- and demand-side factors that have hindered the implementation of strategic management systems in ministries.

Information Sources, Units of Analysis, and Variables

Three main official documents of strategic planning in ministries were analyzed:

1. The annual strategic plan (*direttiva annuale*) containing also the statement of intents on political priorities by the minister (*atto di indirizzo*) and the detailed financial and action plans
2. The annual budget (*nota preliminare*)
3. The final report on performance, which should also inform the budget debate in the parliament

The authors performed an in-depth analysis by reading all the official documents and gathering data that constituted the basis for analyzed variables, as described in the following sections. Several measures were taken to limit the errors inherent in the subjective assessment process. The authors worked independently of each other, and the discrepancy between the assessments was less than 1.5 percent; variables that were rated differently were reviewed once again, discussed, and agreed upon.

Most of these documents were introduced or reformed in 2006, so the analysis starts with documents from 2007. In 2008 there was a change in government that could have influenced the actual execution of the reforms, and for this reason performance reports were no longer issued in 2008. Therefore we based our analysis of the monitoring and reporting stages on the performance information included in the budget.

Our units of analysis are the sixteen Italian ministries of the central government that have governance responsibilities in specific fields, representing all the ministries:

1. Ministry of Social Policy
2. Ministry of Health
3. Ministry of Labor
4. Ministry of Transport
5. Ministry of Universities and Research
6. Ministry of Public Education
7. Ministry of Foreign Affairs
8. Ministry of the Interior
9. Ministry of Defense
10. Ministry of Agriculture, Food, and Forestry Policies
11. Ministry of Economic Development
12. Ministry of Infrastructure
13. Ministry of Environment
14. Ministry of Economy and Finance
15. Ministry of Cultural Heritage and Activities
16. Ministry of Justice

Not included in the study are ministries "without portfolio" (such as the Ministry for Regional Policy and Ministry for Equal Opportunities) that do not prepare a budget and do not have at their disposal a fully structured organizational body.

The variables resemble the classic stages of the strategic management process. Our investigation is document-based and is limited to the coverage of the phases of strategic planning; it provides only limited evidence on the quality of strategic planning. For instance, if the official documentation on strategic management by the Ministry of Social Policy provides evidence that

Box 10-1. *Protocol for Analysis of Variables*

*Group 1: Variables Verifying Documents**

1. Is the document called "Strategic Plan" available for the year 2007?
2. Is the document called "Budget" available for the year 2007?
3. Is the document called "Report on Performance" available for the year 2007?

Group 2: Variables Giving Evidence of Analytical Activities by Ministries

4. Is there evidence of external environment analysis?
5. Is there evidence of internal environment analysis?
6. Is there evidence of stakeholder management activity?
7. Is the connection with the previous strategic planning cycle emphasized?
8. Is there evidence of risk management analysis?

Group 3: Variables Analyzing the Formulation of a Strategic Plan

9. Are there multiyear strategic objectives in strategic plans?
10. Are there cross-cutting strategic objectives, shared with other ministries?
11. Are the strategic objectives linked to the budget management cycle?
12. Is the linkage between strategic objectives and priority of policymakers emphasized?
13. Are consistent indicators connected to strategic objectives?
14. Is an exact deadline determined for the objectives?

* Variables not included in the cluster analysis.

some internal analysis or stakeholder mapping have been performed, we take this to mean that these phases have been carried out, but we have no objective information on the quality of the strategic analysis and we cannot compare it with a similar activity in another ministry. Therefore, we have opted for binary variables and left for a later study research on the quality of strategic management, based on primary data such as interviews.

In order to assess the methodological rigor (coverage of stages) of the strategic management process in Italian ministries we have identified fourteen binary variables, which are classifiable in three groups. Box 10-1 shows the protocol of our analysis, divided into three groups. The first group of variables (group 1) aims at verifying the availability of the documents useful for collecting information on the methodology of strategic management. The objective of this area is to answer the very preliminary question: Is there evidence of strategic planning activity in the Italian ministries studied?

The second group of variables (group 2) aims to locate evidence of analytical activities that should be conducted by strategists prior to the formulation of a strategic plan. To formulate a good strategy, the organization has to be aware of the characteristics of its internal and external environment. Several tools are available for conducting these analyses, such as the SWOT/C analysis, stakeholder management, and risk management. The rationale for these variables is clear, since the environmental analysis is undertaken to make organizations aware of their internal strengths and weaknesses, and this awareness is the starting point for networking with stakeholders and effectively managing risks. It is also important to connect the strategic plan with the previous cycle of strategic planning to ensure the temporal continuity of the strategic decisions and activities.

The third group of variables (group 3) aims to analyze the formulation of the strategic plan, with particular attention to strategic objectives and indicators. We focus on the main characteristics highlighted in the literature, such as the linkage with the budget management cycle, which should ensure financial sustainability; the multiyear time horizon, which represents an indicator of the mid- to long-term orientation; the presence of cross-cutting activities and objectives; and the specification of consistent indicators for performance measurement. The objective of this area is to establish whether the formulation of the strategic plan is methodologically appropriate: that is, are all the stages recommended in the literature covered and are the key features of strategic objectives present?

The Cluster Analysis Method

Besides formulating descriptive statistics for the collected data, we decided to employ cluster analysis to identify similar groups of ministries in terms of their strategic analysis and strategy formulation for the years 2007, 2008, and 2009. Cluster analysis has been a rather popular methodology in the field of strategic management because of the emphasis of strategic management on identifying groups of similar organizations. By taking a sample of organizations or other elements and grouping them such that the statistical variance among the grouped, or clustered, organizations is minimized while between-cluster variance is maximized, cluster analysis permits the inclusion of multiple variables as sources of configuration definition, thus capturing the multidimensionality of constructs of interest in strategy research. Even absent a large observation sample, it can provide rich descriptions of configurations without overspecifying a model.[17] In fact, the identification of clusters is inductive and empirically based, instead of guided by theory. Covering three years in the analysis allows us to compare changes in cluster membership from one year to the other, and to assess the evolution of strategic management practice in that period.

We decided to use cluster analysis for the second group of variables, on strategic analysis, and the third group, on strategy formulation, since the first group merely indicates the formal availability of documentary evidence and is not useful for our analytical purposes. The cases of observation are all sixteen Italian ministries.

We used agglomerative hierarchical algorithms, which the theory indicates as best suiting data sets where the sample is rather small and measures are qualitative. In our case, all the variables are binary. Similarity was measured by calculating binary Euclidean distances and aggregation was conducted by employing Ward's method, as this has been indicated as the best method in the absence of outliers.[18]

The clusterization algorithm was thus run in an SPSS environment using the original eleven variables from the two groups, each comprising sixteen observations, including the three years simultaneously so as to obtain a blocked membership outcome. The visual inspection of the dendrogram result and the coefficient analysis (see figure 10-1) suggested the existence of three separate clusters for the three aggregate years. We then graphically represented the cluster positioning for the whole time interval considered in a scatter plot, which features the percentage of "yes" answers on formulation variables on the X axis and the "yes" answers on analysis ones on the Y axis,

Strategic Management in Italian Ministries: Analysis of the Policy Design and Implementation Guidelines

Managerial reforms in Italy date back to the 1980s, when several public administrations, mainly local governments, introduced some management principles and tools. The results of these experimental programs were modest, but they were useful for testing the tools and preparing those in the field for nationwide reforms such as those included in the main laws that were soon approved. They also showed that efficiency and effectiveness principles did not run counter to more traditional values such as legality and transparency.

During the 1990s, public sector reforms touched almost all functions of public management, not only functions such as financial management, human resources management, and organizational structures but also areas such as regional devolution and transparency. Political reform agendas were clearly inspired by the NPM model, and many of them introduced some of NPM's key features, such as market-type mechanisms and performance management. In practice, however, the reform resembled a different model, one that puts the emphasis on quality and citizens' satisfaction, to be achieved mainly through the creation of a professional culture of quality and service.

Figure 10-1. *Cluster Analysis Coefficients*

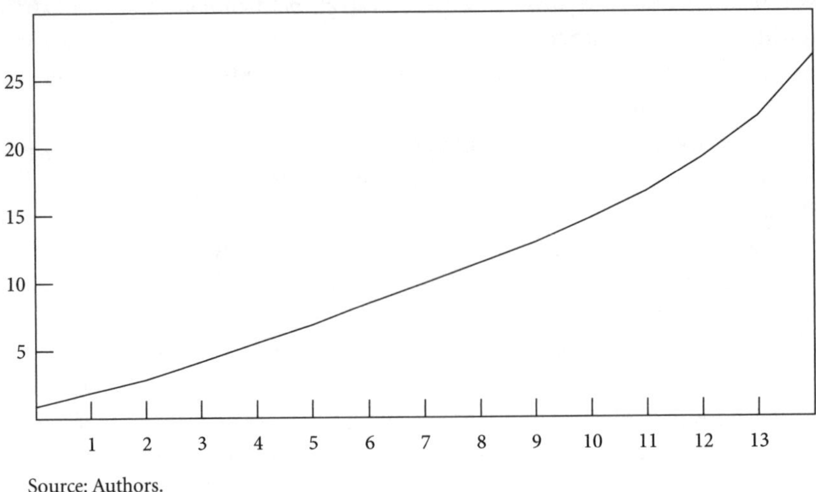

Source: Authors.

The imperative of representative democracy, key to the Weberian model, remained firmly in place while evolving to include a range of devices for facilitating consultation with citizens.[19]

In 1999 the Committee for Strategic Planning (Comitato Tecnico-Scientifico, or CTS) at the Presidency of the Council of Ministers issued a first decree relating to strategic planning with the general goal of achieving efficiency, effectiveness, and economy in the public sector. The interesting point with this first wave of reforms is the sequence of policy implementation that was mandated: The first round of reform was to consist of evaluating the performance of senior civil servants. The second round gave guidance on the introduction of accrual accounting and managerial controls. This first decree proved ineffective because it took place in a vacuum—the absence of any strategic analysis and planning processes.[20]

In 2006 the CTS's mission was revised. Now the focus shifted to strategic management and planning, which was finally acknowledged to be a precondition for any form of strategic control and performance evaluation or performance-related pay. The guidelines issued shortly afterward pursued two main aims: (1) to strengthen the connection between policy formulation—the political program of the government for the legislature—and the strategy of ministries; and (2) to enhance the integration of financial resources planning and the strategic management process within ministries.[21]

The CTS provided detailed guidance on the different phases of the strategic management process, the instruments to be used, the actors involved, and the specific role to be played by the ministerial strategic units, called the Internal Control Services (*Servizi di Controllo Interno*, or SECIN). SECINs were directly embedded at the ministerial top management level to support the implementation of strategic planning. The recommended process resembled a top-down rational planning approach and was heavily regulated. Each minister, after considering the ministerial mission and mandate, had to state the political priorities, which became the basis on which the ministerial top management defined a first proposal of strategic objectives and a budget plan. This proposal was then transmitted to the National General Accounting Department of the Ministry of Economy and Finance (Ragioneria Generale dello Stato—Ministero dell'Economia e Finanze, or RGS-MEF) and had to be revised two times a year, following the Mid-term Expenditure Framework (MTEF) and the approval of the annual financial bill by parliament. After the final approval, the strategic plan had to be implemented. It had to contain operational objectives for each strategic objective, expressed in an action plan comprising a specified time frame; the horizontal or sector-based nature of the objectives; the indicators whereby the objective is measurable and accountable; and the name of the manager responsible for achieving each objective. In addition, the plan was to be monitored and its implementation assessed to correct its execution on a timely basis and to continuously evaluate its relevance and effectiveness. Internal monitoring reports had to be produced every three or four months, and a final report for internal use and a public performance report were to be published, communicating the results achieved and explaining any gap between objectives and results.

In 2009 the government approved a new decree on productivity, efficiency, and transparency in the public sector that introduced relevant innovations in strategic management. It introduced the performance management cycle, strongly based on strategic planning and managerial controls, and changed the profile and the role of strategic planning units. The latter are now required to be independent from the political level (unlike the SECINs) and directly responsible for the quality of strategic management. Furthermore they must meet specific professional and expertise requirements. The decree created a new entity at the level of central government to ensure the implementation of the law and to audit the strategic management and control systems in place (the Commission for Evaluation, Transparency, and Integrity—*Commissione per la Valutazione, la Trasparenza e l'Integrità delle Amministrazioni Pubbliche*, or CIVIT). The CTS continues to exist, but its role and the division of competencies with the CIVIT is unclear.

The analysis of the policy design and implementation highlights an improvement in the approach—while the 1999 reform has a clear instrumental

Figure 10-2. *Strategic Management Policy Design and Implementation*

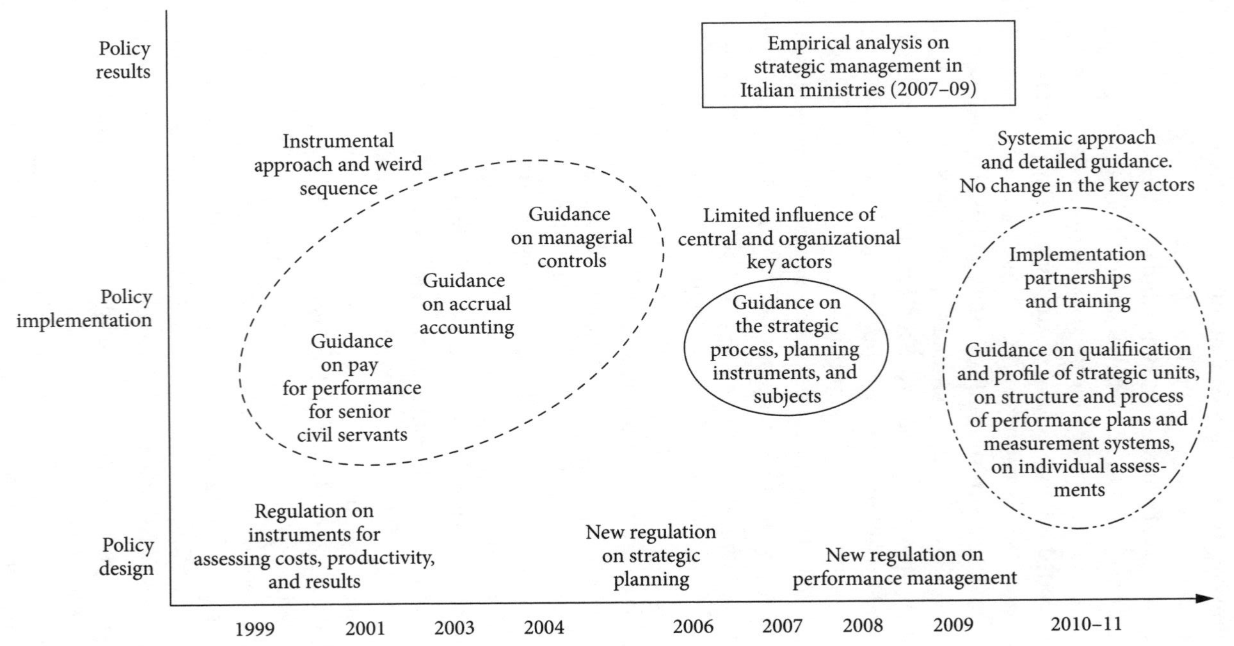

Source: Authors.

approach, the 2006 and 2009 interventions adopt a systemic approach—and a greater attention to implementation aspects. Greater attention is paid to the characteristics of the key actors and their interactions.[22]

As far as the policy results are concerned, our analysis of the adoption of strategic management in Italian ministries, performed using 2007, 2008, and 2009 data, shows a significant implementation gap, with two policy implications, as it provides an early assessment of the impact of the 1999 and 2006 guidance and a kind of feasibility study of the 2009 policy. As it will be highlighted later, several elements of the 1999 and 2006 policies that may have determined the implementation gap endure in the 2009 new law (see figure 10-2).

Policy Results: The Adoption of Strategic Management by Italian Ministries

As already mentioned, our analysis of the years 2007 to 2009 featured an intermediate stage to the two reform waves from 1999 to 2006 and from 2010 to 2011. It consists of a descriptive analysis of documental evidence about the strategic management process in ministries and a final data reduction study through cluster analysis.

Availability and Quality of the Official Documentation

A first phase of our study concerned the availability of the three documents—strategic plan, budget, and performance report—that, according to the law, should be approved and made public. The compulsory requirement is not sufficient; not all the ministries have defined and approved these documents. The publication of the strategic plan has been mandatory since 1999, and in fact it has been adopted by almost all ministries. The budget and the performance report have been compulsory since 2006, but only half of the ministries complied with this legal requirement in 2007; in 2008 there was a significant increase, from eight to fifteen in the number of ministries that prepared the budget document. In 2009 all the ministries complied with the requirement.

Although the focus of our analysis is strongly oriented to the strategic management process, the documents hold their own relevance, especially in terms of internal and external communication of strategic priorities and results, and also in light of the still-dominant legalistic administrative culture of the country.

In some ministries (Defense, University and Research, Public Education) even if the strategic plan is adopted, it consists only of a brief document, less than fifteen pages, of poor quality, and lacks the fundamental phase of identifying strategic objectives. In other cases, specifically the Ministries of Transport, of Agriculture, and of Cultural Heritage, there is only a list of strategic objectives, without any other relevant information on how these have been defined and how they will be pursued.

It is interesting to notice that only two ministries, Interior and Economy, have produced all three required documents relating to strategic management. This is particularly relevant because the process is really effective only if it is iterative and operates systemically. For instance, absent the performance report it is impossible to compare the results achieved with the goals, and strategic management runs the risk of being ineffective and of no practical use. Moreover, the lack of the performance report negatively affects the degree of public accountability.

In eight ministries the budgeting process is still not integrated into the planning process, which is a very negative state of affairs because the 2006 normative framework was introduced with the explicit aim of improving the connection and the coherence of the two processes.

To summarize, strategic management activities are taking place in Italian ministries, but in most cases the ministries are adopting a bureaucratic and compliance-oriented approach rather than a proactive managerial approach.

Coverage of the Strategic Analysis Phases

The picture worsens when we move to an in-depth analysis of the documents for each ministry. In only four ministries—Social Policy, Labor, Foreign Affairs, and Defense—there is some evidence that the internal and external environmental analyses have been done, although these are preconditions for an effective strategy formulation.

Several ministries have done a strategic analysis for just one of the two areas. The Ministry of Health analyzed its internal environment, quantifying the human and financial resources of the various organizational units. Only two ministries, Social Policy and Labor, carried out a stakeholder mapping and engagement analysis; these were two of the four ministries that carried out internal and external environment analyses. This demonstrates that stakeholder management is strongly related to internal and external context analysis. Stakeholders may be other public administrations or groups of interest, and their role and position can influence the strategy of the ministry. The Ministry of Social Policy and the Ministry of Health present a relevant peculiarity: in their action plans, for each objective they include a section detailing predictable barriers to be overcome. This indicates a risks recognition activity and for this reason we can assume that there is a risk management activity in these organizations.

To summarize, most Italian ministries do not pay sufficient attention to the strategic analysis part of the strategic management process. There is no evidence of their collecting relevant information regarding the internal and external context in which the strategic plan will be implemented. This leads to another question: Could a strategic plan be feasible and effective without the implementers' knowing the opportunities and challenges that the context presents, and without their understanding internal strengths and weaknesses? The literature already provides a negative answer; an empirical verification of this would require an in-depth evaluation of the performance of these organizations, in order to determine whether the goals have been achieved, how they have been achieved, and what outcomes they have produced.

Coverage of the Strategic Formulation and Monitoring Phases

The quality and rigor of strategy formulation and monitoring depends greatly on the quality of the strategic objectives. Our analysis shows that most of the Italian ministries have objectives with a lifetime longer than one year. This is a positive feature, since it indicates that the organization has a longer-term focus, but it does make monitoring strategic objectives and defining operational targets more complex. All the ministries except that for Universities and Research establish a clear deadline for their achievement.

Only nine ministries have cross-cutting objectives, meaning that they recognize that the realization of their objectives depends on the action of other ministries. An interesting example is the Ministry of Economy and Finance. In its plan there is a strategic objective called "reducing the deficit and respecting the Internal Stability Pact." This issue is manifestly horizontal because its achievement requires that each public administration reduce its expenses, but technically this strategic objective is not considered cross-cutting because it does not cross ministry boundaries.

Another crucial aspect is the connection between the strategic planning process and the budgeting process, necessary to effectively allocate resources and to enable the implementation of recent performance-budgeting reforms, similar to the United Kingdom's Spending Review and France's LOLF (*loi organique relative aux lois de finances*). Only through an effective strategic planning process is it possible to evaluate the performance and to distinguish between programs that are producing results and those that are not, enabling managers to improve poor-performing programs and decisionmakers to improve resource allocation. In Italian ministries, this approach was totally absent before the reforms. The situation improved in 2007, when eight strategic plans had strategic objectives connected to their spending prevision, and again in 2008, when the number of complying ministries reached fifteen, most probably due to the budgeting reform.

When the strategic process is operating correctly, any citizen should be able to trace the performance chain from the government's priorities to the operational objectives, and to understand the results. Yet currently the linkage between political priorities and strategic objectives is highlighted in the strategic plans of only half of the Italian ministries.

Another element of a good strategy is represented by high-quality and consistent indicators, without which objectives are not measurable and the results cannot be accounted for. Yet as things currently stand, citizens who would like to understand how a public administration or a program is performing can find this information for only three ministries, although it is mandatory to maintain such information.

Ministries seem to be distributed at two clear poles when it comes to strategy formulation: Social Policy; Labor; Agriculture, Food, and Forestry Policies; Infrastructure; Environment, and Economy and Finance present a high quality of strategy formulation across almost all six variables. Transport, Public Education, Foreign Affairs, and Defense present a low quality on almost all variables. Only a few ministries stand in an intermediate position. This draws attention to the high interdependency among strategic management phases and elements.

In sum, the quality of strategy formulation in general and of strategic objectives in particular is very low, with only the Ministries of Social Policy, Labor, and Infrastructure satisfactorily covering all the key aspects.

Impact of Reforms in Advancing Strategic Management in Italian Ministries: Results from the Cluster Analysis

At this point we can try to interpret the findings of the cluster analysis conducted on all of the ministries and on eleven of the fourteen variables considered (but excluding the three variables concerning the presence/absence of documents), which was carried out considering simultaneously the variables from the three years. A scatter-plot representation of the three identified clusters allows us to visually interpret the position of groups with respect to the degree of strategic analysis and formulation and monitoring, on the Y and X axis, respectively. Movements in the scatter-plot view represent the actual difference in the coverage of strategic management activities by cluster members from one year to another. This was made possible by calculating the coverage percentage of activities for each year separately, while blocking the overall cluster composition for the three years combined.

The cluster analysis allows producing an overview of the evolution of strategic management practices in ministries, following the 1999 and 2006 policy decrees.

The main result is that the reforms have produced an impact for just three ministries that already were showing high levels of coverage of strategic management phases in 2007. The reforms have not contributed to improvement in the situation of the by far most populated clusters, 2 and 3, although an increase in the number of documents and formats produced can be observed. Strategic analysis is still a neglected area of strategic management.

As shown in figure 10-3, cluster 1 represents the more "virtuous" ministries—those that steadily carry out more than 50 percent of the strategic activity requirements for each area. It has only three ministries in it, and the impact of the reforms is strongly positive on both the analysis and the formulation sides, ultimately leading to the complete coverage of the main strategic management stages in 2009.

Clusters 2 and 3 stand considerably below cluster 1 in terms of strategic analysis; the reform focused mainly on formulation standards, but it did not produce any remarkable improvement in this regard. A relevant difference between cluster 2 and cluster 3 is the degree of coverage of formulation and monitoring stages. Whereas cluster 2, with six ministries, initially shows a limited analysis and a limited formulation pattern in 2007, almost an absence of strategic management, cluster 3 covers all the stages of strategy formulation, and strategic control even in the absence of any kind of analysis. The second and third years of analysis show a seemingly parallel pattern for the two clusters: a consistent prevalence of the coverage of formulation over analysis, which only shows marginal improvements for both groups.

The analysis of the initial years of application of strategic planning guidelines in ministries points out the diffused adoption of a formal compliance-based approach. Most of the ministries fulfill the minimum legal requirements and few show an active take-up of the strategic management process. There are considerable differences in the quality of strategic documents and in the capacity to carry out context analysis and link it to organizational goals and strategies. Although the Ministries for Social Policy, Health, and Labor rank high in terms of both strategy analysis and formulation and monitoring, the other ministries share a critical issue, which is the generalized lack of internal and external analysis, including stakeholder mapping and engagement and risk management. This is reflected in a very low quality of strategic objectives, and this in turn affects the quality of the indicators and, thus, of monitoring and evaluation. Strategic objectives are usually lists of activities instead of

Figure 10-3. Strategic Management in Italian Ministries: Results of the Three-Year Longitudinal Cluster Analysis

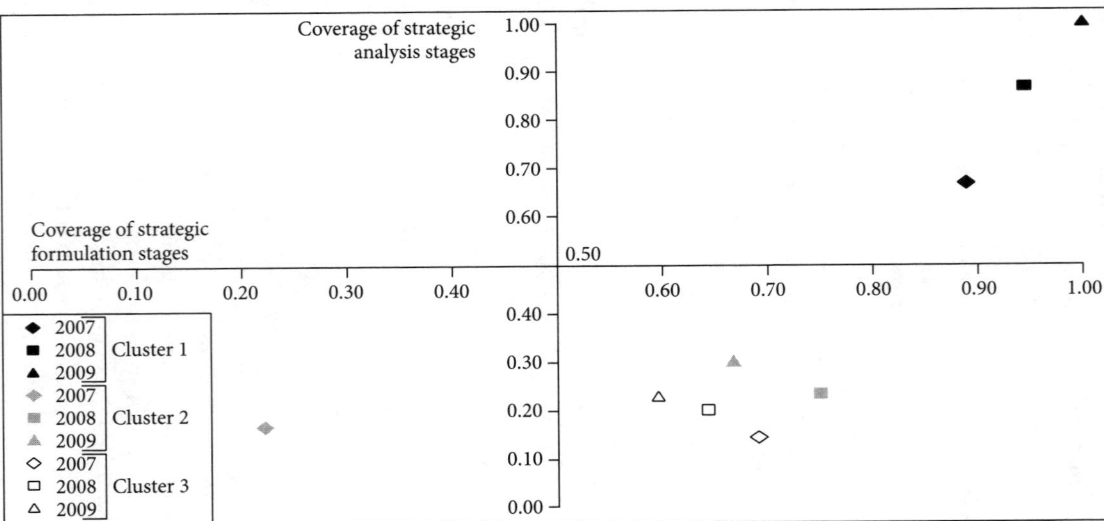

Cluster 1: Social Policy; Health; Labor
Cluster 2: Transport; Public Education; Foreign Affairs; Defense; Cultural Heritage; Agriculture, Food, and Forestry Policies
Cluster 3: Environment; Justice; Interior; Economy and Finance; Infrastructure; Universities and Research; Economic Development

future-directed priorities and outcomes, and indicators often refer to limited aspects of the goals. A persistent focus on outputs and even on the control of inputs is observed, instead of outcomes.

In other countries one of the aims of introducing strategic planning has been to increase horizontality within government, but cross-cutting issues are rare in Italian ministries' strategic planning. Relevant causes include the difficulty of pooling budgets and a lack of interministerial coordination.

Another lingering weakness, in spite of recent reforms, is the integration with the budget process, which was achieved only pro forma, by aligning the timing of both processes, and not substantially, by means of the substantive content of strategic and financial planning.

Conclusions and Policy Implications

Our findings as reported here show that the results of the reform processes regarding strategic management in the Italian central government have been unsatisfactory so far. Even in the best cases, a formal compliance-oriented approach prevails. Identifying and analyzing potential determinants is relevant not only for assessing past policies but also for predicting implementation barriers to the current ones, including both supply-side factors such as the characteristics of the central policy and demand-side factors such as organizational characteristics.

The focus of the laws and of the central policy guidance—the role played earlier by the CTS and now by CIVIT—has been and continues to be on strategic documents. Ministries' behavior has been entirely oriented to formally producing and adopting these documents according to the letter but not to the spirit of the law. The actual use of the strategic management system has not been a priority of either the central actors or the ministries.

There has been no cooperation among the key central stakeholders, the CIVIT (and previously the CTS), responsible for the strategic management process, and the RGS–Ministry of Economy and Finance, responsible for the budget process. (In France, the Ministry of Finance bears both responsibilities, which brings evident advantages in terms of policy coordination.) There is also an overlapping of roles and responsibilities as the previous technical committee, CTS, continues to exist along with the new authority, CIVIT. Most notable, however, is that the creation of a new independent authority, CIVIT, has not solved the weak authority problem, as was demonstrated by a recent episode: as a consequence of two recent decisions, one by the Ministry of Economy and Finance as part of its anticrisis package and the other by the trade unions as part of their national agreement with union representatives on public employment,

Box 10-2. *Barriers to Strategic Management in Italian Ministries*

Supply-side elements that have led to an implementation gap

Focus of laws and policy guidance on documents. Strategic analysis neglected.

Lack of cooperation among the key central stakeholders, overlapping of roles and responsibilities, and weak authority of the main actors.

Sporadic participation of ministerial strategic units in the policy design and implementation process.

Insufficient financial and human resources dedicated to policy implementation.

Demand-side elements that have led to an implementation gap

Low competencies of the ministerial strategic units.

Low motivation and reward expectation of public managers and human resources managers.

Persistence of a legalistic administrative culture and no renewal of personnel in the public sector.

Strategic management system is not tied to other management functions.

Weak autonomy of public managers in Italy does not provide incentives to change the formalistic approach.

Source: Authors' compilation.

the wage of civil servants cannot be raised or lowered before 2014, which means that the performance-related pay component of the reform cannot be implemented, at least in the next three years.

Other factors hindering cooperation have been the sporadic participation of ministerial strategic units in the policy design and implementation process and the insufficient financial and human resources dedicated to policy implementation.

On the demand side, obstacles that have determined a compliance-oriented behavior can be attributed to characteristics of top public managers and human resource managers in Italian ministries. The ministerial strategic units called SECIN, since 2010 referred to as *organismi indipendenti di valutazione* (independent evaluation bodies), or OIV, displayed weak competences and a do-the-minimum, compliance-oriented attitude. Formal requirements on strategic units' composition and profile were introduced in 2009 by decree no. 150/2009 but have been largely ignored by the ministries.[23]

Public sector managers who do not enjoy strong autonomy from the political leaders have evidenced low work motivation. Lower-level staff, too, have low motivation because they have low expectation of reward for doing more. This specific situation is a symptom of the general persistence of a legalistic administrative culture and of low staff turnover in the public sector.

Finally, the strategic management system is not tied to other management functions, which weakens the ownership and internal acceptance of innovations by the whole organization, not just the strategic planning unit. (See also box 10-2, "Barriers to Strategic Management in Italian Ministries.")

A comprehensive evaluation for the 2009 reform is still premature and beyond the scope of this study. However, some of the policy design and implementation flaws identified for the 2006 reform persist in the new decree. There is a lack of awareness of the state of strategic management in ministries, which hinders the effectiveness of the reform. This chapter is a first attempt to provide evidence on what has worked and what has not.

Notes

1. Donald P. Moynihan and Sanjay K. Pandey, "The Big Question for Performance Management: Why Do Managers Use Performance Information?" *Journal of Public Administration Research and Theory* 20, no. 4 (2010): 849–66; Mark H. Moore, *Creating Public Value: Strategic Management in Government* (Harvard University Press, 1995); Theodore H. Poister, "The Future of Strategic Planning in the Public Sector: Linking Strategic Management and Performance," *Public Administration Review* 70, Supplement S1 (2010): s246–s254.

2. Benjamin L. Crosby, "Strategic Planning and Strategic Management: What Are They and How Are They Different?" Technical Notes (Washington: USAID, Implementing Policy Change Project, 1991), p. 1.

3. John M. Bryson, *Strategic Planning for Public and Nonprofit Organizations: A Guide to Strengthening and Sustaining Organizational Achievement,* 3rd ed. (San Francisco: Wiley, 2004).

4. Richard M. Walker and George A. Boyne, "Public Management Reform and Organizational Performance: An Empirical Assessment of the UK Labour Government's Public Service Improvement Strategy," *Journal of Policy Analysis and Management* 25 (March 2006): 371–93; George A. Boyne and Richard M. Walker, "Strategic Management and Public Service Performance: The Way Ahead," *Public Administration Review* 70, Supplement S1 (2010): s185–s192.

5. Rhys Andrews, George A. Boyne, and Richard M. Walker, "Strategy Content and Organizational Performance: An Empirical Analysis," *Public Administration Review* 66 (January 2006): 52–63.

6. Tony Bovaird, "Strategic Management in Public Sector Organizations," in *Public Management and Governance,* edited by Tony Boivaird and Elke Löffler, 2nd ed. (London: Routledge, 2009).

7. Bryson, *Strategic Planning for Public and Nonprofit Organizations*, p. 6.

8. John M. Bryson, Fran Ackermann, and Colin Eden, "Putting the Resource-Based View of Strategy and Distinctive Competencies to Work in Public Organizations," *Public Administration Review* 67, no. 4 (2007): 702–17; Paul Joyce, *Strategic Management for*

the Public Services (Milton Keynes, UK: Open University Press, 1999); Paul Joyce, "The Strategic and Enabling State: A Case Study in the UK, 1997–2007," *International Journal of Leadership in Public Services* 4, no. 3 (2008); Jan-Erick Lane and Joseph Wallis, "Strategic Management and Public Leadership," *Public Management Review* 11 (January 2009): 101–20.

9. The latter is particularly relevant in the private sector. See "Strategic Planning in a Crisis: A *McKinsey Quarterly* Survey," *McKinsey Quarterly* 2, 2009 (www.mckinseyquarterly.com/Strategic_planning_Three_tips_for_2009_2340?pagenum=2).

10. George A. Boyne and others, "Problems of Rational Planning in Public Organizations: An Empirical Assessment of the Conventional Wisdom," *Administration & Society* 36 (July 2004): 328–50.

11. Barry Bozeman, *All Organizations Are Public: Bridging Public and Private Organizational Theories* (San Francisco: Jossey-Bass, 1987).

12. Rhys Andrews and others, "Strategy, Structure and Process in the Public Sector: A Test of the Miles and Snow Model," *Public Administration* 87 (December 2009): 732–49.

13. Donald F. Kettl, "Management Matters?" *Journal of Policy Analysis and Management* 25 (Spring 2006): 491–510; Norma M. Riccucci, *How Management Matters: Street-Level Bureaucrats and Welfare Reform* (Georgetown University Press, 2004).

14. Amy C. Edmonson and Stacy E. McManus, "Methodological Fit in Management Field Research," *Academy of Management* 32, no. 4 (2007): 1155–79.

15. The national context of studies is relevant because strategic management is a highly context-dependent phenomenon. The political and administrative culture and other public sector reforms influence its take-up. Therefore, unfortunately, only a very limited use can be made of the vast literature on strategic planning in other countries, such as the United States.

16. Lane and Wallis, "Strategic Management and Public Leadership."

17. David J. Ketchen Jr. and Christopher L. Shook, "The Application of Cluster Analysis in Strategic Management Research: An Analysis and Critique," *Strategic Management Journal* 17, no. 6 (1996): 441–58.

18. F. Kent Kuiper and L. Fisher, "A Monte Carlo Comparison of Six Clustering Procedures," *Biometric* 31 (September 1975): 777–83; Craig S. Edelbrock, "Mixture Model Tests of Hierarchical Clustering Algorithms: The Problem of Classifying Everybody," *Multivariate Behavioral Research* 14, no. 3 (1979): 367–84.

19. Denita Cepiku and Marco Meneguzzo, "New Public Management and Beyond: Comparing Italy and the United States," *International Journal of Public Administration* 34, no. 1 (2011): 19–25.

20. Compare the annual guidelines and reports of the Committee for Strategic Planning in Central Administrations for the years 2001, 2003, and 2004 (www.governo.it/Presidenza/controllo_strategico/direttive.html).

21. The budgeting process, meanwhile, is undergoing relevant reforms very similar to the French LOLF and, to a lesser extent, the U.K. spending reviews.

22. Jeffrey L. Pressman and Aaron Wildavsky, *Implementation* (University of California Press, 1973).

23. Detailed information on the current composition of the strategic planning units is found on the CIVIT website (www.civit.it/?page_id=1501). Fifty-two percent of the units' members have a legal background and their average age is fifty-four; these parameters are far from complying with those required by decree no. 150/2009, which indicated a prevalence of managerial competencies and an average age of no more than fifty for units' members.

PART V

International Perspectives on Public Sector Reforms

MICHAEL BARZELAY

11 The Study of Public Management: Reference Points for a Design Science Approach

This chapter's focus is on the study of public management itself, rather than on this field's substantive concerns. The issue is how to conceive of good work within this field of study, where the functional role of such work is to contribute to research knowledge or to education about public management. In approaching this issue, I examine the argument that the form of the study of management should be that of a design science. I then elaborate and offer a qualified endorsement of this argument.[1]

Design science approaches to the study of management are fairly elusive. Herbert Simon discussed the idea of design science in his *Sciences of the Artificial.* More recently, van Aken, a management professor in the Netherlands, published a much-cited article in 2004 that elucidated the idea of a design science approach to the study of management.[2] Van Aken's article is not about the design process, but rather about properties of domain knowledge, where the domain is management. Van Aken described the form of such domain knowledge as grounded, field-tested heuristic technological rules. Van Aken's argument, though abstract, can serve as a reference point for a design science approach to the study of public management.

On Domain Knowledge in Management: Van Aken's Account

I begin with an exposition of van Aken's "Management Research Based on the Paradigm of the Design Sciences: The Quest for Field-Tested and Grounded Technological Rules." He presented "design science" as a label for a distinctive approach to carrying out the research function of fields of management. An important facet of this approach (like any approach to carrying out a function) is its characteristic goals. Under the design science approach, the goal of research is to remedy deficiencies in formal expert knowledge about *classes of problems*. The handling of *particular* problems falls outside the immediate concerns of a design science approach to research.

Van Aken characterized formal expert knowledge in terms of *grounded and field-tested heuristic technological rules about classes of problems*. All the component terms built into this expression are helpful in coming to grips with the idea of a design science approach to the study of management: we simply have to cope with the expression's elongated string of nouns and adjectives. A coping strategy is to break the formula down into two pieces. The phrase "heuristic technological rules about classes of problems" corresponds to the idea of formal expert knowledge; this idea points to the *kind* of knowledge sought. The adjectives "grounded and field-tested" point to the *quality* of formal expert knowledge sought. Let's consider each part of van Aken's overall formulation in turn.

As noted, the phrase "heuristic technological rules about classes of problems" is the design science approach's expert term for "formal expert knowledge." From this standpoint, what is *not* formal expert knowledge? Three concepts are useful as contrast cases. One is ordinary, or layman's, knowledge, which is not expert. A second is tacit, or personal, craft knowledge, which may be expert, but is not formal. A third is formal expert knowledge about theoretical objects in the study of society (for example, culture, exchange rate movements, and revolutions). Mentioning these contrast cases is not intended to deprecate them in any way. Tacit, or personal, craft knowledge plays a necessary role in the handling of particular challenges in managing organizations, businesses, or programs. Equally, under the design science approach, formal expert knowledge about theoretical objects in the *study of society* plays a role in research about heuristic technological rules. Van Aken retrieved the concept of "technological rules" from a modest line of philosophical analysis written in the mid-1960s, concerned with comparing scientific, technological, and other categories of knowledge. The pursuit of technological knowledge was seen as directed toward establishing stable norms of successful human behavior.[3] Technological rules were defined as algorithms, that is, instructions to perform a finite number of acts in a given order to accomplish a given aim. Van Aken used the concept of technological rules to press the point that a design science approach to developing management theory is not the same as an explanatory social science approach to developing organization theory. Technological knowledge about management and explanatory theories of organizations were framed as categorically different bodies of knowledge, whatever their common sources.

In introducing the term "heuristic" as an adjective of technological rules, van Aken made it clear that literal instructions for pursuing given goals—which he called algorithms—are not the usual form of management theory. For one thing, the problems with which management theory would be concerned involve deliberation about goals; for another, the outcome of a particular course of action of a managerial character is normally influenced by a host of site-specific conditions. The term "heuristic" then meant that the research target became "chunks" of technological knowledge about classes of situations where operational goals may remain ambiguous or contested, rather than rules of action for realizing given goals.

The idea of heuristic technological rules about classes of problems should be seen as an important marker in evolving academic argumentation about the design science approach to the study of management. The advantage of van Aken's specific choice of words is its backward compatibility with philosophical distinctions among different kinds of knowledge. This advantage, however, may be outweighed by other considerations. One is that use of the term "technological rules" fosters the impression that research strives to provide solutions for problems, rather than reference points within the study of management that educated practitioners may find advantageous to draw upon as they respond to challenges facing the enterprises they manage. Another is that van Aken's introduction of "heuristic" as a modifier of "technological rules" seems like a reformulation.

I see no good reason to give priority to preserving the idea's backward compatibility with philosophical interests in the 1960s, while I also see compelling reasons to give priority to maintaining the idea's congruence with strands of contemporary academic discourse. A candidate substitute formulation is "usable knowledge about managerial challenges." Readers familiar with the literature on social science and social problem solving will know the distinguished source of the term "usable knowledge."[4] In the present context, "usable knowledge" corresponds to "technological knowledge" but leaves aside the problematic background idea that the study of management is an applied science, like parts of both engineering and medicine. The seemingly vague term "managerial challenges" corresponds to what van Aken called "classes of problems." Implicit in the idea of both classes of problems and managerial challenges is that they are theoretical objects within a field of study whose relation to problems encountered and acted upon in real-world situations is one of analogy. Consequently, in what follows the phrase "usable knowledge about managerial challenges" will often be used in place of the phrase "heuristic technological rules about classes of problems." However, this substitution is only motivated by its presentational advantages: much can be gained by referring back to van Aken's more elaborately stated formulation.

This first such occasion is now. Recall that the term "heuristic technological rules about classes of problems" expressed only part of the goal of the study of management; the other part was indicated by the term "grounded and field-tested." Heuristic technological rules do not qualify as usable knowledge about managerial challenges unless such webs of belief are grounded and field-tested. Some specification of these concepts is needed at this juncture. The term "grounded" comes directly out of the philosophical analysis of technological knowledge. In that context, "grounded" meant that a technological rule was covered by one or more established scientific laws. Once the concept of technological rules is extracted from this philosophical mind-set, what qualifies as adequate technological knowledge becomes an open question.

Van Aken's choice of explanatory approach is generally known in sociology and elsewhere as a mechanism-based one.[5] His chosen expository device was to summarize a landmark book on evaluation research about public programs, *Realistic Evaluation*, written by two British academics, Ray Pawson and Nick Tilley.[6] Since program evaluation research happens to intersect the study of public management, we might as well take the time to grasp the role played by Pawson and Tilley's methodological argument in van Aken's account of design science.

Pawson and Tilley's overall argument is best seen as dialectically opposed to the first generation of program evaluation research, which sought to address the practical issue of whether particular programs were effective by attempting to quantify the causal effect of a given program's operation on the program's targeted outcomes. The authors' key reservation about this so-called quasi-experimental approach to program evaluation was that it repeatedly asked an inapt question, namely, whether outcomes for target groups could be *singularly* attributed to the treatment represented by the program's operation. This form of the research question was seen as inapt because case-oriented research had shown that when program interventions work, it is typically because conditions in the program context played enabling causal roles. This conceptualization of the role of programs in social betterment implies that little is to be gained, scientifically or practically, from testing whether program conditions are *singularly* responsible for changes in target conditions.

Pawson and Tilley characterized "realistic evaluation" as an alternative approach. In a nutshell, realistic evaluation research seeks to craft cogent explanatory arguments about particular interventions meant to solve public problems on a host of different scales—from assaults and vandalism in car parks on up to the British National Health Service. The lodestar is to understand how and why (not just to what extent) interventions generate effects that prevent or remedy public problems. This question loudly echoes the historical aspiration for technological knowledge, while leaving aside the idea that any such knowledge is covered by valid scientific laws.

According to *Realistic Evaluation,* the form of any cogent evaluation research argument involves relations among three theoretical concepts: context, mechanisms, and outcomes—which Pawson and Tilley branded as the CMO approach. Fundamentally, mechanisms characterize programs, context characterizes problem situations across multiple levels of analysis, and outcomes characterize the cumulative changes of target conditions during interventions. An intervention design is said to be *grounded* if it stands to reason that the interplay of mechanisms and context conditions is a cause of improved outcome conditions. As Pawson and Tilley put it in the book's introductory chapter:

> The realist research design employs no one standard "formula," other than the base strategy of producing a clear theory of program mechanisms, contexts, and outcomes, and then using them to design the appropriate empirical measures and comparisons. . . . What is under test in realist evaluation are theories of how programs work.[7]

The idea of groundedness is the conceptual link between van Aken's account of design science and Pawson and Tilley's account of evaluation research methods. To make the link somewhat thicker, it is helpful to introduce another concept making an appearance in *Realistic Evaluation,* that of program theory. In brief, a program theory is an expert argument about how the design of a program, if implemented, would bring about the betterment of targeted conditions. Program theories are meant to travel between specific interventions with similar purposes; in this sense, they resemble the sort of generalizations that van Aken calls heuristic technological rules. At the risk of oversimplifying, we can say that a program theory is grounded if research has explained cross-case variation in outcomes resulting from the operation of the same kind of program, provided that the explanatory argument's (umbrella) causal factors are mechanism and context. Likewise, then, heuristic technological rules about classes of managerial problems can be said to be grounded if they reflect a cogent argument—in mechanism, context, and outcome terms—of the conversion of problematic conditions into better ones.

A near-final step in analyzing van Aken's account of the design science approach is to comment on the second criterion of adequacy of formal expert knowledge about management, reflected in his applying the adjective "field-tested" to the noun phrase "heuristic technological rules." Unlike groundedness, this criterion does not appear to have a direct counterpart in the philosophy of technological knowledge; we can take it to have the same wide meaning as in ordinary discourse. The specific point that van Aken makes is that the causal role of context conditions in managerial problem situations is so substantial that we should be skeptical about heuristic technological rules that, even if grounded, are not field-tested. Here, field-testing means drawing conclusions from theoretically informed comparative field studies.

In sum, van Aken has provided a highly serviceable account of the design science approach to studying management; accordingly, we can go forward on the basis of the exegesis just provided. This account, as we have seen, characterizes management theory as technological knowledge, whose component parts are bundles of grounded and field-tested heuristic technological rules about classes of managerial problems. Any given bundle of heuristic technological rules should not be presumed to qualify as formal expert knowledge unless it has been grounded and field-tested by systematic investigation. A grounded rule employs mechanism-based causal analysis to conceptualize how a stylized response to a challenge, such as a planned line of managerial action, would potentially change given conditions into preferred ones. As bundles of formal expert knowledge, grounded rules are essential but not fully satisfactory because outcomes necessarily result from the interplay of mechanism and context, with the latter conditions inevitably varying significantly from situation to situation. Accordingly, heuristic technological rules should be field-tested through field research, using comparative methods familiar in case-oriented sociology.

Herbert Simon's Pure Theory of Artificial Systems Design as Genealogy

Simon's *Sciences of the Artificial* weaves an argument about creating useful artifacts, optimizing the behavior of sociotechnical systems, and attempting to better social conditions through public policy or reform. From Simon's standpoint, a proper theory of design is concerned with the abstract matter of searching for and selecting means to satisfy collective goals on any scale. Included within the theory of design Simon favored are scientific accounts of human cognition, distillations of systems theory, and conceptual accounts of the design process itself. As part of presenting the "sciences of the artificial," Simon argued that education for practice should consist of means to enable experts and societal institutions to be far more capable of generating and testing solutions to problems than they would be if educators, inclined to teach analysis based on their research disciplines, gave no more than lip service to the intelligence needed to synthesize solutions to complex problems.

The flavor of Simon's argument comes across in a few lines from the conclusion of the key chapter, entitled "The Science of Design: Creating the Artificial." Simon wrote: "I have called my topic 'the theory of design' and my curriculum a 'program in design.' I have emphasized its role as complement to the natural science curriculum in the total training of a professional engineer—or of any professional whose task is to solve problems, to choose, to synthesize, to decide."[8] In an earlier passage in the same chapter, Simon presented the sciences of the artificial in the following way:

> Everyone designs who devises courses of action aimed at changing existing situations into preferred ones. The intellectual activity that produces material artifacts is no different fundamentally from the one that prescribes remedies for a sick patient or the one that devises a new sales plan for a company or a social welfare policy for a state. Design, so construed, is the core of all professional training; it is the principal mark that distinguishes the professions from the sciences. Schools of engineering, as well as schools of architecture, business, education, law, and medicine, are all centrally concerned with the process of design.[9]

What Simon had to say about a theory of design, on the one hand, and about a design curriculum, on the other, was highly intertwined. For a curriculum on design to find its way into university departments, the subject had to be seen as entirely worthy in an intellectual culture that had come to prize theoretical knowledge of natural and social phenomena. Simon therefore presented the curriculum on design as educating practitioners in theoretical knowledge about *artificial phenomena*. Thus was born the idea of a theory of design, a conceptual innovation intended to foster the impression that a curriculum on design would be "intellectually tough, analytic, formalizable, and teachable" at research universities.[10]

Simon says everybody should learn something about the artificial world, including many of the same tough, formalizable, and teachable aspects about the design process. One supporting argument along these lines is that practitioners need to be educated about the theory of design in order to adapt their actions as means for innovation. In other words, everyone should know some of the same parts of the theory of design if they truly want to see their efforts integrated with others in an innovation process. That said, domain knowledge is important, too. While the form of reasoning involved in designing may be similar across fields of practice, the content is as dissimilar as between, say, electrical engineering and public health. Simon's pure theory of design is more than an exercise in conceptual clarification, but it certainly is that. The direct implication is that a curriculum on design must enable learners to reason and communicate about the two main topics of Simon's theory: artificial phenomena (artificial systems and objects) and design processes. Just reading through the book is not enough to understand what it means, however. Although the style is plain, ambiguities are inevitable, not least because the chapters in Simon's volume originated as invited lectures spanning decades. We pause here, then, to present an exegesis of relevant parts of the text, for purposes of getting clear about Simon's theory of design, which, as noted, could be used in educating any kind of practitioner about this subject.[11]

We start with a focus on the part of the theory of design concerned with artificial phenomena, whether called artificial systems, artificial objects, or artifacts. In delineating the characteristics of artificial phenomena, Simon's "contrast case" was natural phenomena.[12] Artificial phenomena exist in relation to goals whereas natural phenomena simply exist. Although natural phenomena serve as a conceptual contrast case for "the artificial," the two are not parallel universes. In Simon's words, "Those things we call artifacts are not apart from nature. They have no dispensation to ignore or violate natural law. At the same time they are adapted to human goals and purposes. They are what they are in order to satisfy our desire to fly or to eat well."[13] Artificial phenomena become adapted to natural ones by design. To make this point, Simon gives the example of an airplane wing, an artificial object that is part of an artificial system for flight. Airplane wings are adapted to the natural systems of the outer environment (understood in terms of the physics of atmospheric gases). The inner environment of an airplane wing includes the natural systems characterizing their component materials. From this standpoint, artificial objects and systems are not separated from natural systems; rather, the former are adapted to natural systems by design activity for the sake of serving goals.

Box 11-1 offers a conceptual analysis of Simon's discussion of artificial phenomena. It results from applying a technique called frame-semantic analysis, which originated with the linguist Charles Fillmore, at the University of California, Berkeley, and has been employed in philosophy by George Lakoff and Mark Johnson.[14] Under this technique, the unit of analysis is a conceptual domain. The theory of meaning involved is that people understand statements by inferring their conceptual structure, with little awareness that they are doing so when such conceptual structures are conventionalized in their thought communities or wider cultures. The typical use of frame-semantic analysis is to make people aware of how they reason about various experiential domains. However, the use in the present application is different, as the

Box 11-1. *Frame-Semantic Analysis of Artificial Phenomena*

Conceptual Scheme

Artificial phenomena	Outer environment
Theory	Interface
Artificial system	Adapted
Artificial object (or artifact)	Functions
Organization	Behavior
Inner environment	Goals

Domain knowledge

An *artificial system* is designed so that its *behavior* accomplishes *goals.*

An *artificial system* is designed so that its *functions* are performed.

A well-designed *artificial object* is adapted to its *outer environment* as means to accomplish *goals.*

The *functions* of an *artificial system* are performed in the course of contact between an *artificial object* and its *outer environment.*

An adequate theory of an *artificial system's* behavior centers on analyzing the *interface* between an *artificial object* and its *outer environment.*

An *adequate theory* of an *artificial object* analyzes the organization of its *inner environment.*

aim is rather to incorporate the unconventional frame of "artificial phenomena" into practitioners' explicit knowledge.[15]

The unit of analysis in frame-semantic analysis is a conceptual domain. In applying the technique, a step is to identify the concepts within the domain. Listing concepts belonging to a domain's conceptual scheme is a step toward understanding its conceptual structure. The next step is to analyze the roles played by individual concepts within the frame as a whole. The background idea is that meaning in language comes from conceptual organization (in other words, the relations of concepts within the frame), not from the "definition" of any single concept.[16] Accordingly, the standard way to analyze the roles played by concepts within a frame is to construct a battery of statements about the domain, each of which includes two or more items in the conceptual scheme. The function of the body of statements is to characterize the domain's conceptual structure. With a domain's structure represented, it is easier to communicate and reason in its terms.

Box 11-1 includes a body of statements that characterizes the conceptual structure of artificial phenomena. This characterization is consistent with Simon's text—and, it is hoped, somewhat more clearly stated than the way it was presented textually in such passages as the following:

Box 11-2. *Frame-Semantic Analysis of Design Process as Decisionmaking*

Conceptual Scheme

Decisionmaking	Alternatives
Process	Goals
Problem	Choice
Solution	Constraints
Search	Optimizing
Selecting	Satisficing

Domain Knowledge

Decisionmaking is a *process* of selecting paths for generating *alternatives.*

A *choice* is typically made by selecting among *alternatives* assessed in terms of *goals.*

Optimizing is discovering the best solution to a problem, defined in terms of *goals* and *constraints.*

Satisficing is a *search process* that stops when an acceptable *solution* is found.

> An artifact can be thought of as a meeting point—an "interface" in today's terms—between an "inner" environment, the substance and organization of the artifact itself, and an "outer" environment, the surroundings in which it operates. If the inner environment is appropriate to its outer environment, or vice versa, the artifact will serve its intended purpose.[17]

To further this effort to discern the conceptual structure of Simon's theory of design, let us now turn to a discussion of his second topic: the design process. I see Simon attempting to bridge two conceptual domains: decisionmaking and engineering (see boxes 11-2 and 11-3).

There are points of conceptual contact between artificial phenomena and the design process. The most evident one is that the concept of goals plays roles in each. In artificial phenomena, the role of the concept of goal is in explaining why such phenomena exist and thereby also offers a contrast with the case of natural phenomena. In design process, the concept of a goal plays a role in giving meaning to the idea of testing design solutions and of choosing among alternatives. Another point of contact involves the concept of functions. In artificial phenomena, the concept of performing functions plays a role in explicating what an artificial system does to achieve the goals it is meant to serve. In design process, by contrast, the concept of functions plays a role in reasoning about how to break down the overall design problem into parts, so that design solutions can be more readily devised, and it plays a role

Box 11-3. *Frame-Semantic Analysis of Design Process as Engineering*

Conceptual Scheme

Engineering	Design solutions
Process	Integrating
Factoring	Generating
Functions	Testing
Design problems	Synthesizing

Domain Knowledge

Engineering is a process of factoring design problems into parts, such as *functions*, and synthesizing *solutions* to each part of the problem.

Engineering is a process of integrating design solutions for parts into a design solution for the *design problem* as a whole.

Engineering is a process of *generating* and *testing design solutions* to design problems.

A design *choice* is typically made by *selecting* among *alternatives* assessed in terms of *goals*.

in reasoning about how design solutions for the parts can be integrated into a design solution at the level of the whole artificial system. As can be seen, the same concept, whether goals or functions, plays different roles in the two respective frames. More specifically, in artificial phenomena, goals and functions characterize the ontology of this domain in contrast with that of natural phenomena, whereas in design process the same concepts characterize heuristics for reasoning within an intentional process to create artificial objects and shape artificial systems.

Simon's text does important philosophical work on behalf of a theory of design, whose goals (here I am paraphrasing Simon) include fostering an impression that a curriculum on design would be "intellectually tough, analytic, formalizable, and teachable" at research universities. In fostering this impression, it is helpful that Simon's own credibility remains strong beyond his lifetime. However, I do believe that the substance of his theory of design could be significantly strengthened.

Public Management's Own Reference Point for a Design Science

Let us stand on the shoulders of a more contemporary figure to take a few important steps in this direction. The shoulders we stand upon are those of Eugene Bardach, emeritus professor of public policy at the University of California, Berkeley. The statement of Bardach's perspective that we retrieve for this purpose is a published lecture, entitled "The Extrapolation Problem," based on his 2003 presidential address to the largely academic Association of Public Policy Analysis and Management.[18]

An extrapolation problem is a scenario that begins when an elected official or public manager has become aware of another jurisdiction's or organization's reputed success in some area of policy or management and wishes to know what lessons can be learned and applied locally. The wish becomes a command to an available analyst. The scenario includes analyzing the reputedly good practice of the source site and thinking through the resulting analysis's implications for the local or target site. The analysis of the source site's practices is concerned not only with whether its practices deliver as reputed but also with why it behaves or performs as it does.

The scenario of "extrapolation problem" corresponds to Simon's concept of the design process, but it is a special case involving the use of analysis of a source site to search for alternatives for a target site. A common name for a source site practice, once it has been analyzed, is a "design exemplar."[19] The analysis and use of design exemplars is a relevant topic for a theory of design; Simon even provides a hint of its relevance: "One way to solve a complex problem is to reduce it to a problem previously solved."[20]

Bardach likens analyzing why a practice works the way it does to the reverse engineering of existing physical products. As it happens, what is involved in reverse engineering strongly resembles Pawson and Tilley's recommended approach to evaluation research. In particular, mechanisms play a role in researched explanations of the behavior of a source site practice. Bardach's examination of the reverse engineering aspects of responding to the extrapolation problem can be used to strengthen the core of Simon's theory of design. First, Bardach's text is concerned directly with design solutions that are social in form, whereas Simon's pure theory of design is concerned with contrasting artificial and natural phenomena.[21] In fact, Bardach's running example to illustrate his theoretical argument is a practice for educating public policy practitioners—sometimes called the integrated policy exercise—an example that differs considerably from airplane wings. Second, Bardach—perhaps surprisingly—draws on engineering in a more substantial way than Simon did. This aspect of Bardach's theory of design of practices is exhibited in the following attention-getting passage:

> I want to say something more abstract about the idea of a "mechanism." "Mechanism" is obviously a metaphor, and there is no escaping the use of metaphors when dealing with issues of ontology. I will add a second metaphor: the sort of basic mechanisms I have in mind tap into "reser-

voirs" of what might be thought of as energy, or potentiality, in "social nature." These reservoirs are sitting around free, nature's gifts to us, like the energy stored in hydrocarbon molecules that can be extracted and then channeled into useable mechanical force. . . . To extend the metaphor further, obviously, a mechanism that "taps natural reservoirs" must have a way of doing the tapping, some system of human contrivance that manages to draw on this reservoir of energies and channels them to some productive purpose.[22]

As is evident from reading other passages, the central idea here is that a practice represents a good design if it "takes advantage" of "social nature" to achieve goals "on the cheap." The idea that a good design takes advantage of physical nature is central to engineering design. In Bardach's analysis of practices, the concept of advantage stands for a cause-effect relation between, for example, the features of a practice and the functions it performs, and this relation can be usefully conceived in terms of activated social mechanisms. Likewise, the concept of advantage can stand for the cause-effect relation between the behavior of a practice and preferred conditions (or outcomes) in the outer environment.

Curiously, advantage does not enter clearly into Simon's conception of artificial phenomena. In the passage quoted earlier, Simon uses the concept of appropriateness. It stands to reason that a conception of artificial systems that includes the idea of taking advantage of social nature is more compelling than one that does not. The theory of design taught to practitioners should be revised accordingly.

With this thought in mind, let's perform some additional frame-semantics analysis to formalize these observations. The top half of box 11-4 sets up an array of correspondences between Simon's frame for artificial phenomena and Bardach's frame for the conceptual domain we can call practices. As presented, the two domains have a fairly similar structure. Each of the two schemas incorporates the same concepts of theory, goals, and functions, and they also play similar roles in the two. Box 11-4 also indicates where the concepts are different, although their roles in their respective frames are similar: these correspondences are between physical and social nature, artificial objects and practices, inner system and interlocking features, and outer environment and context.

The Morphology of the Study of Public Management

One of the properties of the design science approach to studying public management that needs to be pinned down sooner or later is the classes of managerial problems. In my view, it is better to adopt a conservative posture in

Box 11-4. *Frame-Semantic Analysis of Artificial Phenomena and Practices*

Conceptual Scheme

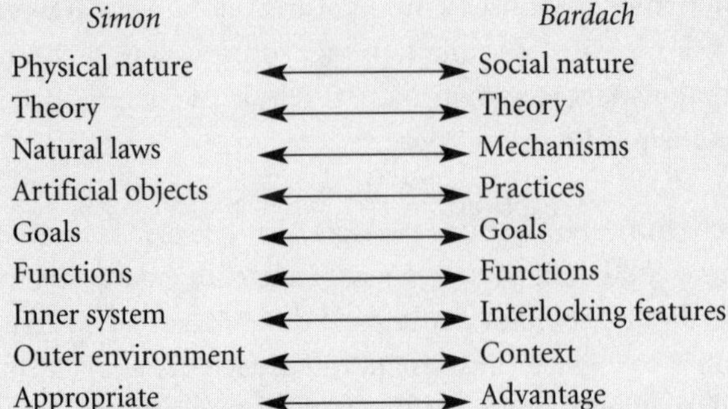

Domain Knowledge (for Artificial Social Phenomena)

A practice's behavior is a means for attaining *goals.*

The mainsprings of a practice's advantage lie in *social nature.*

A practice creates advantage by tapping in to *social nature.*

Mechanisms are theories of processes in *social nature.*

A practice's features are devices to activate mechanisms and place them in service of a practice's *goal.*

doing so. Although this prudent stance makes sense in principle, its application requires some finesse due to the variable geometry of public management's relationship to the study of management and public policy.[23] To accommodate this institutional reality, the principle needs to be applied in more than one way. I discuss two candidates here.

The first selected reference discipline is management (or, traditionally, administration) as distinguished from public policy. Before the study of management became internally differentiated, researchers and educators shared expert accounts of administration. No such account was more standard during the formative period of the study of management than that credited to Henri Fayol as the author of *Industrial and General Management.*[24] Fayol's book offered a conceptual outline of the overall task of administering a company that delineated various functions, including planning, organizing, commanding, coordinating, and controlling. From the 1920s on, progenitors of the study of public administration in the United States modified this scheme so that it would serve as a core account of the work of appointed officials playing administrative roles within governments that had been reformed and reorganized in the Progressive era or later. The outline version of the modified account was compressed into the acronym POSDCORB, which stood for the functions of planning, organizing, staffing, directing, coordinating, reporting, and budgeting.

The POSDCORB scheme is so closely associated with a bygone era that it cannot be used to construct a face for the design science approach to studying public management. However, it is worth reflecting on how to derive some of the same field-defining and analytic benefits that once flowed from the use of this scheme in the past.

The field-defining benefit was to provide a broadly inclusive definition of the role of an administrator with general responsibility for a business or other enterprise. POSDCORB named the whole as a well as the parts of the administrator's role; likewise, it provided a useful whole-parts scheme for the study of administration. The analytic benefits flowed from the avowed functional conception of administration. To say that planning is part of the administrator's role is also to say that planning is a function. According to this line of argument, if planning or any other function were not performed, the business or organization would presumably perform below its potential or worse. Likewise, the argument holds that carrying out any and all functions is presumably "required" if the business or organization as a whole is to operate and develop satisfactorily. As conceived, the functional conception of administration neither necessitates nor rules out specific characteristics of managerial responses to functionally defined challenges, allowing choices instead to be assessed argumentatively within an evolving expert framework of practical reasoning.

Even though the functional approach may afford the field-defining and analytic advantages just claimed, the specific POSDCORB scheme is not completely adequate. Simply put, POSDCORB is about administrative effectiveness, whereas public management is concerned with more than this. An indication of public management's broader concerns is the doctrinal claim that public value creation is the purpose of managerial work in government.[25] Another indication is that the study of public management is heavily concerned with service delivery considered in its totality. In addition, the study of public management remains concerned, to some degree, with the challenge of developing innovative technologies and practices to enable future program delivery. However, neither production nor innovation was strongly implied, let alone declared, within the POSDCORB's outline of administrative functions.

The reasons are easy to discern: functions of administration were understood as covering only part of what was required for a successful enterprise. Production was seen as being what administration was not. Developing innovative physically embodied technologies as well as work methods was seen as the domain of engineers rather than administrators. For their part, the historical figures in American public administration found it rhetorically convenient to present the field in terms similar to Fayol's.[26] The implication for us, however, is that stylized managerial problems in the study of public management should include not only functions of administration but also non-administrative functions that are integral to the satisfactory operation and development of organizations and "enterprises" in the public sector.

What functions presumably must be carried out, individually and severally, for longer-term program and organizational performance? For what it is worth, I will respond by summarizing what I say to my students when introducing the study of public management and what I say to public officials when portraying the managerial challenges that my field knows how to approach. The script goes more or less as follows.

I begin by asking whether, for our immediate purposes, we can simply agree that public organizations need to accomplish two main things if they seek to be effective and efficient over the longer run: delivering in the present and preparing for the future. Absent delivering in the present, the organization will court failure. Absent preparing for the future, delivering will be done less effectively and efficiently at a later point than would otherwise be the case. The reception to this formulation has never been problematic. I then ask whether we can also agree that this formulation is just *too* simple; no resistance to this move has been encountered, save once. I then go on to suggest that for purposes of studying public management we would find it advantageous to distinguish two challenges within "preparing for the future" as well as another two within "delivering in the present."

Transitioning into an expert account, I indicate that one challenge in preparing for the future is to develop strategy, whereas another is to develop capabilities for future use in delivering programs or services. The first is about intentions; the second is about realizing intentions in the form of human, organizational, social, or physical capital. Likewise, in delivering in the present, one challenge is production—actually converting inputs into outputs—while another challenge is to control the delivery process. Having introduced these terms, I then ask whether we can agree that no fewer than four key functions need to be carried out for effective and efficient performance in the public sector: developing strategy, creating capabilities for future delivery, controlling the delivery process, and production. Completing this account, I then argue that it would be rewarding to use this scheme of functional challenges in structuring and building expert knowledge about public management.

In making this case, I often go through the exercise of comparing and contrasting it with the historical POSDCORB scheme; in showing continuity I relate planning in POSDCORB to strategy development in the four-fold scheme as well as "reporting" and "budgeting" to "controlling the delivery process." Depending on the audience and occasion, the script varies, as does the ensuing dialogue, but I can say that I find myself confident in using the scheme for its field-defining and analytic characteristics. On the basis of this experience, I believe that this four-fold functional scheme, which can be rolled up into "preparing for the future" and "delivering in the present," is serviceable as an account of stylized managerial challenges with which a realistic design science of public management can be centrally concerned. Some who participate in the study of public management identify at least as strongly with a particular policy field than with either management or public administration. Programs have always been a common interest for all manner of specialists (including management) in numerous areas of public policy. I have recently come to believe that Pawson and Tilley's realistic approach to evaluation research offers a way to think in some detail about pursuing this common interest. The main intellectual reason is that the realistic approach to evaluation research is conceived similarly to the research function under the design science approach to studying public management. Specifically, conducting research under either rubric is oriented toward understanding of both the problem and solution sides of challenges—in other words, not just knowledge about problems but also about how responses to them play causal roles in their treatment.[27] In both cases the scientific aim is for "theoretical" knowledge about a world that exhibits an analogical relationship to the real world of particular entities and events. Still, the vocabularies of public management and program evaluation research are not well articulated with one another.

To bridge the two research enterprises requires an appreciation of how their respective concepts and their terminology correspond with each other. What is the corresponding concept in realistic evaluation research for van Aken's concept of "heuristic technological rules about classes of problems"? Pawson and Tilley adopt the term "program theories" to refer to the expert knowledge that comes from realistic evaluation research. They envision program evaluation research as yielding families of program theories, each of which is concerned with a class of challenges defined in terms of public problems and mechanisms configured to remedy them. Program theories express knowledge about those challenges, arrived at through the "methodology" of realistic evaluation research.

To me, a "program theory" and "heuristic technological rules" for stylized managerial problems share conceptions of expert knowledge. However, the terms are not equivalent because they refer to different knowledge domains: program theories are about kinds of public problems and would-be solutions to them, whereas the study of public management is centrally concerned with expert knowledge about managerial problems defined in relation to organizational functions, such as controlling the delivery process. This difference in the definition of knowledge domains, however, is not hard to bridge, because research interests in the field of public policy by public management specialists easily fall under both descriptions.

Consider the example of air traffic control programs. A function within this program, related to production, is monitoring and coordinating the movement of aircraft from the time they enter a control center's airspace until the time they leave it. Likewise, another function within the same program, related to controlling the delivery process, is to respond administratively to declared errors arising (by definition) if two aircraft come closer to each other than permitted under rules of separation. As indicated, these program functions correspond closely to two of the organizational functions in the study of public management. Thus, all that's really needed to forge a clear connection between the respective knowledge domains of program evaluation research and public management research is to envision overall programs as intrinsically decomposable into functional parts. The connection would be strongest when the functional parts of programs are conceived as stylized managerial challenges within the study of public management, as in the example of air traffic control.

The question then arises as to how someone interested in research to refine expert knowledge about accomplishing programs' functional parts would label such knowledge, at least for presentational purposes. The term "program theory" could be used; however, its normal meaning is centrally concerned with expert knowledge about programs as a whole, and in particular with the issue of impact or outcome. A simple workaround for this linguistic inconvenience can be derived from literature on evaluation research on which Pawson and Tilley themselves draw. In a venerable evaluation textbook, Peter H. Rossi, Mark W. Lipsey, and Howard Freeman argued that in the interest of researching program realization, evaluators should examine "program processes" that, if not carried out, would diminish the effectiveness of the program (as a whole), possibly to the point of failure.[28] In other words, "program processes" play the role of responses to the managerial challenges of carrying out functional parts of programs. For reasons of parallelism and convention, it is highly convenient to label expert knowledge about such program-function challenges and their corresponding responses as "program process theories."

Conclusion

To recap, the "classes of problems" with which the study of public management is concerned can be presented in different ways, depending on whether management or public policy is considered as the principal reference discipline. When management is the reference discipline, the research interest is in obtaining usable knowledge about managerial challenges, such as developing strategy, creating capabilities for future delivery, controlling the delivery process, and production. When public policy is the reference discipline, the research interest is in obtaining program process theories about challenges in carrying out program functions that favor program realization. This conception of the value of a field of study's heuristic technological rules entails a view about what makes for the adequacy of research. In general, a piece of research needs to have an adequate research problem: in design science, a research problem is not adequate unless it relates to serious defects in research knowledge about solving classes of problems.

As previewed, the argument in this chapter is that the design science approach to the study of public management is worth making clear. Doing so includes connecting the dots of "back region" arguments such as those presented by Simon, van Aken, and Bardach. Formulating a design science approach to the study of public management involves complementary efforts by researchers and educators to frame the study of public management for practitioners. Without such framing techniques, the design science approach will never become sticky, for either practitioners or the intellectual community involved in the study of public management.

Notes

1. For an earlier and briefer account of this argument, see Michael Barzelay and Fred Thompson, "Back to the Future: Making Public Administration a Design Science," *Public Administration Review* 70 (Supplement 1) (December 2010): s295–s297.

2. Herbert A. Simon, *The Sciences of the Artificial,* 3rd ed. (MIT Press, 1996); Joan Ernst van Aken, "Management Research Based on the Paradigm of the Design Sciences: The Quest for Field-Tested and Grounded Technological Rules," *Journal of Management Studies* 41 (March 2004): 219–46.

3. Mario Bunge, "Technology as Applied Science," *Technology and Culture* 7 (1966): 329–47.

4. Charles E. Lindblom and David K. Cohen, *Usable Knowledge: Social Science and Social Problem Solving* (Yale University Press, 1979).

5. Jon Elster, *Nuts and Bolts for the Social Sciences* (Cambridge University Press, 1989); Peter Hedström and Richard Swedberg, eds., *Social Mechanisms: An Analytical*

Approach to Social Theory (Cambridge University Press, 1998); Douglas McAdam, Sidney Tarrow, and Charles Tilly, *Dynamics of Contention* (Cambridge University Press, 2001); Peter Abell, "Narrative Explanation: An Alternative to Variable-Centered Explanation?" *Annual Review of Sociology* 30, no. 1 (2004): 287–310; Renate Mayntz, "Mechanisms in the Analysis of Social Macro-Phenomena," *Philosophy of the Social Sciences* 34 (June 2004): 237–59; Peter Hedström, *Dissecting the Social: Principles of Analytic Sociology* (Cambridge University Press, 2005).

6. Ray Pawson and Nick Tilley, *Realistic Evaluation* (London: Sage, 1997).

7. Ibid., pp. xv–xvi.

8. Simon, *Sciences of the Artificial*, p. 135.

9. Ibid., p. 111.

10. Ibid., p. 112.

11. The word and concept of exegesis mentioned here is taken from Douglas Walton, "Examination Dialogue: An Argumentation Framework for Critically Questioning an Expert Opinion," *Journal of Pragmatics* 38 (2006): 745–77. More to the point, in what follows I seek to live up to Walton's suggested standards for exegesis and critical assessment of expert opinions.

12. I borrow the concept of the contrast case from Thomas F. Gieryn, "Boundary-Work and the Demarcation of Science from Non-Science: Strains and Interests in Professional Ideologies of Scientists," *American Sociological Review* 48 (December 1983): 781–95. Coincidentally, Gieryn's study was about efforts by natural scientists to differentiate science from both engineering and philosophy in Victorian England.

13. Simon, *Sciences of the Artificial*, p. 3.

14. George Lakoff and Mark Johnson, *Metaphors We Live By* (University of Chicago Press, 1980); George Lakoff and Mark Johnson, *Philosophy in the Flesh* (New York: Basic Books, 1999).

15. I remain forever indebted to George Lakoff for teaching me how to do frame-semantic analysis back in the mid-1990s, when we wrote a paper for a research conference on whether customer satisfaction should be the goal of public organizations. Note that I follow the convention he uses in his books of capitalizing names of conceptual domains under analysis.

16. Behind this is the psychological idea of gestalt perception. See George Lakoff, *Women, Fire, and Dangerous Things: What Categories Reveal about the Mind* (University of Chicago Press, 1987).

17. Simon, *Sciences of the Artificial*, p. 6.

18. Eugene Bardach, "The Extrapolation Problem: How Can We Learn from the Experience of Others?" *Journal of Policy Analysis and Management* 23 (Spring 2004): 205–22.

19. Donald A Schön, *The Reflective Practitioner* (New York: Basic Books, 1983).

20. Simon, *Sciences of the Artificial*, p. 213.

21. It is true that *Sciences of the Artificial* includes a chapter on social reform and discusses organizational design, but it does not reexamine the fundamental idea.

22. Bardach, "Extrapolation Problem," p. 210.

23. Nathan Glazer, "The Schools of the Minor Professions," *Minerva* 12 (July 1974): 346–64.

24. Henri Fayol, *Industrial and General Management* (London: Pitman, 1949).

25. Mark H. Moore, *Creating Public Value: Strategic Management in Government* (Harvard University Press, 1995).

26. Alasdair Roberts, "Demonstrating Neutrality: The Rockefeller Philanthropies and the Evolution of Public Administration, 1927–1936," *Public Administration Review* 54, no. 3 (1994): 221–28.

27. On the distinction between the problem and solution side of challenges within an undeclared design science approach, see Eugene Bardach, "The Problem of Best Practice Research," *Journal of Policy Analysis and Management* 13 (Spring 1994): 260–68.

28. Peter H. Rossi, Mark W. Lipsey, and Howard E. Freeman, *Evaluation: A Systematic Approach,* 7th ed. (Thousand Oaks, Calif.: Sage, 2004).

ELAINE CIULLA KAMARCK

12 *Government Reform and Innovation: A Comparative Perspective*

In this chapter I examine central aspects of government reform in the contemporary era, surveying and analyzing developments and patterns in four separate historical contexts:

1. The late-twentieth-century revolution in governance in advanced Information Age democracies
2. The late-twentieth-century revolution in governance in the world's developing nations
3. The postbureaucratic state in advanced Information Age democracies
4. The challenge of government capacity building in the developing world

The Late-Twentieth-Century Revolution in Governance in Advanced Information Age Democracies

Twentieth-century government conducted its business through the governmental equivalent of the assembly line. For most of that time, in the United States and in other developed countries, the organizational structures of the private sector and the public sector were pretty much the same. The absence of information technology—especially large computers for storing and analyzing records and data—meant that public sector organizations spent much of their time collecting and organizing records. The employees of these large organizations consisted largely of clerks and those who supervised them. The U.S. federal government and most state and local governments were, for most of the century, governments of clerks.

But by the end of the twentieth century the private sector was changing, and those changes were having an effect on the way citizens saw their governments.

This manifested itself in a paradox. In the world's most advanced democracies, citizens who lived in countries that had, by many objective measures, done a pretty good job of delivering on public goods, were getting more and more critical of government.[1] Nowhere was this as apparent as in the United States, where, over a period of four decades in which the United States was prosperous and mostly at peace, Americans grew less and less trustful of government.

In an entire book of essays on this topic called *Why People Don't Trust Government* various explanations are tried and found wanting.[2] An examination of this decline reveals that it persisted in the face of changing economic fortunes, it persisted in the face of real governmental accomplishments, and it persisted in the face of changes in political parties and policies.[3] As one looks at the persistence of these data across so many decades and so many different political situations, it is hard to avoid the conclusion that there was something about government—its form, its behavior—that made late-twentieth-century Americans mad, regardless of government's purposes and regardless of its leaders.

These changes were evident in other mature democracies as well, and politicians were not oblivious to them. Ronald Reagan (the American president from 1980 to 1988) Brian Maloney (the Canadian prime minister from 1984 to 1993), and Margaret Thatcher (the British prime minister from 1979 to 1990) made impressive careers out of dissatisfaction with late-twentieth-century government.[4] "Stupid government stories" fueled both conservative political revolutions and late-night television. Distaste for the bureaucratic state got to the point where people could not imagine that anything they liked and valued was actually done by the government. President Bill Clinton used to tell of meeting an old woman who pressed his hands intensely in hers and pleaded with him, "Please, please, Mr. President, don't let the government ruin my Medicare" (Medicare is the government-run health care program for Americans aged sixty-five and older).

Dissatisfaction with government manifested itself in more concrete ways in a tax revolt that spread across the United States beginning in 1978. Even left-of-center politicians became reluctant to raise taxes, and right-of-center politicians, in the United States especially, came to use lower taxation as a panacea for all the ills that ailed the country. In the meantime, however, no one seriously suggested that government should actually do less. Local governments were expected to fix potholes and run school systems, state governments were expected to manage public health systems and fund universities. When the conservative, antigovernment movement in America finally bore fruit in 1994 with Newt Gingrich's Republican takeover of the House of Representatives from the Democrats for the first time in more than forty years, conservative political elites hoped for great changes, and liberal political elites feared them.

But even then, with the wind at their backs and fueled by decades of pent-up antigovernment sentiment, the conservative revolution failed to deliver any substantial reduction in government. A conservative, antitax, antigovernment majority governed Congress from 1994 to 2006, and with the exception of changes related to 9/11 such as the creation of the Department of Homeland Security, the government does not look appreciably different now than it did then. In fact, ironically enough, it has gotten bigger in both the number of personnel and in its total expenditures.

So how can we explain the growth in citizen distrust of government that so permeated politics in the last decades of the twentieth century? One explanation is that as the century wore on, citizens began to perceive a disconnect between the aspirations of policymakers and the realities of policy implementation.[5] By the 1990s continuing dissatisfaction with policy implementation had contributed to the growth of a powerful critique of bureaucracy. The traditional public administration literature, which focused either on "top-down" or "bottom-up" analysis, gave way to a new set of concerns focused on performance.[6] In *Breaking through Bureaucracy*, published in 1992, Michael Barzelay showed how the modern bureaucratic paradigm had managed to turn bureaucracies into organizations that were often dysfunctional even when—or especially when—operating according to the rules.[7] By the end of the century authors such as Derek Bok, Christopher Pollitt and Geert Bouckaert, Neal Ryan, Cheryl Barnes and Derek Gill, and Harvey Sims, representing a cross-section of the Anglo-American world of public administration, were all arguing what the politicians had intuited all along: citizen mistrust of government had its roots in failing government performance.[8]

In the meantime, in the face of citizen distrust and doubts about policy implementation, elected politicians and civil servants still had to govern. Late-twentieth-century political culture presented those who governed with an interesting dilemma: How do you govern in an era when the public yells "Do something!" at regular intervals about problems ranging from bad meat in hamburgers to terrorists in the subways, yet are quickly yelling yet again, "And don't let the government do it!"

This barrage of contradictory messages begat one of the most creative periods in the history of governance. The movement to "reinvent government," as it was dubbed in the United States, or the "new public management," as it was called in the other Anglo-American countries who were at the forefront of this movement, began in Great Britain in 1982, in New Zealand in 1984, in American state houses in the 1980s, and in the American federal government in 1993. In Great Britain, the first part of the so-called Thatcher Revolution involved the privatization of state-owned industries. As Great Britain began undoing the accomplishments of its quasi-socialist past, other countries watched and followed suit. In fact, through much of the 1980s government reform consisted of privatizing previously state-owned industries. (Although the American president at the time, Ronald Reagan, was a fellow conservative and great friend of Margaret Thatcher, the American government didn't change very much during this period, mainly because industries that had been nationalized in other parts of the world had never been nationalized in the first place in the United States.)

Having endured the political response to the brutal politics of privatization, the Thatcher government turned next to the operations of the core government. There, under Minister Michael Heseltine, Thatcher established the Efficiency Unit, a revolutionary office that began the process of bringing private market accountability for results to the civil service. The eventual report of this unit argued that to solve the management problem,

> the government would have to separate service-delivery and compliance functions from the policy-focused departments that housed them—to separate steering from rowing. Second, it would have to give service-delivery and compliance agencies much more flexibility and autonomy. And third, it would have to hold those agencies accountable for results, through performance contracts.[9]

As Britain was remaking its large government bureaucracies into more entrepreneurial organizations, New Zealand was undergoing an even more dramatic revolution. In the mid-1980s New Zealand faced an economic and political meltdown of striking proportions. As the new Labour government took over in 1987, it published a postelection briefing paper described as the "manifesto" of the New Public Management.[10] The New Zealand experience was unique for its boldness, for its continuity, and for its intellectual coherence. It is no wonder that for many years at the end of the twentieth century government reform seemed to have outstripped lamb as the most popular New Zealand export.

Like the Thatcher reforms, the New Zealand reforms injected the language of competition, incentives, and performance into public administration. These reforms were remarkable in absolute terms, and viewed against the quasi-socialist dogmas of previous governments they were extraordinary. They called for getting the government out of activities that could be more effectively carried out by nongovernmental bodies. They called for a clear separation of the responsibilities of ministers and departmental heads—giving the traditional civil service both more autonomy and more responsibility for results than ever before. And perhaps the most revolutionary aspect of all was the directive that *everything* that was publicly funded—even policy advice—was to be made "contestable and subject to competitive tendering."[11] Cabinet ministers "purchased" government outputs from what used to be the bureaucracy, and the bureaucracy was forced to "compete" with other public and private organizations to do the work of the government.[12] New Zealand broke the public monopoly of government on governance. At a time when officials in the United States were still asking "What is a core governmental function?" New Zealand had decided on the answer: essentially, nothing.

Whereas reinvented government started at the national level in Britain and New Zealand, in the United States this revolution in government management started at the state and local level. Unlike the federal government, state governments cannot print their own money. Mayors and governors in the 1970s and 1980s—forced to live within their means and buffeted by tax revolts on the one hand and continued demands for services on the other—had no choice but to try and do more with less, even if it meant stepping on some toes. For American state and local officials, and for British and New Zealand national officials in the 1980s, reinvented government was the only way out of an impossible governing situation, but what had begun as an adaptation to budget crises evolved into a more or less coherent philosophy. In countries close to the United Kingdom and other Commonwealth countries and in western Europe, it came to be called the New Public Management; in America it came to be called "reinventing government." This movement hit the U.S. federal government in 1993, when Vice President Al Gore, at the request of President Bill Clinton, inaugurated the National Performance Review.[13]

Along the way, these government reform efforts in first world countries were inspired and reinforced by the information revolution going on in the private sector. Beginning in the 1980s the private sector rushed to use new information technology tools. These created a new and more profound ability to be "customer-friendly." Convenience—banking at ATM machines, shopping on the telephone, and, later, shopping on the Internet—and customization in the private sector stood in sharp contrast to the one-size-fits-all, rigid, and inconvenient public sector. To citizens accustomed to the new customer service efforts of the 1980s, the public sector looked hopelessly obsolete and unresponsive. The situation was the same in Europe and in the United States and Canada.

> In the early 1980s, service industries in Europe became more competitive. Relaxation of restrictive practices in industries such as banking and airlines forced companies to compete for customers, not just through price but also through customer service. This had two impacts on the public sector. First it started to raise the expectation of citizens about

> how well services could be provided. . . . Secondly, it showed that there were better ways of providing services than simply having bureaucracies working for their own convenience.[14]

At the same time that information technology was remaking the customer side of business, it was also remaking the organizational side of business. Businesses began to cut product cycle times at dizzying rates. They also began to cut middle management, back office operations, and hierarchical forms of organization. As the Information Age economy began to replace the Industrial Age economy, the failures of traditional bureaucracy seemed more and more apparent, and interest in customer choice, organizational reform, and innovation grew accordingly.

By the beginning of the twenty-first century the Anglo-American experiments in postbureaucratic government were well documented and had become the topic of several international conferences.[15] That government policy should be implemented through "nonbureaucratic" means was taken for granted in many of the world's most advanced democracies. In England, Tony Blair's "New Labour" kept most of the important Thatcher innovations and expanded upon them by paying more attention to electronic government (government delivered over the Internet instead of on paper or in official offices), by pushing the government toward "joined-up" government (an effort to get government agencies to work across agency boundaries), and by introducing competition and contestability into the provision of public services.[16] To the intense discomfort of the privileged British civil service, the Blair government centralized policymaking in Number 10 Downing Street in what was deemed a "presidential system" in order to more closely control policy. This was a necessary measure because among the policies he wanted to drive were changes in the civil service itself.[17]

In the United States, the Bush administration retained many if not most of the Clinton-Gore reforms and added to them their own "President's Management Agenda." This included a renewed emphasis on electronic government and a management agenda that emphasized, among other things, performance and goal setting, a mandate on competitive sourcing or having agencies ask carefully whether a function should be done in-house or contracted out, and an award-winning addition to the Office of Management and Budget (OMB) performance process called PART, for Performance Assessment Rating Tool, which is used to assign scores to government programs in order to rate their effectiveness.[18] And in New Zealand, the dramatic reforms of the 1980s persisted throughout a series of governments of both political parties, although they, too, have now been modified by the addition of "circuit breaker teams, a new emphasis on partnerships, managing for outcomes . . . [which are] an understandable response to the excesses of earlier reforms."[19]

The Late-Twentieth-Century Revolution in Governance in the World's Developing Nations

In the advanced Information Age demand for change in the world's democracies usually started with the citizens and impacted their political leaders. In addition, conservative partisan politics and the fiscal demands on the states of the European Union as they moved toward creation of the euro kept pressure for reform intense throughout the 1990s and into the new century. In the rest of the world, however, when there was impetus for reform of the state more often than not it originated from the international institutions involved in economic development on which those countries relied when they got into economic trouble.

Starting in the 1990s, the development banks turned their attention and their funding to "governance issues." The World Bank, the International Monetary Fund, the Inter-American Development Bank, and the Organization for Economic Cooperation and Development all developed extensive programs offering aid and financial resources to countries interested in developing "state capacity."[20] The United Nations established a program in Public Administration and Civil Service Management Reform under the auspices of its Development Program's section. Over the years program staff have coordinated external assistance in promoting a professional civil service, transparency, the use of information and communication technology, and other areas of government reform.

The development advice of these large institutions (often linked to funding) was not aimed at recreating the bureaucracies of the twentieth century. Instead, because their staffs were influenced by the revolution in governance going on in the more developed economies, their advice was often couched in the language of the New Public Management and reinventing government movements that were popular in those countries. For instance, the World Bank offered the following advice in its *World Development Report 1997*:

> It [state capacity] means subjecting state institutions to greater competition, to increase their efficiency. It means increasing the performance of state institutions, improving pay and incentives. And it means making the state more responsive to people's needs, bringing government closer to the people through broader participation and decentralization.[21]

The second big driver for government reform in developing countries was the fall of communism. With it fell the one large alternative paradigm to free market democracy. The result was a global celebration of free market virtues that echoed the rhetoric around government reform in the 1990s. And the result of that was that, fairly or unfairly, when the efficiencies of free markets in the private sector were applied to bureaucracies in the public sector, the public sector inevitably came up looking inefficient, slow to adapt new technology, and slow to reflect citizen demands.

Finally, the end of the cold war removed the overlay of geopolitics from international relations and opened up a new era of global economic competition. Recognizing this, many countries embarked on serious and often painful government reform movements out of a desire to attract international business and investment. As various World Bank reports have shown, there is a high correlation between economic performance and reliable governmental functioning.[22] As Jeff Garten, an international trade expert and a former dean of the Yale School of Management, said, "The world needs to walk away from countries unwilling to make serious changes."[23] And Thomas Friedman, in his popular best-seller *The Lexus and the Olive Tree,* put the need for government reform in the global economy even more starkly: "And the Supermarkets and the Electronic Herd really don't care what color your country is outside any more. All they care about is how your country is wired inside, what level of operating system and software it's able to run, and whether your government can protect private property."[24]

Global economic competition placed a high premium on tackling the twin problems of deficits and corruption. When the European Union decided to expand its membership, the establishment of governance-related criteria for joining the EU became one of the biggest motivators for public sector reform ever seen. Thus, for a host of different reasons, most of the world's governments embarked on one or more serious efforts at government reform at the same time in history. The timing of all these changes made it inevitable that the models ascendant in the first world countries, the donor countries, would be applied to developing countries as well. We have now had nearly two decades of experience, and it is time to evaluate the use of these models in the developing world.

The Postbureaucratic State in Advanced Information Age Democracies

As a result of the reform movements just described, twenty-first-century government in many advanced Information Age economies has moved beyond bureaucracy into a post-bureaucratic form. Much of this has been made possible by the information revolution. For example, citizens of the world's advanced democracies are accustomed to paying their taxes online. With every passing day more and more transactions between citizens and government move to the Internet. Governments of clerks have been replaced by governments of computers.

But technology is just the tip of the iceberg. Twenty-first-century problems do not fit neatly into the bureaucratic boxes of the twentieth century. Citizens in advanced, Information Age democracies expect a high degree of responsiveness and performance from their governments, and they want that performance at the lowest possible tax rate! The result is that political and civil service leaders throughout the world have been experimenting with new ways of implementing policy.

The world's most advanced democracies now implement policy in a wide variety of ways. To be sure, traditional bureaucracies still exist, but they exist alongside new and reformed bureaucratic structures, and alongside an array of public-private partnerships—contracting out, networked government, and coproduced government, to name but a few. Finally states have begun to use state power to create incentives for certain behaviors where there were none before. In other words, twenty-first-century government is a messy blend of old-fashioned bureaucracy and partially privatized and fully privatized government and markets.

To summarize the characteristics of the postbureaucratic state: reinvented government, government by network, and government by market. These are not exclusive of each other; rather, they are meant to describe general tendencies in the postbureaucratic approach to government.

Reinvented Government

I use the term "reinvented government" to refer to public sector organizations that operate without the trappings of traditional bureaucracy. In these organizations, performance measures act as market proxies, allowing government to compete against measures set for it and against other similarly situated governments (or in some cases against similar private sector institutions). In theory in these organizations, central control mechanisms such as budget rules, personnel rules, and procurement rules are replaced by performance measures in exchange for enhanced flexibilities. In practice in many governments, performance management has been added on top of old-fashioned means of control. The downside to this is that there is another layer of management; the upside is that performance is now at least one criterion in the evaluation of bureaucratic functioning. Examples abound. In these organizations customer service is used as a model for organizational behavior vis-à-vis the citizen, even though it is clear that the citizen is not exactly a "customer." In these organizations information technology is used to increase productivity. In other words, reinvented government is government that has incorporated the technological and organizational productivity revolution pioneered in the private sector and adapted it for the public sector, using performance measures as proxies for the market.

Government by Network

In government by network, the bureaucracy is replaced by a wide variety of other kinds of institutions—a network of institutions. In government by network, the government stops trying to do everything itself and funds other organizations to do the actual work that the government wants done. The variety of organizations that can be a part of government by network is immense. Churches, university research labs, private research labs, nonprofit organizations, for-profit organizations—all have been called upon to perform what has been seen as the traditional work of the government. When the state opts to create a network it is because its leaders want things to happen that would not occur to the same extent absent the resources and direction and intervention of the state. Networks can be composed of other governmental organizations such as state and local governments, or they can be composed of nongovernmental organizations. The defining characteristic is that they are all being contracted with by a state entity, using state money, for the production of something that the private market would not produce, to the extent required, on its own initiative. Government by network presupposes the existence of a vibrant private sector or "third sector" (nonprofit sector). Among developed countries the United States has had the most robust "third sector," in part because it had a less robust public sector.

Government by Market

Reinvented government and government by network are both different from bureaucratic government, and yet they both involve a significant amount of traditional government as we know it. In reinvented government departments and local governments, the public's work is done by people who work for the government. In government by network much of the public's work is paid for by the government, even though it is not performed by people who work for the government and is not constrained by all of government's protocols and central control mechanisms. In the third category of implementation, government by market, the work of government involves few if any public employees and little or no public money. In government by market, the government uses state power to create a market that fulfills a public purpose. By definition that kind of market would not exist in the private sector. Often this involves taking into account what economists call "externalities." For instance, "bottle bills" that require charging a fee for every drink container, to be refunded when the container is returned, is an instance where the state used its power to incentivize a public good. If reinvented government is government all dressed up to look like the private sector and government by network is government that hides behind much more popular organizations, government by market is so well disguised that most people are not even aware that it is government in operation. Because of this it is the model furthest removed from traditional bureaucratic government.

The Challenge of Government Capacity Building in the Developing World

In the past two decades the world has spent a great deal of time and effort on increasing the quality of governance in developing nations. For instance, between 1990 and 2006 the World Bank spent about $20 billion, or 5.4 percent of the fund lent by the bank, on public sector reform activities.[25] The working assumption has been that quality governance is important to economic development. Progress on both fronts, however, has been painfully slow and often impossible to see. And this has led scholars and practitioners to ask themselves some hard questions about the challenge of building government capacity in the developing world.

Frauke de Weijer, a fellow at Harvard's Institute for International Development, argues that the problem stems from the fact that the development community, with its members' Western bias, has tended to treat complex socioeconomic problems as merely technical problems:

> The West has managed to "tame" many of its adaptive problems, and turned them into technical problems. The knowledge is acquired, definitions and solutions agreed upon to a relatively high degree, and unintended side effects have been acknowledged and mitigated, or they led to a reformulation of the problem and the solution. In the end, they were tamed. Operational procedures were devised and institutional mechanisms established, and these formed the foundation for our bureaucratic organizational structures that currently dominate the West.[26]

Lant Pritchett and his colleagues at both Harvard and the World Bank argue that the attempt to import modern government techniques from the developed countries to less developed countries constitutes a "technique of failure":

> What are the techniques of failure? Two stand out. First, "big development" as modernization encourages progress through importing standard responses to predetermined problems. This encourages *isomorphic mimicry* as a technique of failure: the adoption of the *forms* of other functional states and organizations which camouflages a persistent lack of *function.* Second, an inadequate theory of developmental change reinforces a fundamental mismatch between expectations and the actual capacity of prevailing administrative systems to implement even the most routine administrative tasks. This leads to *premature load bearing* in which wishful thinking about the pace of progress and unrealistic expectations about the level and rate of improvement of capability lead to stresses and demands on systems that cause capability to *weaken* (if not collapse).[27]

If development failure stems from "isomorphic mimicry," as Pritchett and others point out, what is it that is lacking in developing countries that accounts for the inability to map techniques and processes of government from the first world to the developing world? What accounts for the persistence of failure? Answering this question is a central challenge for all who seek to understand the current state of public administration in a global context. Some of the best insights come from the work of the Peruvian economist Hernando de Soto, who became famous for introducing the world to the existence of an informal economy in many of the world's poorest countries. In *The Mystery of Capital,* de Soto traces the sources of poverty to the lack of an infrastructure (my term) that allows for the formalization of economic activity. He points out that poor people around the world are economically active and entrepreneurial. The difference between their activity and the equivalent activity in first world countries comes down to the fact that this activity is captured by a legal system in the first world but not in the developing world.

> But they hold these resources in defective forms: houses built on land whose ownership rights are not adequately recorded, unincorporated businesses with undefined liability, industries located where financiers and investors cannot see them. Because the rights to these possessions are not adequately documented, these assets cannot readily be turned into capital, cannot be traded outside of narrow local circles where people know and trust each other, cannot be used as collateral for a loan, and cannot be used as a share against an investment.
>
> In the West, by contrast, every parcel of land, every building, every piece of equipment, or store of inventories is represented in a property

> document that is the visible sign of a vast hidden process that connects all these assets to the rest of the economy. Thanks to this representational process, assets can lead an invisible, parallel life alongside their material existence. They can be used as collateral for credit.[28]

De Soto's insights about the failure of capitalism in many poor countries provide a point of departure for understanding the failure of government in many poor countries as well and especially the failure of modern government reforms. Just as economic activity in poor countries absent a structure that allows them to lead a "parallel life" keeps economies mired in poverty, so government in poor countries absent structures that permit accountability keeps government weak, ineffective, and unable to assist in economic development. The infrastructure of effective governance is missing in most developing countries, thus reform politicians come and go, international lending organizations come and go, consultants from the first world come and go—and basically nothing changes.

The first step in unraveling the infrastructure of effective modern government is to ask, "What is it that citizens of the first world take for granted in their governance systems that is missing in the governance environments of the developing world?" The answer lies in six areas that I shall briefly describe.

1. Reliable Information

Strong statistical agencies have made it possible for first world countries to reinvent government by enacting performance measures and performance management systems that decrease bureaucracy and increase efficiency and accountability.

Many development agencies have championed the creation of performance management systems in developing countries, but the establishment of performance measurement is made infinitely more difficult if there are no basic statistics—on social well-being, on tax compliance, on criminal behavior—from which to derive appropriate targets for performance improvement. The existence of reliable and nonpartisan statistics makes possible the sorts of innovations in policing that made New York City's police reform program (known as COMPSTAT) so successful and that made the measurement and accountability innovations in city management in Baltimore (known as CITISTAT) so successful.

Of course, the temptation to try and cheat or "game" performance metrics is powerful everywhere they have been used. From the National Health Service in Great Britain to educational testing in the United States, government officials have tried to make the numbers come out in ways that seem to spell progress. But overall, the use of performance metrics in first world countries has contributed to greater efficiency and accountability, and attempts at cheating are uncovered quickly. In part this is because first world countries generally have multiple sources of reliable data—both public and private. For instance, in the area of automobile safety, the government's statistics exist alongside statistics gathered by and for the insurance industry. If government officials do try to mislead with statistics, the depth and variety of sources of data are such that no one can get away with this for long.

In developing countries the problem is just the opposite. Many countries do not even have archival laws requiring government officials to turn over records and data to the state when they leave office. Nor can most countries afford the extensive collection of reliable data that characterizes, for instance, the Bureau of Labor Statistics in the United States and its extensive monthly surveys on the state of labor markets. It is extremely difficult to find even reliable census data for most of the countries in Africa. The absence of reliable statistical data—both public and private—means that it is nearly impossible to execute effective performance management systems. When the data themselves are of poor quality they are subject to political interpretation and manipulation.

2. Information Technology

In developed countries information technology can create huge cost savings through reengineering and the conversion of paper-based systems to electronic systems, whereas in developed countries the cost savings are illusory because the paper-based systems are often substandard to begin with.

Most advanced democracies now process a large proportion of their tax returns online. This has meant enormous improvements in productivity and in the accuracy of tax payments. It has also gotten rid of the need to increase the budget for wages as the number of tax returns to be processed increases. Information technology plays an important role in nearly every innovation at the federal, state, and local level, and increasingly in first world countries technology is ubiquitous in all citizen-to-government transactions.

But in poor countries data are usually so poor to start with that information technology is of little help. For instance, using computers to streamline government's personnel systems is no good if the government's records contain hundreds of "ghost workers" and other inaccuracies. When it comes to information technology, the temptation in developing countries has been to think that government could "jump over" the bureaucratic stage right to e-government. But time and time again those hopes have been dashed because the fundamental records and processes have proved to be so poor that information technology was no help. Not only is gaining access to computers difficult for most citizens in developing countries, but most of the economies of the world today are still "unbanked," meaning that they are cash economies. Information technology is of little use in economies where most transactions are still cash-based.

This situation is most dire in the area of property ownership. In many of the world's developing countries comprehensive and accurate information about land ownership is absent, owing to war, communism, or other problems. Without being legally registered, land cannot become a source of economic growth and progress. Information technology can cut the cost of such record keeping enormously; in most jurisdictions in the United States, for example, land ownership records and tax records are easily available online. But information technology is no help in the absence of reliable information. According to the Hungarian land expert András Osskó, in developed countries the cadastre and legal registry work well. But in developing countries it is common for there to be no well-functioning land administration and thus no secure land tenure.[29]

3. Established Civil Service

In the first world there is a strong class of permanent civil servants who make implementation of reform possible.

The involvement of civil servants in the design of reform efforts has been critical to the success of these movements, especially in the United States, Great Britain, and other Commonwealth countries. At times the strength of the "permanent government," as these civil servants are often referred to in their own countries, has meant that they have often impeded reform efforts more than have elected politicians. But when reform efforts have involved the civil service in design and implementation, its active involvement has been an important factor in the success and longevity of those movements. Government reform takes time, and if political power changes hands every few years, absent a "permanent government" there is no one to nurture reforms to maturity.

Too many developing countries have weak pools of civil servants who change with the change in political regime. This means that there is no cadre with the strength to carry out reform. The result: poor countries all too often bounce from one reform effort to another and from one reform regime to another, contributing to the well-known "reform fatigue" syndrome.

4. Adequately Compensated Public Employees

In developed countries public employees tend to be paid well enough that relatively few are tempted into corruption.

Small-time corruption—where civil servants try to extract bribes in return for providing common public goods such as passports, driver's licenses, or building permits—is relatively unusual in most first world systems and in most advanced democracies. It is almost unheard of for low-level civil servants to regard bribes and graft as a legitimate means of enhancing their salaries. In the United States this kind of corruption, regular bribery, "no show" or "ghost worker" jobs, and other petty corruption was prevalent from the end of the Civil War (1864) to the advent of the Progressive movement in the 1920s. Since then, however, the civil service has been paid well enough and policed well enough that the kind of regular and accepted corruption so common in most developing countries is rare.

This is not to say that there is no corruption in American government, but it tends to occur in the acquisition of large contracts or in the gaming of large benefit systems. At this point in time American citizens are so accustomed to honest and straightforward government that most would be outraged if they were expected to pay a bribe for a basic service such as getting a driver's license renewed. The absence of low-level corruption turns out to be central to political reform efforts because it creates expectations of honesty among the public.

In the developing world everyone (including those working in government reform) has become accustomed to everyday instances of petty corruption. To be sure, these are often small and do not add significantly to expense. In fact, some economists argue that they are actually efficient because they augment the civil servants' low salaries. However, they contribute to an attitude of tolerance toward corruption that then undermines the public and therefore the political will to take on larger examples of public sector corruption.

5. High Expectations of Government

In the first world citizens have high expectations of their government. In the developing world too many citizens accept that they are powerless.

The result is that the grassroots political nature of reform movements in developed countries stands in contrast to the experience of administrative reform in many developing countries. In the developing world the impetus for reform of the state has come, more often than not, from the development institutions on which those countries relied when they got into economic trouble. In the absence of citizen expectations for improvement, reform efforts lag and vanish, often without a trace.

6. Rule of Law

In countries where there is weak or non-existent rule of law, especially contract law, the government cannot reliably extend its reach and innovative capacity by creating networks or markets to do the government's work.

The absence of effective contract law and also of a robust third sector—the nonprofit sector—means that government by network (as described earlier) is not an option for most developing countries. Of course, NGOs operate extensively in these countries, but unlike the organizations that participate in government by network in the United States and in other first world countries, the NGOs that operate in developing countries are not accountable to the governments of those countries. They are accountable either to other governments, development banks, or international donors of great wealth such as Bill Gates.

Although it has not been without its problems, in first world countries the expansion of government capacity to include the third sector has been a source of both creativity and innovation as well as a means of increasing government legitimacy by making private sector actors part of the public project. A robust third sector that competes for government work and therefore seeks to improve on the provision of government services cannot thrive in a country where weak contract law means that few entrepreneurs can rely on the government to pay them if they do compete for government work.

In the absence of a strong rule of law, government by market (as described earlier) becomes yet another invitation to corruption on the part of the ruling class. Markets need to be policed by the state in order to work properly. First world countries with long and robust regulatory histories often fail to police their markets, as was clear in the 2008 financial crisis that spread from Wall Street to the rest of the world. But this regulatory failure was addressed by the American political system in a series of reforms enacted in 2010 and 2011. Though not ideal, the regulatory structures that govern the New York and London financial markets succeed in creating enough trust and transparency that no other markets are likely to catch up with them in the near future. Government by market cannot work outside the framework of a strong rule of law and an effective regulatory regime, a pair of problems that most developing countries are still struggle to solve.

Conclusion: The Infrastructure of Modern Government

It is easy to see how and why the revolution in governance taking place in the first world affected so strongly the techniques transferred to the developing world. In this chapter I argue that in the attempt to understand the poor results of government reform efforts in developing countries, too little attention has been paid to the infrastructure of modern government and its role in making government reform possible. This infrastructure is taken for granted by donor countries, and yet it is often weak or nonexistent in developing countries.

Notes

1. See Donald Inglehart, "Postmodernization Erodes Respect for Authority but Increases Support for Democracy," in *Critical Citizens: Global Support for Democratic Governance,* edited by Pippa Norris (Oxford University Press, 1999).

2. Joseph S. Nye Jr. and others, eds., *Why People Don't Trust Government* (Harvard University Press, 1997).

3. On the absence of a clear relationship between economic performance and declining trust, see Robert Z. Lawrence, "Is It Really the Economy, Stupid?" in *Why People Don't Trust the Government*, edited by Nye and others, chapter 4. For a discussion of government accomplishment in the face of declining trust, see Derek Bok, "Measuring the Performance of Government," in *Why People Don't Trust the Government,* edited by Nye and others, chapter 2.

4. For a wonderful history of these leaders, see Donald Savoie, *Thatcher, Reagan and Mulroney* (University of Pittsburgh Press, 1994).

5. As distrust grew, political scientists turned their attention to problems in policy implementation. Much of this distrust had been fueled by unhappiness with Great Society programs. In 1973 (updated in 1984) Jeffrey Pressman and Aaron Wildavsky took on the problem in a book whose subtitle says it all: *Implementation: How Great Expectations in Washington Are Dashed in Oakland; Or, Why It's Amazing That Federal Programs Work at All, This Being a Saga . . . on a Foundation* (University of California Press, Oakland Project Series, 1984).

6. See Paul A. Sabatier, "Top-Down and Bottom-Up Approaches to Implementation Research: A Critical Analysis and Suggested Synthesis," *Journal of Public Policy* 6 (January 1986): 21–48.

7. Michael Barzelay, *Breaking through Bureaucracy* (University of California Press, 1992).

8. See Derek Bok, *The Trouble with Government* (Harvard University Press, 2001); Neal Ryan, "Public Confidence in the Public Sector," discussion paper prepared for the Office of the Auditor General of Western Australia, *Journal of Contemporary Issues in Business and Government* 6, no. 1 (May 2000): 20–32; Cheryl Barnes and Derek Gill,

"Declining Government Performance? Why Citizens Don't Trust Government," working paper 9 (Wellington: State Services Commission, 2000) (www.ssc.govt.nz/wp9); Christopher Pollitt and Geert Bouckaert, *Public Management Reform: A Contemporary Analysis* (Oxford University Press, 2000); Harvey Sims, "Public Confidence in Government and Government Service Delivery" (Ottawa: Canadian Center for Management Development, 2001).

9. David Osborne and Peter Plastrick, *Banishing Bureaucracy: The Five Strategies for Reinventing Government* (Reading, Mass.: Addison-Wesley, 1997), p. 25.

10. Jonathan Boston and others, *Public Management, the New Zealand Model* (Oxford University Press, 1996).

11. Ibid., p. 5.

12. See Tim Irwin, "An Analysis of New Zealand's New System of Public Sector Management," in *Public Management in Government: Contemporary Illustrations*, OECD Occasional Papers 9 (Paris: Organization for Economic Cooperation and Development, 1996).

13. Elaine Kamarck was senior policy adviser to Vice President Gore and had primary responsibility for creating and managing the National Performance Review.

14. Norman Flynn and Franz Strehl, eds., *Public Sector Management in Europe* (New York: Prentice-Hall Europe, 1996), p. 3.

15. The first international conference on reinventing government, held in Cambridge, Massachusetts, in 1999, was sponsored by the Kennedy School of Government at Harvard and the United States government. Since then, international conferences focusing on government reforms have been held in Brazil, Italy, Morocco, Mexico, and Korea; the United Nations' Office of Public Administration has played an important role in these conferences.

16. Vernon Bognador, *Joined Up Government* (Oxford University Press, 2005).

17. Peter Hennessy, *The Prime Minister: The Office and Its Holders Since 1945* (London: Allen Lane, 2000), pp. 476–93. See also Prime Minister's Strategy Unit, *The UK Government's Approach to Public Service Reform* (London: June 2006).

18. This program won the Innovations in Government Award in 2005, which is sponsored by the Kennedy School of Government at Harvard University (www.innovations.edu).

19. Tim Tenbensel (University of Auckland, Department of Political Studies), personal communication (e-mail), March 22, 2004.

20. See, for example, Michael Pinto-Duschinsky, "The Rise of Political Aid," in *Consolidating Third Wave Democracies: Regional Challenges*, edited by Larry Diamond and others (Johns Hopkins University Press, 1997).

21. World Bank, *The State in a Changing World; World Bank Development Report 1997* (Washington: 1997), p. 3.

22. Ibid., p.42.

23. Jeffrey E. Garten, "Lessons for the Next Financial Crisis," *Foreign Affairs*, March–April 1999.

24. Thomas Friedman, *The Lexus and the Olive Tree* (New York: Doubleday/Anchor, 2000), p. 201.

25. World Bank, Independent Evaluation Group, *Public Sector Reform—What Works and Why?* (Washington: 2008).

26. Frauke de Weijer, "A Systems Perspective on Tackling Complex Problems: With an Eye on Afghanistan," working paper (Harvard University, Center for International Development, November 2010).

27. Lant Pritchett, Michael Woolcock, and Matt Andres, "Capability Traps? The Mechanisms of Persistent Implementation Failure," working paper (Harvard University, Kennedy School of Government, May 2010).

28. Hernando de Soto, *The Mystery of Capital* (New York: Basic Books, 2000), p. 3.

29. András Osskó, "Advantages of the Unified Multipurpose Land Registry System" (www.fig.net/pub/proceedings/korea/full-papers/pdf/session6/ossko.pdf).

MARIO IANNIELLO, PAOLO FEDELE,
AND LUCA BRUSATI

13 *Stakeholders' Inclusion: Measuring the Performance of Interactive Decisionmaking*

Interactive decisionmaking has become an established practice, especially in local governments.[1] Many administrations involve citizens, social organizations, and, broadly speaking, stakeholders in the early stages of policymaking, before concrete policy proposals are developed.[2] The goal of what has come to be called interactive decisionmaking is to adopt better and more democratic policy decisions and to avoid recurrent problems that are encountered in usual "go it alone" decisionmaking by public officials. There are many pluses with interactive decisionmaking. It may enhance public administrations' intangible assets and establish bridging relationships with their citizens.[3] Generally speaking, stakeholders can provide decisionmakers with information they would otherwise lack, leading to more informed solutions. Conflicts and use of veto powers may be avoided through timely information and consultation. Citizens and social organizations may support the implementation of policies that are regarded as more democratic and legitimate.[4] Interaction can take place through many organizational arrangements: public hearings, referenda, participatory planning procedures, citizens' juries, and others.[5]

Interactive policymaking is not without risks, however. Decisions as to who or what group constitutes a stakeholder group to be consulted and included in the process can lead to problems of democratic accountability;

This chapter presents the preliminary results of a research project partly supported by a grant awarded to Udine University, Gorizia, by the provincial administration of Gorizia, Italy. An earlier version of this chapter was presented at the seventeenth BledCom International Public Relations Research Symposium on Government Communication, held in Bled, Slovenia, July 2–3, 2010.

vested interests may end up affecting decisions; and decisionmaking processes may become too time consuming.[6]

Although interactive policymaking has been widely debated, how to evaluate its effects is still underanalyzed.[7] In this chapter our goal is to make a conceptual and empirical contribution to this debate. Our main research question is: How do organizational arrangements influence the outcomes of interactive decisionmaking? We propose that the organizational structures adopted in practice to manage an interactive process significantly influence its results, although they are mediated by some contextual factors. We base our analysis on two assumptions: the importance of network management and the influence of formal organizational structure in shaping behaviors.[8] We have developed a model for qualitative analysis that builds on some previous contributions in the public administration literature. We then use the model to analyze five case studies, with minor adaptations suggested by the data collected during the research. The chapter presents the conceptual model and the results of five case studies.

Theoretical Framework: Governance Networks, Interactive Decisionmaking, and Evaluation

The work refers, broadly speaking, to the governance literature, and more specifically to the mainstream of that literature that focuses on governance networks.[9] Interactive policymaking implies, in fact, that public policies are the outcome of interactions between interdependent actors.[10] Other disciplinary fields have dealt with this subject, among them public relations studies, which here complement the previously mentioned governance mainstream.

Governance and governance networks have been so widely debated that the concepts have become subject to conceptual stretching.[11] In this chapter we focus on a specific aspect of this academic debate: the evaluation of networks. The matter can be viewed as simple: networks affect decisions on public policies and public spending. Is there a way to evaluate networks? As Robin Keast and his colleagues put it: are networks only about drinking a cup of tea, or are they about performance?[12] If networks have to be evaluated, then criteria for evaluation need to be proposed.

Interactive decisionmaking is different from traditional hierarchical approaches, but it is still, though not exclusively, about "making decisions." Consequently, the adoption of a shared decision is one of its main purposes and can therefore be considered a relevant, although very rough, evaluation criterion.

On the other hand, evaluation against a set of objectives spelled out beforehand, which is the most recurrent practice in public management, can hardly apply to networks, for widely acknowledged reasons: setting ex ante objectives requires some form of hierarchical authority, which is by definition absent in a network; impacts of collaboration are hardly measured through performance measures; and learning through interaction by the parties involved in the process can render ex ante formulated objectives obsolete.[13] So, how to further evaluate networks? The answer provided by many is that what has to be evaluated is the interaction, for this is the distinctive feature of interactive decisionmaking. Thus, level of satisfaction or actor contentment, with regard both to process and decisions, have been proposed as evaluation criteria. Satisfaction has been largely debated in public relation studies; broadly speaking it implies that a satisfying relationship occurs when each party believes the other is engaging in positive steps to maintain the relationship.[14]

Satisfaction is often adopted as an evaluative criterion, yet as a measure for evaluating interactive processes it has many pitfalls, and other evaluating factors matter.[15] In particular, interactive policymaking can create and consolidate an intangible asset: increased trust between governments and citizens.[16] This is why we assume that consolidation of trust is another evaluative criterion against which interactive policymaking should be measured. At the core of the concept of trust there is the confidence level that actors have in each other and their willingness to open themselves to others.[17]

If shared decisions, contentment, and trust are the dependent variables, many factors might be considered antecedents of these outcomes. Organizational designs have an influence on how decisions are taken: since actors cannot make fully rational choices, they need selection mechanisms to guide their decisionmaking behaviors. The formal organizational structure provides them with some selecting mechanisms.[18] This is why, in our analytical model, we study the relationship between the previously mentioned outcomes of the interactive process and the organizational arrangement adopted to manage the process.

Methodology

The research was carried out by means of a multiple-case study. The strengths and weaknesses of this approach are well known, and we adopted an iterative approach aiming at literal and theoretical replication.[19] We adopted a "structured" approach to case studies data analysis, in order to identify and measure constructs.[20] This approach has been criticized by some authors, who say that such procedures just try to replicate hypothesis-testing research methods and do not consider the richness of data emerging from any single case study. We were aware of this potential bias and explicitly also employed some of the information "lost" in the operationalization process in the phase of interpretation of empirical evidence.

Case Selection

Previous empirical studies examined interactive decisionmaking processes with a common focus taking place in different geographical locations.[21] In this case, though, mimetic isomorphism is likely to play a role in shaping organizational designs, thus reducing the meaningfulness of the comparison.[22] Moreover, interactive decisionmaking patterns in different locations are likely to be shaped by different traditions of civic engagement, and these in turn are influenced by a wide range of variables, such as demography or economic structure. We chose instead to study decisionmaking processes with different focuses taking place in a single geographic location, the province of Gorizia, in northeastern Italy. Our reasoning is that this choice allows a better control of external variables and a clearer understanding of the link between the formal-structural organizational design of interactive decisionmaking processes and their outcomes.

Using a purposeful sampling approach we selected five cases of interactive decisionmaking processes initiated and carried through to the end by local administrations in Gorizia. Cases were selected on the basis of data richness and relevance, including both successful and unsatisfactory experiences. Two cases were chosen for a pilot phase, in order to test the appropriateness and relevance of the analytical model as well as to fine-tune the structure of the interviews. (See the appendix for examples of interview questions.)

For each case study, we initially collected the documents immediately available to the general public: reports, press releases, and newspaper articles. Subsequently, local administrations granted permission for accessing the official documents. Afterward, semistructured interviews with key informants were scheduled and conducted. We decided to adopt two different sets of questions as guidelines reflecting the categories of the theoretical model: one set of questions was used with politicians, bureaucrats, and professional facilitators involved in the design and management of the process; the other was used with process participants. Finally, we planned a series of observations from the field by participating in some of the inclusive processes. Different data collection techniques allowed triangulation of the evidence and strengthened the relevance of the findings as well as reduced the risk of errors in the original records.[23]

A Qualitative Model for Analysis

The qualitative model assumes that it is possible to assess how the organizational arrangements of the interactive process—the way the process is designed before the event—influence its results, given the influence of a range of contextual factors. The starting point is the structure designed by Jurian

Edelenbos and Erik-Hans Klijn, which explores the potential influence of organizational arrangement on the effect of the interactive processes. It was adapted to the task of studying interactive decisionmaking processes dealing with a range of different issues.[24]

To do this three macro-categories were identified, along three variables: organizational arrangements, contextual factors, and results (as suggested by Keith G. Provan and H. Briton Milward and by Provan and Julianne G. Sebastian.[25] We then specified each macro-category in single subcomponents, and for each of the latter we defined a measurement scale. For organizational arrangements, each subcomponent was specified in more detail.

The organizational arrangements component and contextual factors component were defined by positioning them on a scale ranging from a minimum value of 0 to an intermediate value of 0.5 to the maximum value of 1.

To define the results of inclusive decisionmaking processes is by far the biggest challenge: there is always the risk of becoming either tautological (the result is the decision itself) or inconsistent (the result is participation per se). We decided to assess the preliminary result through the dichotomy "decision taken: yes or no." Then the main results were graduated on a four-values scale: ++, +, –, —. The middle value (0) was purposefully excluded in order to ensure a better understanding and a clearer identification of differences (see figure 13-1).

Organizational Arrangements

This category was divided into three subcomponents of the process: formalization, accessibility, and internalization. Each subcomponent was divided into items. Each item was then evaluated and given a score of 0, 0.5, or 1.

The degree of formalization of the decisionmaking process specifies the level of structuring or destructuring of the inclusive process. The items we considered are:

FORMALIZATION OF PROCESS DESIGN. Edelenbos and Klijn reflect on organizational arrangements through "the degree of formalization of the interactive process through process design and process management."[26] We originally took into consideration only the process design. Maximum formalization corresponds to processes that for legal normative reasons or by custom or choice have a predefined design and are rigidly followed, allowing for neither flexibility nor adaptation. These processes received a score of 1. An intermediate level of formalization corresponds to an "open" design, which takes its final shape during process implementation, either suggested by the process manager or as a contextual need (a score of 0.5). Minimum formalization means there was no preexisting process design (value 0).

Figure 13-1. *The Model for Analysis*

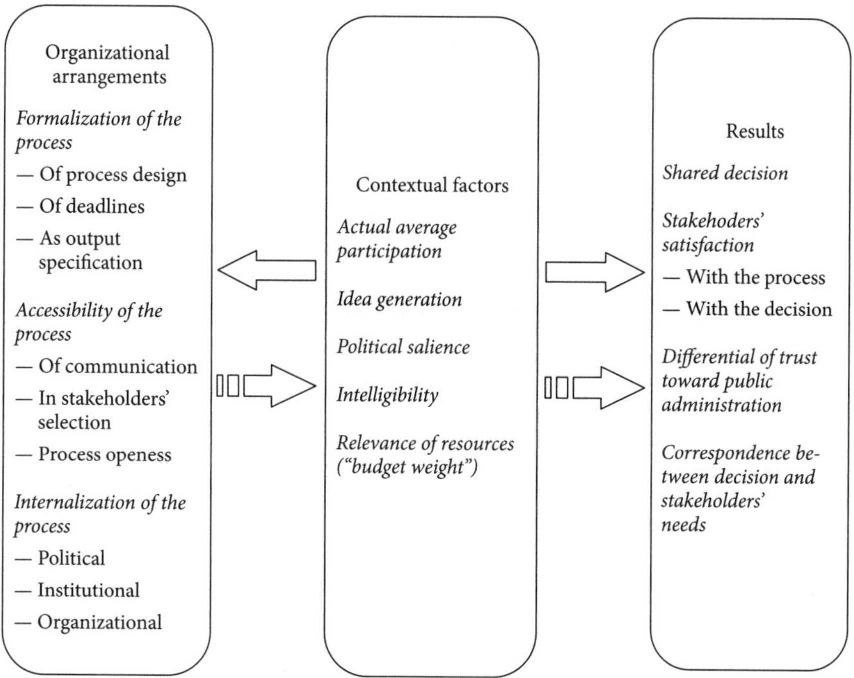

Source: Authors.

FORMALIZATION OF DEADLINES. Clear deadlines, related to some or all the phases of the process, are one of the most self-evident indicators of formalization. Maximum formalization corresponds here to fixed predetermined deadlines (value 1); an intermediate level of formalization corresponds to flexible deadlines, either suggested by the process manager or negotiated by participants (value 0.5); minimum formalization is when no deadlines are set (value 0).

FORMALIZATION AS OUTPUT SPECIFICATION. This item refers to the expected outputs and contributes to defining the formalization level of the process inasmuch as it establishes ex-ante that a predetermined output is expected, requiring specific content and procedures, as a maximum of formalization (value 1). A generic output is expected at an intermediate level of formalization, when the process binds the participants to a specific result, without specifying content and procedures (value 0.5). A minimum of formalization means there is no output expected other than the inclusive process in itself (value 0).

The second subcomponent of organizational arrangements is accessibility of the decisionmaking process. Accessibility is defined here as the openness to authentic stakeholders' participation.[27] The relevant items are:

ACCESSIBILITY OF COMMUNICATION. The transparency of an administrative process is strictly related to its accessibility and contributes to create trust.[28] Here we consider the contribution of communication that the local administrations have put in place throughout the inclusive decisionmaking process. Maximum accessibility corresponds to a dialogic approach, two-way and targeted communication that goes along the whole process (value 1). An intermediate level of accessibility corresponds to a communication approach that is one way, generic, and limited to the main steps of the process (value 0.5). Minimum accessibility corresponds to communication limited to compulsory information and that uses standard tools (value 0).

ACCESSIBILITY IN STAKEHOLDERS' SELECTION. The gate-keeping role in respect to the process is by far one of the most significant dimensions of accessibility. Many authors have indicated participants' selection as one of the main organizational arrangements that influence the results of inclusive decisionmaking processes.[29] In this category we also include the "width" of participation suggested by Edelenbos and Kljin.[30] Maximum accessibility here is represented by the lack of selection (value 1); intermediate accessibility corresponds to a selection made on a representational basis or on self-candidature (value 0.5); minimum accessibility indicates a selection made by choice (value 0). In this case we will try to highlight the criteria used and, specifically, whether representativeness or internal democracy is requested of organizations that are to be selected for participation.[31]

PROCESS OPENNESS. The effective role of participants within inclusive decisionmaking processes has been depicted through many typologies.[32] Here we maintain the basic model that differentiates among codecision, consultation, and information. Considering the peculiar context, however, it would be difficult to find codecision in its strict sense. We suggest active engagement, based on the concept of coproduction introduced by Edelenbos as the highest level of process openness (value 1). The intermediate level is consultation, where participants' opinions are considered in the decisionmaking process but are not binding for the local public administration (value 0.5). The minimum level of process openness is merely informing participants of decisions (value 0).[33] This item includes as well the "depth" of participation indicated by Edelenbos and Klijn.[34]

The third subcomponent of organizational arrangements is process internalization. Its specificity and importance lie in its capacity to highlight the commitment toward inclusive decisionmaking by the administration concerned—in other words, to spell out whether they believe in this approach to the point of actively participating, making new rules, and changing organizational roles.[35] The relevant items considered are:

POLITICAL INTERNALIZATION. This item considers the "roles of politicians," in that it describes the role politicians take within the inclusive decisionmaking process.[36] The highest level of political internalization corresponds to the case of politicians taking on a formal role in the process and following it actively and on a regular basis (value 1); the intermediate level is defined as a participation by politicians that take on de facto public visibility and accountability, without direct involvement in the discussions (value 0.5); the minimum level corresponds to the lack of participation of the politicians, without any direct visibility or accountability toward the process (value 0).

INSTITUTIONAL INTERNALIZATION. This subcategory refers to formal regulations mandating the use of interactive decisionmaking.[37] For instance, in Italy, some administrations, mainly at the intermediate tier of government (the region), have passed laws regulating the inclusion of citizens in the process. Maximum institutional internalization corresponds to the presence of norms or rules compelling public administrations to take a strategic approach to inclusive decisionmaking (value 1). The intermediate level is represented by the existence of a regular praxis of inclusive decisionmaking that might find some acknowledgement in a variety of formal acts, such as council reports, conventions, or official statements (value 0.5). The minimum level corresponds to the complete lack of institutionalization of inclusive processes (value 0).

ORGANIZATIONAL INTERNALIZATION. This item refers to organizational changes in the structure of the public administration concerned. The highest level of organizational internalization ("complete") corresponds to the presence of units or posts solely dedicated to the management of inclusive decisionmaking processes and of dedicated financial resources in the annual budget (value 1). The intermediate level ("mixed" organizational internalization) corresponds to a substantial involvement of internal resources and structures, with temporary tasks assigned to existing units and posts or the involvement of external consultants (value 0.5). The minimum level is a form of ad hoc internalization, with processes entirely entrusted to external consultants and no consistent involvement of internal resources and structures (value 0).

Contextual Factors

Some mediating factors have a substantial influence on the relationship between organizational arrangements and results. More specifically:

ACTUAL AVERAGE PARTICIPATION. Participation is not considered a result in itself, but a precondition for the success of an inclusive decisionmaking processes. This is why participation is included in the model as a mediating factor between organizational arrangements and results. At the same time, two dimensions seem to be relevant to fully describe the phenomenon at hand: how many people actually took part in the process and how active their participation was.[38] Instead of referring to the size of the population concerned, we deemed it more insightful to consider average attendance at meetings as a share of the number of stakeholders initially selected.[39] The highest value of participation is when the average is more than 50 percent (value 1). The intermediate value is between 49 and 25 percent (value 0.5). The minimum value is between 24 and 0 percent (value 0).

IDEA GENERATION. We assessed the "quality" of participation also by looking at the participants' contributions in terms of idea generation, advice, and initiatives.[40] The highest value of idea generation corresponds to participants' contributions that are substantially innovative and unique in respect to the initial proposal (value 1). The intermediate value corresponds to participants' contributions that significantly complement the public administration's proposal (value 0.5). The minimum value corresponds to the lack of ideas and initiatives initiated by participants (value 0).[41]

POLITICAL SALIENCE. The concept of salience can refer to an organization within the public sector or to a policy area.[42] An issue or policy area is salient if it is of relevance for public opinion and interest groups and if it often attracts the attention of the media. Maximum salience is the situation when all major stakeholders are active in the process or oppose it from outside and the process is discussed in the media on a regular basis (value 1). An intermediate level of political salience corresponds to a minority of active stakeholders and to a presence in the media limited to main events (value 0.5). The minimum value of salience corresponds to the substantial lack of stakeholders' or media attention (value 0).

INTELLIGIBILITY. This refers to the ease with which issues are understood by the general public. Not all the issues are easily understandable by the general public; some of them require specialized knowledge. We assume that this is a relevant feature when an issue is debated through an interactive process.[43] The highest value of intelligibility corresponds to the processes that do not require any kind of technical or specialized knowledge (value 1). The middle value corresponds to the issues that demand a training phase by subject experts, even if just an introductory session (value 0.5). The minimum level of intelligibility corresponds to the issues that require not only a training phase but also continuous support throughout the process (value 0). The demand for training was assessed in terms of the perceptions of stakeholders.

RESOURCE RELEVANCE ("BUDGET WEIGHT"). "Budget weight" refers to the budgetary implications of a policy, project, or decision. Budget weight can be logically included as a component of political salience. It can be reasonably assumed that the budgetary implications of main issues will come under strict scrutiny by government and citizens because these issues' course of development can massively affect the overall public budget and impact society at large.[44] At the same time, it seems legitimate to assess budget weight through two different components: the simple monetary component and its local relevance, that is, the capacity to influence the long-term policy issues relevant to the community. The latter component was assessed according to information provided by local administrations. For practical purposes, in our case studies we adopted the following brackets: the maximum level of relevance includes processes involving more than 500,000 euros or having a substantial impact on the majority of the local community in the long term (value 1). The intermediate level of relevance includes processes with budgets of between 500,000 and 100,000 euros or having a significant impact on an important part of the community in the medium term (value 0.5). The minimum level of relevance includes the processes whose budgets are less than 100,000 euros or have limited consequences for a part of the local community in the short term (value 0).

Results

We considered that the primary and minimum result for an inclusive decisionmaking process would be to reach a shared decision. Other results are the level of stakeholders' satisfaction with the decision taken and the process itself, the increased or decreased trust toward the local administration involved, and, finally, the increased or decreased consistency between the decisions taken and the needs expressed by the stakeholders. A detailed description follows, including the scale adopted for measurement.

SHARED DECISION. At the risk of being reductionist, we can say that since interactive decisionmaking is still a form of decisionmaking, the first outcome to consider is the adoption of a shared decision (value yes/no).

STAKEHOLDERS' SATISFACTION. There is a clear connection between actors' satisfaction and their perception of a positive result of the process.[45] We take into account the most common criticism to this evaluative criterion: effectiveness. Namely, the suggestion of an alternative focus (effectiveness, efficiency, and equity of the decision) put forward by Coglianese is partly retrieved here through the dimensions of trust highlighted in the interviews. More specifically, as concerns satisfaction, we asked interviewees about their contentment with the decision taken (to what extent do stakeholders accept and support a policy decision) and with the process itself (which reflects the quality of the interaction).[46] The answers were classified according to the following criteria:

— ++: Very satisfied; most interviewees express satisfaction without reservation.

— + : Satisfied; most interviewees express satisfaction, even with some reservations about specific aspects of the decision or of the process.

— –: Unsatisfied; most interviewees express dissatisfaction, although with some appreciation for specific aspects of either the decision or the process.

— —: Very unsatisfied; most interviewees express dissatisfaction and no appreciation for the decision or for the process.

DIFFERENTIAL OF TRUST TOWARD PUBLIC ADMINISTRATION. Many authors claim that any form of inclusion might lead to greater trust in government by the public, regardless of any other results, since participation implies ownership of public policy.[47] Trust has been operationalized according to James E. Grunig, that is, insulating the dimensions of integrity, dependability, and competence in two ways.[48] First we included in the interviews three questions meant to assess the level of stakeholders' trust toward the local administration concerned. These questions were:

"Would you describe anything that the local administration has done to treat the participants fairly and justly, or unfairly and unjustly?" (focusing on integrity)

"Would you describe things that the local administration has done that indicate it can be relied on to keep its promises, or that it does not keep its promises?" (dependability)

"How confident are you that the local administration has the ability to accomplish what it says it will do? Can you provide examples of why you feel that way?" (competence)

Second, we cross-checked stakeholders' perceptions with those of administrators and managers and with documental analysis. The answers were classified according to the following criteria:

— ++: very trustful; most interviewees express trust in all their answers to the questions

— +: trustful; most interviewees express their trust in a majority of their answers to the questions, even with some reservations.

— –: distrustful; most interviewees express distrust in a majority of their answers to the questions even with some appreciation.

— —: very distrustful; most interviewees express distrust in all their answers to the questions.

CORRESPONDENCE BETWEEN DECISION AND STAKEHOLDERS' NEEDS. Stakeholders' inclusion should allow governments to incorporate measures to meet citizens' needs in decisionmaking processes, thus increasing legitimacy. Most relevant were their answers to the questions "Do you think that the local administration has taken the participants' point of view into account in its decision? Can you provide any examples?" The answers were classified according to the following criteria:

— ++: complete; most interviewees express a positive opinion in all their answers to the questions.

— + : good; a majority of interviewees express a positive opinion in their answers to the questions, but with some reservations.

— – : poor; a majority of interviewees express a negative opinion in their answers to the questions, but with some appreciation.

— — : absent; a majority of interviewees express a negative opinion in each of their answers to the questions.

Case Studies

The analytical model described in the previous section was applied to five case studies of decisionmaking in public policy, all of them in the province of Gorizia.

—Agenda 21 "Elettrodotto": the construction of a high power line, the Elettrodotto Redipuglia-Udine, to serve the province of Gorizia.

—Agenda 21 Comune di Sagrado: the use of a quarry near the town of Sagrado as a waste collection site.

—Agenda 21 Comune di Cormons, Progetto "Prendi Posto!": deciding the future use of the former army barracks area in the historical center of the town of Cormons.

—Agenda 21 Programma provinciale rifiuti urbani: the urban waste management program of the Gorizia provincial administration.

—Bilancio Partecip@attivo San Canzian d'Isonzo: the participatory budget process of the municipality of San Canzian d'Isonzo.

The cases are summarized in tables 13-1, 13-2, and 13-3.

Results, Conclusions, and Ideas for Further Research

The validity of the model was mainly confirmed by the field research. Empirical evidence was easily organized through the conceptual framework of the model, and interviewees confirmed that most relevant topics were covered.

Table 13-1. *Comparative Table on Case Studies' Organizational Arrangements*

	Organizational arrangements								
	Formalization			*Accessibility*			*Internalization*		
Case	*Of process design*	*Of deadlines*	*As output specification*	*Of communication*	*In stakeholders' selection*	*Process openness*	*Political*	*Institutional*	*Organizational*
Agenda 21 "Elettrodotto"	0.5	1	1	0.5	0.5	0.5	1	0.5	0.5
Agenda 21 Comune di Sagrado	0.5	0.5	0.5	0.5	0.5	1	0.5	0.5	0.5
Agenda 21 Comune di Cormons	0.5	1	1	1	0.5	1	0.5	0.5	0
Agenda 21 Programma provinciale rifiuti urbani	1	1	1	0.5	0	0	1	1	0.5
Bilancio Partecip@ attivo San Canzian	1	1	1	0.5	0.5	0.5	1	1	0.5

Source: Authors' compilation.

Table 13-2. Comparative Table on Case Studies' Contextual Factors

	Contextual factors				
Case	*Average actual participation (percent)*	*Ideas generation*	*Political salience*	*Intelligibility*	*Relevance of resources ("budget weight")*
Agenda 21 "Elettrodotto"	0.5 (22,3 — 38)* 0 (22,3 — 6)**	1	1	0	1
Agenda 21 Comune di Sagrado	0.5 (15 - 29)	1	1	0.5	1
Agenda 21 Comune di Cormons	1 (84 — 58)	1	1	0.5	1
Agenda 21 Programma provinciale rifiuti urbani	0.5 (15,3 — 26.4)* 0 (15,3 – 2.7)***	0.5	1	0.5	1
Bilancio Partecip@attivo San Canzian	0.5 (17—34)****	1	0.5	0	0.5

Source: Authors' compilation.

* The average has been calculated by dividing the number of participants for the number of stakeholders that initially signed up to local Agenda 21 of the province of Gorizia.

** This calculation has been made on the basis of 350 stakeholders identified at the beginning of the process (data emerging from the interviews).

*** This calculation has been made on the basis of 560 stakeholders identified at the beginning of the process (data emerging from the interviews).

**** This refers to the number of associations involved.

Table 13-3. *Comparative Table on Case Studies' Results*

		Results			
Case	*Shared decision*	*Stakeholders' satisfaction for the decision*	*Stakeholders' satisfaction for the process*	*Differential of trust in the public administration*	*Correspondence between decision and stakeholders' needs*
Agenda 21 "Elettrodotto"	YES	+ satisfied	– unsatisfied	– mistrusting	+ good
Agenda 21 Comune di Sagrado	YES	+ satisfied	– unsatisfied	+ trusting	– scarce
Agenda 21 Comune di Cormons	YES	++ very satisfied	++ very satisfied	+ trusting	++ complete
Agenda 21 Programma provinciale rifiuti urbani	NO	– unsatisfied	+ unsatisfied	+ mistrusting	+ scarce
Bilancio Partecip@attivo San Canzian	YES	– unsatisfied	– unsatisfied	+ trusting	– scarce

Source: Authors.

ORGANIZATIONAL ARRANGEMENTS. There was a general high level of formalization throughout the cases, especially in relation to deadlines and output specification. Accessibility was generally good in formal terms, but there was a tendency to use narrow, traditional communication tools and to fail to establish good-quality, long-term relationships with stakeholders. The role of stakeholders in the decisionmaking process was seen as ancillary: there is no evidence of real codecisionmaking in any of the processes, and good consultation seems the best that can be done at the moment. Internalization is a complex subcomponent: the main findings seem to be the predominant role of politicians and the minimal involvement of administrators.

CONTEXTUAL FACTORS. Participation is generally low: in only one case did more than 50 percent of the stakeholders initially selected by the administration participate. Idea generation, political salience, and resource relevance is high in four cases out of five, but there is not one case of high intelligibility.

RESULTS. In one case no shared decision emerged from the interactive decisionmaking process. As a rule stakeholders were more satisfied with the decision than with the process. Despite this result, in most cases interactive decisionmaking resulted in an increased trust in local public administrations.

The main findings are:

The highest levels of formalization correspond to the lowest levels of stakeholders' satisfaction, both toward the decision and the process. This relationship seems to be confirmed by the low level of correspondence between the decisions made and stakeholders' needs.

A closer scrutiny of this finding through the data collected in the interviews suggests that the main reason for dissatisfaction is that decisions that had already been taken somewhere else were brought to the stakeholders' table. This seems to be confirmed by a corresponding low level of participation and of process openness. There is an emerging connection among decisionmaking processes with stakeholders' active role, participation levels, and satisfaction.

Accessibility—the openness of the process—appears to determine stakeholders' satisfaction, especially when it is combined with the strategic use of communication and strong political control.

In this research we set out to study the relationship between the organizational arrangements of inclusive decisionmaking put in place by local administrations and the results of the decisionmaking process itself, taking into account a series of possible mediating factors. Our findings appear to make a relevant contribution to the debate on governance networks and inclusive decisionmaking.

The first finding is a confirmation of a remark made by Edelenbos and Klijn (working in the Netherlands context): "One can better afford no participation at all than bad participation."[49] In fact, despite the specific entangled cultural, political, and administrative environment in which the research took place—very different from that in the Netherlands—Italian stakeholders' attitudes are similar.[50] They often refer to participation as a good thing per se, and most of them consider any attempts toward inclusion made by public administrations as positive, but at the same time they declare their dissatisfaction with those processes that are only formally inclusive, that do not accept them as fully empowered actors, that call on them only to ratify what has been already decided.

Another contribution draws on inclusive decisionmaking from a managerial perspective and the role of politicians in the process: the key factor enabling these processes to show their real value—which might finally lead to their more thorough evaluation—seems to be the willingness of politicians to relinquish control over the process and negotiate the decisionmaking process with the stakeholders from the very start, coupled with the capacity for strategic management of stakeholders' relationships.

Our research also confirmed that inclusive decisionmaking plays a role in conflict reduction. The closer the correspondence between the decisions taken and stakeholders' needs, the higher their satisfaction toward the decision taken is, even if they are not completely satisfied with the process itself.

The research findings reveal a need for further empirical research on inclusive decisionmaking processes. The direct relationship between elected officials and citizens at the local government level seems to justify the apparent lack of influence of organizational internalization on the results of the cases observed. There are preliminary indications, however, that the full involvement of the bureaucratic structure might be a key component of sustainability and success, especially of a wider adoption of inclusive approaches to decisionmaking. This implies a growing influence of these processes on policy decisions. This leads to new problems: The limited participation of citizens and the poor level of representativeness and accountability of many associations at the local level raise concerns about the risk that these processes could be taken over by and turned into a mouthpiece for already active interest groups (or even individuals), sidelining citizens' more general interests. Last, the better results achieved by the interactive decisionmaking processes started at municipal rather than at the provincial level suggest a possible connection between the effectiveness of inclusive decisionmaking processes and the proximity of the government level where interactive decisionmaking is initiated to individual citizens.

APPENDIX 13A
§1 Interview Format for Politicians, Public Officials, and Managers

Note: The interviews were semi-structured: the interviewers were free to change the order in which the questions were asked, and information besides answers to the questions was collected during the interviews when available.

1.1. Presentation of the research; explanation of the interview's structure; collection of basic information about the interviewee

1.2. Introductory questions (grand-tour questions)

1. What is your overall impression of the process?
2. What was your role within this initiative?

1.3. Central questions

1.3.1. Organizational arrangements

Formalization

3. Were the phases and the steps of the (interactive/participatory) process formally designed and regulated since the beginning? By whom? How?
4. Did the process include exact deadlines? Could you provide an example?
5. What output was the process intended to produce? Was this formalized since the beginning?

Accessibility

6. How were the stakeholders (participants) kept informed about the process?
7. How were stakeholders (participants) selected?
8. How was the stakeholders' (participants') point of view taken into account in shaping the final decision? Can you recall any related examples?
9. Did you report to stakeholders (participants) about the process through any means (reports, public events)? Can you recall any related examples?

Internalization

10. Did any politicians participate in the process? How? On what occasions?
11. Did the administration issue any formal act to establish and regulate the process?

12. Who was in charge of following the process among unelected officials? Was there any dedicated organizational unit?

1.3.2. Contextual factors

13. How many people participated in the process (in the different phases)? Are any data available?
14. Did the stakeholders (participants) contribute with new ideas and new solutions to the issues at stake? Can you recall any related examples?
15. Do you remember any relevant political/administrative event occurring in the same period? (Elaborate.)
16. What was the size of the budget that the process was supposed to decide on? Are any related data available?

1.3.3. Results

17. Was a shared decision reached at the end of the process? Are you satisfied with the decision taken?
18. Could you describe positive and negative aspects of the process? Do you consider yourself satisfied with the process? Can you recall any examples that support your answer?

1.4. Closing questions

19. What recommendations would you formulate for further processes?

Summary and review

Do you think that your answers reflect correctly your position? Is there any important point missing or something that you feel you want to add before closing the interview?

§2 Interview Format for Participants (Stakeholders)

2.1. Presentation of the research; explanation of the interview's structure; collection of basic information about the interviewee

2.2. Introductory questions (grand-tour questions)

1. What is your overall impression of the process?
2. What was your role within this initiative?

2.3. Central questions

2.3.1. Organizational arrangements

Formalization

3. Were the phases and the steps of the participatory process formally designed and regulated since the beginning? By whom? How?
4. Did the process include exact deadlines? Do you remember which ones?
5. What output was the process intended to produce? Was this formalized since the beginning?

Accessibility

6. How were you informed (kept informed) about the process?
7. How were you selected to participate in this process?
8. How was your personal point of view taken into account in shaping the final decision? Can you recall any related examples?
9. Did you report to the administration about the process through any means (reports, public events)? Can you recall any related examples? Did the administration report to stakeholders (participants) about the process through any means (reports, public events)? Can you recall any related examples?

Internalization

10. Did any politicians participate in the process? How? On what occasions?

2.3.2. Contextual factors

11. How many people participated in the process (in the different phases)? Are any data available?
12. Did you contribute with new ideas and new solutions to the issues at stake? Can you recall any related examples? Did other stakeholders (participants) contribute with new ideas and new solutions to the issues at stake? Can you recall any related examples?
13. Do you remember any relevant political/administrative event occurring in the same period?
14. What was the size of the budget that the process was supposed to decide on? Are any related data available?

2.3.3. Results

15. Was a shared decision reached at the end of the process? Are you satisfied with the decision taken?

16. Could you describe positive and negative aspects of the process? Do you consider yourself satisfied with the process? Can you recall any examples that support your answer?
17. Do you think that the administration has taken the participants' point of view into account in the final decision? Can you recall any examples that support your answer?
18. Could you describe anything that the local administration has done to treat the participants fairly and justly, or unfairly and unjustly (integrity)?
19. Could you describe things that the administration has done that indicate that it can be relied on to keep its promises or that it does not keep its promises (dependability)?
20. How confident are you that the local administration has the ability to accomplish what it says it will do (competence)? Can you provide examples of why you feel that way?

2.4. Closing questions

21. What recommendations would you formulate for further processes?

Summary and review

Do you think that your answers reflect correctly your position? Is there any important point missing or something that you feel you want to add before closing the interview?

Notes

1. Jurian Edelenbos, "Design and Management of Participatory Public Policy Making," *Public Management Review* 1, no. 4 (1999): 569–78; Erik-Hans Klijn, "Governance and Governance Networks in Europe," *Public Management Review* 10, no. 4 (2008): 505–25.

2. Walter J. M. Kickert, Erik-Hans Klijn, and Joop F. M. Koppenjan, eds., *Managing Complex Networks: Strategies for the Public Sector* (London: Sage, 1997); Peter McLaverty, ed., *Public Participation and Innovations in Community Governance* (Aldershot, UK: Ashgate, 2002).

3. Jurian Edelenbos and Erik-Hans Klijn, "Managing Stakeholder Involvement in Decision Making: A Comparative Analysis of Six Interactive Processes in the Netherlands," *Journal of Public Administration Research and Theory* 16 (July 2006): 417–66; Cary Coglianese, "Is Satisfaction Success? Evaluating Public Participation in Regulatory Policymaking," KSG Working Paper RWP02-038 (Harvard University, Kennedy School of Government, 2002) (http://ssrn.com/abstract=331420); Renée A. Irving and John Stansbury, "Citizen Participation in Decision Making: Is It Worth the Effort?" *Public Administration Review* 64, no. 1 (2004): 55–65; Frans A. J. Van den

Bosch and Cees B. M. Van Riel, "Buffering and Bridging as Environmental Strategies of Firms," *Business Strategy and the Environment* 7 (February 1998): 24–31.

4. Luigi Bobbio, "La democrazia deliberativa nella pratica" [Deliberative democracy in practice], *Stato e Mercato* 73 (April 2005): 67–88.

5. Organization for Economic Cooperation and Development, *Citizens as Partners* (Paris: OECD Publications Service, 2001); Bobbio, "La democrazia deliberativa nella pratica."

6. Marian Barnes and others, "Constituting the Public in Public Participation," *Public Administration* 81 (June 2003): 379–99; Irving and Stansbury, "Citizen Participation in Decision Making."

7. Joop F. M. Koppenjan, "Creating a Playing Field for Assessing the Effectiveness of Network Collaboration by Performance Measures," *Public Management Review* 10, no. 6 (2008): 699–714.

8. Kickert, Klijn, and Koppenjan, *Managing Complex Networks*; Klijn, "Governance and Governance Networks in Europe"; Morten Egeberg, "How Bureaucratic Structure Matters: An Organizational Perspective," in *Handbook of Public Administration*, edited by B. Guy Peters and Jon Pierre (London: Sage, 2003), pp. 116–26.

9. For an overview on governance literature in public administration studies, see Rod A. W. Rhodes, "The New Governance: Governing without Government," *Political Studies* 44 (September 1996): 652–67, and Klijn, "Governance and Governance Networks in Europe."

10. Kickert, Klijn and Koppenjan, *Managing Complex Networks*; Klijn, "Governance and Governance Networks in Europe."

11. Giovanni Sartori, "Comparing and Miscomparing," *Journal of Theoretical Politics* 3 (July 1991): 243–57.

12. Robin Keast and others, "Network Structures: Working Differently and Changing Expectations," *Public Administration Review* 64 (May 2004): 363–71.

13. Koppenjan, "Creating a Playing Field for Assessing the Effectiveness of Network Collaboration by Performance Measures."

14. Erik-Hans Klijn and Geert R. Teisman, "Strategies and Games in Networks," in *Managing Complex Networks: Strategies for the Public Sector*, edited by Kickert, Klijn, and Koppenjan, pp. 98–118; also see Linda C. Hon and James E. Grunig, "Guidelines for Measuring Relationships in Public Relations" (Gainesville, Fla.: Institute for Public Relations, 1999) (www.instituteforpr.org/topics/measuring-relationships); Stephen D. Bruning, "Relationship Building as a Retention Strategy: Linking Relationship Attitudes and Satisfaction Evaluations to Behavioral Outcomes," *Public Relations Review* 28 (February 2002): 39–48; Stephen D. Bruning and John A. Ledingham, "Perceptions of Relationships and Evaluations of Satisfaction: An Exploration of Interaction," *Public Relations Review* 26 (Spring 2000): 85–95; James E. Grunig, "Qualitative Methods for Assessing Relationships between Organizations and Publics" (Gainesville, Fla.: Institute for Public Relations, 2002) (www.instituteforpr.org/wp-content/uploads/2002_AssessingRelations.pdf).

15. For a review, see Coglianese, "Is Satisfaction Success?"

16. Ibid.; see also Irving and Stansbury, "Citizen Participation in Decision Making."

17. Grunig, "Qualitative Methods for Assessing Relationships between Organizations and Publics"; Mirna P. Mandell and Robin Keast, "Evaluating the Effectiveness of Interorganizational Relations through Networks," *Public Management Review* 10, no. 6 (2008): 715–31.

18. For an overview of different streams in organization theory for the study of the public sector, see Tom Christensen and others, *Organization Theory and the Public Sector: Instrument, Culture and Myth* (London: Routledge, 2007); Herbert A. Simon, *Administrative Behavior* (New York: Macmillan, 1947).

19. Kathleen M. Eisenhardt, "Building Theory from Case Study Research," *Academy of Management Review* 14 (October 1989): 532–50; Robert K. Yin, *Case Study Research: Design and Methods* (Thousand Oaks, Calif.: Sage, 2003).

20. Eisenhardt, "Building Theory from Case Study Research."

21. See, for example, Edelenbos and Klijn, "Managing Stakeholder Involvement in Decision Making."

22. Paul J. DiMaggio and Walter W. Powell, "The Iron Cage Revisited: Institutional Isomorphism and Collective Rationality in Organizational Fields," *American Sociological Review* 48 (April 1983): 147–60.

23. Robert E. Stake, *The Art of Case Study Research* (Thousand Oaks, Calif.: Sage, 1995), p.114; Robert E. Stake, "Qualitative Case Studies," in *The Sage Handbook of Qualitative Research*, edited by Norman K. Denzin and Yvonne S. Lincoln (Thousand Oaks, Calif.: Sage, 2005), p. 453; Yin, *Case Study Research: Design and Methods* (Thousand Oaks, Calif.: Sage, 2003) p. 97.

24. Edelenbos and Klijn, "Managing Stakeholder Involvement in Decision Making."

25. Keith G. Provan and H. Brinton Milward labeled these variables "network structural characteristics," "network context," and "network effectiveness." See Keith G. Provan and H. Brinton Milward, "A Preliminary Theory of Interorganizational Network Effectiveness," *Administrative Science Quarterly* 40 (March 1995): 1–33; Keith G. Provan and Julianne G. Sebastian, "Network within Networks: Service Link Overlap, Organizational Cliques, and Network Effectiveness," *Academy of Management Journal* 41 (August 1998): 453–63; Alex Turrini and others, in "Networking Literature about Determinants of Network Effectiveness," *Public Administration* 87 (June 2010): 528–50, rely on the same framework for their review of the literature about network effectiveness.

26. Edelenbos and Klijn, "Managing Stakeholder Involvement in Decision Making," 421.

27. Cheryl Simrell King, Kathryn M. Feltey, and Bridget O'Neill Susel, "The Question of Participation," *Public Administration Review* 58 (July–August 1998): 317–26; Vivien Lowndes, Lawrence Pratchett, and Gerry Stoker, "Local Political Participation: The Impact of Rules-in-Use," *Public Administration* 84 (August 2006): 539–61.

28. Irving and Stansbury, "Citizen Participation in Decision Making," p. 61.

29. See, for example, Organization for Economic Cooperation and Development, *Citizens as Partners*, p. 60; Bobbio, "La democrazia deliberativa nella pratica,"

pp. 72–76; Edelenbos and Klijn, "Managing Stakeholder Involvement in Decision Making," p. 421; Gloria Regonini, "Paradossi della democrazia deliberative" [Paradoxes in deliberative democracy], *Working Papers* (Milano: University of Milan, Department of Social and Political Studies, 2005), pp. 8–11; Daniela Cristofoli and Giovanni Valotti, "Corporate governante e processi decisionali" [Corporate governance and decisionmaking processes], in *Management pubblico: Temi per il cambiamento* [Public management: themes of change], edited by Giovanni Valotti (Milan: Egea, 2005), pp. 67–86.

30. Edelenbos and Klijn, "Managing Stakeholder Involvement in Decision Making," 428–29.

31. Darren R. Halphin, "The Participatory and Democratic Potential and Practice of Interest Groups: Between Solidarity and Representation," *Public Administration* 84 (December 2006): 923–24.

32. Sherry R. Arnstein, "A Ladder of Citizen Participation," *Journal of the American Institute of Planners* 35 (July 1969): 216–24; Organization for Economic Cooperation and Development, *Citizens as Partners*; Edelenbos and Klijn, "Managing Stakeholder Involvement in Decision Making"; Daniela Pillitu, *La partecipazione civica alla creazione del valore pubblico* [Civic participation in the creation of public value] (Milan: Franco Angeli, 2009).

33. See Edelenbos and Klijn, "Managing Stakeholder Involvement in Decision Making": "Together politicians, administrations and those involved determine a problem-solving agenda in which they search for solutions together. Politicians are committed to these solutions with regard to the final decision making, after having tested this outcome in terms of a priori conditions" (429).

34. Ibid., 428–29.

35. Cristofoli and Valotti, "Corporate governante e processi decisionali"; Jurian Edelenbos, "Institutional Implications of Interactive Governance: Insights from Dutch Practice," *Governance* 18 (January 2005): 115–16; Edelenbos and Klijn, "Managing Stakeholder Involvement in Decision Making," 421.

36. Edelenbos and Klijn, "Managing Stakeholder Involvement in Decision Making," 431–32.

37. See, for instance, the following regional laws: L.R. n. 4/2006 (Lazio), L.R. n. 69/2007 (Toscana), L.R. n. 3/2010 (Emilia Romagna), L.R. n. 14/2010 (Umbria).

38. See Cristofoli and Valotti, "Corporate governante e processi decisionali"; Edelenbos and Klijn, "Managing Stakeholder Involvement in Decision Making," 428–29; Koppenjan, "Creating a Playing Field for Assessing the Effectiveness of Network Collaboration by Performance Measures." This last aspect is described in the next section, "Idea Generation."

39. This approach raises the problem of evaluating the "quantity" of participation in the processes that are accessible to all citizens, absent any form of selection. The percentage of citizens participating in relation to the number of residents does not seem to be a relevant factor, primarily because different topics are likely to stimulate different degrees of interest and engagement.

40. Cristofoli and Valotti, "Corporate governante e processi decisionali"; Edelenbos, "Institutional Implications of Interactive Governance," 115–16; Edelenbos and Klijn, "Managing Stakeholder Involvement in Decision Making," 421.

41. We include in this value the so-called "zero option"—that is, the possibility of taking no decision at all.

42. Christopher Hood and Andrew Dunsire, *Bureaumetrics: The Quantitative Comparison of British Central Government Agencies* (Farnborough, UK: Gower, 1981); Christopher Pollitt and others, *Agencies: How Governments Do Things through Semi-Autonomous Organizations* (New York: Palgrave Macmillan, 2004); Christopher Pollitt, "Performance Management in Practice: A Comparative Study of Executive Agencies," *Journal of Public Administration Research and Theory* 16 (January 2005): 29.

43. Pollitt, "Performance Management in Practice," p. 36.

44. Ibid., p. 37.

45. Edelenbos and Klijn, "Managing Stakeholder Involvement in Decision Making," 424.

46. Coglianese, "Is Satisfaction Success?" p. 3.

47. Megan Tschannen-Moran and Wayne K. Hoy, "A Multidisciplinary Analysis of the Nature, Meaning, and Measurement of Trust," *Review of Educational Research* 70 (Winter 2000): 547–93; Mark Callanan, "Institutionalizing Participation and Governance? New Participative Structures in Local Government in Ireland," *Public Administration* 83 (December 2005): 912; Xiaohu Wang and Montgomery Wan Wart, "When Public Participation in Administration Leads to Trust: An Empirical Assessment of Managers' Perceptions," *Public Administration Review* 67 (March–April 2007): 265–78.

48. Grunig, "Qualitative Methods for Assessing Relationships between Organizations and Publics"; Sandro Castaldo, *Le relazioni distributive* [The distributive relationship] (Milan: Egea, 1995); Bruno Busacca and Sandro Castaldo, *Il potenziale competitivo della fedeltà alla marca e all'insegna commerciale. Una metodologia di misurazione congiunta* [The competitive potential of brand fidelity: a methodology for measurement] (Milan: Egea, 1996); Hon and Grunig, "Guidelines for Measuring Relationships in Public Relations"; Tschannen-Moran and Hoy, "Multidisciplinary Analysis of the Nature, Meaning, and Measurement of Trust."

49. Edelenbos and Klijn, "Managing Stakeholder Involvement in Decision Making," 46.

50. The province of Gorizia is characterized by the typical traditional Italian administrative structure in a region that has a strong multicultural background and a center-left political majority.

GIOVANNI VALOTTI

14 Public Sector Reforms: State of the Art and Future Challenges

During the meeting of Organization for Economic Cooperation and Development ministers held in Venice on November 15, 2010, chaired by Renato Brunetta, the Italian minister for public administration and innovation, the most crucial concern was productivity in the public sector. As stated in the conference proceedings: "Boosting public sector productivity and maximizing returns on investment in technology will be key to governments playing their part in restoring economic growth."[1] This sentiment is supported by everyone, but what managerial guidelines and devices can be put in place to boost public sector performance?

The basic assumption, which also triggered the recent reforms in public administration in Italy, is that improvements in public sector performance are underpinned by the following pillars: measuring performance, using adequate tools and methodologies; making public sector performance transparent; and boosting performance through leadership and motivation.

The most feasible starting point for a discussion of public sector reform is the adjustment of the systems used for measurement and assessment (part IV of this volume provides an exploration of the importance of performance measurement and management in the public sector). The reasons for poor performance are often unclear—or they are perceived as unclear—because evaluators do not have enough basic information to carry out a detailed evaluation. In such a situation it is inevitable that the actual quality of performance will be filtered by the subjective perceptions of citizens, politicians, and managers.

The configuration of any performance measurement model must clearly be linked to the specific nature of the institution's mission as well as its operations. However, it is crucial that the general architecture be common to all public administrations, to ensure both the scope and comparability through benchmarking.[2]

Measurement systems should be an essential factor for supporting decisions instead of just being considered a way to collect and represent data and information, as in the past.[3] Once performance has been assessed and measured, it is possible to examine the second pillar underpinning the recovery of productivity: the transparency of performance.

Transparency is crucial. Public sector agencies should be obligated to keep reports of their performance on the basis of clearly identified parameters and to use various media, including websites, annual reports, and public meetings.[4] Institutions should not be able to pick and choose whether to publish how their performance has been rated or be able to select which results they want to publish. Administrators, managers, and employees should be obliged to put their credibility to the test and allow a comparison of themselves with other government agencies.

It is unlikely that this will happen if institutions are given too much autonomy and freedom to select how their own performance is represented and interpreted (see chapter 2). Consequently, it is essential to develop a common device for reporting performance in detail—a "performance report" replacing subjective and often poorly coordinated, partial, and fragmentary reviews of financial statements that are currently issued by public administrations.[5] The establishment of truly independent assessment agencies would also be a welcome move, whether they provide in-house auditing services or are independent, public (compartmental and system), or private agencies specializing in certification and accreditation procedures (see chapter 1 in this volume). The significant element is that these agencies are explicitly responsible for their work; they certify the performance of an institution and notify it of any shortcomings, mistakes, or omissions in the documentation they produce. There is a distinct need to "clear the fog" currently obscuring the true status of the performance of public administration, to make the relevant information easily accessible and understandable to anyone, including third parties.[6]

Thus it is essential to measure and assess public sector performance by any means available and to make this information available without any prior selection or concealment. This is a performance-oriented approach. Once this step has been completed, the third fundamental pillar can be taken into consideration: boost public sector performance through leadership and motivation. As discussed in part II, there is a strong need to rethink what leadership skills are required to implement managerial reforms and to improve performance in the public sector and to find a way to reframe the concept of motivation in the public sector and align the human resources management tools with it.

My coeditor's and my aim with this book is to explore the main issues and features of reforming the public sector today. This conclusion proposes a set of guidelines to reform the public sector: some six easy suggestions to make government work better for the practitioners' community and for all those who share important responsibilities in the public sector. In other words, this last chapter aims to provide a diagnosis of what's wrong with public sector reforms—what did not work and why. Following the analytical review is the remedy: a list of very practical suggestions that can be easy implemented.

The Right People Doing Fewer Things While Exposed to Real or Simulated Competition

Can we really imagine any modernization of the public sector if people continue to do the same old things? Is it possible to turn an army of public employees into a professional organization consisting of specialized, highly performing personnel?

What are the actual tasks required of public administration and what are the skills needed to carry them out properly?[7] These are core questions that the reforms carried out in recent decades have failed to answer completely, since they have always tried to strike a compromise between the expectations associated with acquired rights and established positions and the need to manage consent.

The question as to what the public sector should do is a typical problem of strategic positioning, designing the "portfolio of activities," and defining the network of relationships to be developed with all other subjects, be they public or private.

A public agency should focus on its core functions, pursuing standards of excellence and abandoning the concept of "doing a bit of everything adequately." Actual core functions cannot be defined in general terms for the public sector as a whole or for institutional subcategories. We must ask: which of an agency's functions determine its actions and give it a fundamental role in decisionmaking processes that affect the development of the social and economic system? Are its functions considered essential for defending basic rights and safeguarding the standards of community welfare? Are they simply tasks that are important and cannot be undertaken by the market or the private sector because they are not profitable or could lead to the creation of dominant or monopolistic positions? Do they imply exercising authority to regulate conduct and defend public rights? Are they connected with the deployment of collective resources in order to improve infrastructures, support research activities, or promote the development of business or nonprofit organizations?

Basic theory says that any public institution should consider its mission and position with care, identifying its essential and crucial functions and dismissing everything that is not strategic as quickly as possible.[8]

It is clear that the institution's history, structure, configuration, and the environment where it operates all play crucial roles in this process—which is precisely why its "core" functions cannot generally be defined a priori.[9] Instead, institutions should identify, define, and focus on core functions once this process of surveying the institution's existing profile has been completed.

And one more basic element is needed: the introduction of elements of competition to the public sector and the strengthening of citizens' power of choice and voice.[10]

Public organizations have improved wherever forms of competition have been developed. It is quite clear, however, that competition is not always either possible or desirable. As a result, it is important to promote forms of direct competition in the market and in the public services market wherever possible. If this objective cannot be pursued, it is necessary to operate indirect forms of competition via mechanisms of detection, comparison, and publication of performance.

Finally, appropriate measures need to be developed in order to enhance citizen power (see chapter 13 in this volume).[11] As we know, the option of providing a "choice" is preferable, namely, the option of choosing a private or public supplier. If this objective cannot be pursued, it is once again crucial that a citizen's basic rights, associated with policies of good quality and service, are guaranteed and can be exercised. Past experience with public participation agencies, service charters and the associated relief mechanisms, enhancement of service accessibility, and the simplification of dialogue with public institutions illustrate the difficulties and importance of achieving significant results in this direction.[12]

Revolutionizing Organizational Models and Staff Structure

"Flexibility" can be considered another element that denotes the good intentions of reform.

What is "flexibility" and to what extent has it been implemented? Flexibility implies that burdensome regulations and lengthy procedures are no longer an issue and that a certain degree of organizational disorder should be accepted in the interest of encouraging innovation and enhancing performance. Flexibility implies simplifying a department's organization, professional profiles, and organizational levels; and decentralizing decisionmaking processes and the transfer of human resources within the organization and to other institutions. These procedures are often announced in intricate and complex language and as a result are seldom implemented. Nonetheless, it is an acknowledged fact that there is no such thing as an ideal organizational model. It all depends on what public institutions intend to do: if they aim to become the "brains" of the system or a "pole of excellence," they need to resemble a professional studio team of creative, reliable, and performance-oriented professionals. If their focus is primarily on executing traditional functions, then the good old bureaucratic model, permeated by order, rules, and authority, is the most appropriate.

If we accept the notion that the road toward evolution is the one described earlier, that puts the focus on the salient "core functions," there can be no doubt that greater flexibility has to be pursued.

From this perspective, the issue of in-house mobility should be also discussed. A person's job should not be determined by a clearly defined, circumscribed position in terms of time and location but rather by a "working environment" where individual employees have the potential to benefit from development and upgrading primarily through ongoing changes to their job description as time goes by.

Flexibility also leads to greater mobility among institutions when it is not restricted by burdensome procedures and preconditions for getting consent but is promoted correctly as being in the specific interest of institutions and the public sector as a whole.

However, flexibility alone is not enough.

If the future of the public sector and of public sector organizations is to focus on skills, it becomes crucial to invest in professional expertise. Failure to do this may be the main factor behind any slowness in the modernization process. It takes time, money, coherence, and continuity of action to transform an organization's professional skills, create new professional roles and figures, or simply integrate professionals recruited from other work environments.

Obviously, expertise must be remunerated appropriately, but it is hard to contemplate the idea of general pay increases, and not only because of the poor state of public funds. Salary differentiation is not a principle in itself: the need for fair wages demands that the most productive and talented employees be rewarded. If this approach is conveyed properly, it will induce virtuous circles of emulation and guarantee a general improvement in performance. However, the significant increases of wages reported in the last decade, especially at medium-high levels in public administration, didn't produce such an outcome, often as a result of the application of explicit or concealed mechanisms. Organizations must also change direction at these levels. If public institutions are to have a future, they need to become workplaces that attract the best professional resources in the job market. They must be perceived to be interesting environments where it is possible for employees to do a good job but also to grow professionally, pursue a brilliant career based on their merits, and build up a body of experience and knowledge that they can use in other sectors. This scenario does not reflect the situation today, however, and employees who are devoted to public administration and identify with their job run the risk of professional obsolescence.

It would be useful to start by reviewing the traditional methods used for recruitment and selection when new employees are hired. The normal, competition-based recruitment mechanisms are too limiting and restrict the faculty of institutions to hire individuals with the best skills and attitude to handle the various positions, in the name of ensuring that appropriate safeguards are in place and candidates have equal opportunities. In turn, assessment processes are deformed by too many formalities and concerns for objectivity and often degenerate into bureaucratic procedures that are designed to ensure that candidates have the required qualities but that fail to determine their actual skills and above all their development potential. The entire career and incentives system should be redesigned in order to deliver a limited number of clear messages regarding the qualities required by the organization and the conduct and performance that the organization will reward.[13]

The responsibility for redesigning and ensuring the ongoing updating of skills is inevitably divided into several levels. The governing bodies in the public sector are in charge of promoting and supporting investments in training, controlling its quality and effects, and creating the "rules of the game" in order to guide the development of particular skills. Individual agencies have to define innovative policies, identify specific needs, and then implement a plan of action. Employees, whatever their role and level, are responsible for their own commitment to honing particular skills on a regular daily basis as well as in response to unusual challenges, which should naturally be acknowledged and rewarded by agencies.

Turning Bureaucrats into Managers

As in any organization, in the public sector the quality of results is closely linked to the quality of the managerial staff. This is certainly not the only prerequisite; indeed, managers in the public sector often point out the difficulties of operating in an environment that is "hostile" from numerous points of view: regulations, policies, constraints, controls, and so on.

Nevertheless, when other factors are equal, the quality of management makes a difference between different agencies nowadays.

The debate about managerial responsibilities and the need to separate these from political responsibilities started a long time ago. A lot of progress has been made, but there is still a long way to go. It is certainly not possible to retreat or backpedal. Public administrations need a strong, independent, professional, and conscientious management team.

It is the manager's responsibility to implement policies, make efficient use of resources, develop the organization's skills, build a collaborative atmosphere and motivating work place, and safeguard correct administration practices.

Is this an impossible task? Perhaps not, but it is difficult and requires great dedication, skill, and integrity.

Have the results of giving management more autonomy been completely satisfactory to date? Were public managers incapable of taking on such responsibility and are they still unable to do so? Do managers have different qualities and skills leading to differences in the quality of the results they produce? Does their formal independence from politics actually conflict with their often collusive behavior? Is formal decisionmaking noncongruent with actual decisionmaking, so that the person who signs an order may not be the person who actually makes the decision? Are public sector managers generally less inclined to involve their staff and delegate responsibility to them?

We could go on forever. These are real, weighty issues that point to the difficulties in implementing the transition to a new administrative model. However, there can be no doubt that this is the right direction to go.

It is vital to continue efforts to increase the quality, autonomy, and conscientiousness of managerial staff. Once again, individual organizations can do a lot in this direction by completely redesigning the architecture and brief of their management; defining and applying innovative rules for the assignment of managerial duties and the conditions for their renewal and withdrawal; and introducing credible salary mechanisms and incentives that are truly capable of rewarding performance.

In-House Processes of Change

Genuine processes of change in an organization are not the same as reengineering or simply updating tools and techniques. Instead, they are primarily based on intangible and immaterial aspects. Significant changes in direction are usually accompanied by symbolic elements, which are very important for signaling the end of one phase and the start of a new one. Public agencies generally underestimate the importance of this step, often offering a formal interpretation verging on a bureaucratic announcement—once the reorganization has been completed, they organize an event to inform people, and that's that!

In actual fact, the reorganization process starts when models and proposals are finally defined. A project for change has to be deployed and this requires informing and involving the entire organization to take an active and emotional part.

Contrary to this scenario, however, in most cases useful projects for innovation stay at the top-management level and involve managers alone without being passed on, and thus remain unfamiliar or misunderstood by those at lower levels, and feeding misapprehension and often inaccurate hypotheses. At the end of the day, they do not affect the organization as a whole and have no impact on working methods and conditions. They do not provide direction for individual employees nor help them understand their priorities; they do not help to create a new system of values and modify the entrenched culture in the organization. They do not feed a sense of confidence and enthusiasm that is necessary to overcome obstacles and do not help to signal real change and the need for all employees to work together in order to achieve it.

Clearly, investing in "soft" organizational aspects becomes crucial in order to carry out a project for change. A new system of values has to be built that is credible and shared as much as possible; in-house socialization should be promoted, developing a sense of belonging to the agency and identification with the challenges associated with projects aiming at development and change. Individuals have to give themselves a stake in the change; they should feel as though they are an important and active part of a big project and must understand that its success also depends on them.

In order to make this happen, it is essential to invest in in-house communications, which is ultimately what binds a group of people together and is the prerequisite for sharing and participation. How many public administrations have assessed this problem seriously? It is the nature of "announced reforms" to produce formal documents, and very often they do not go much beyond this. These documents are seen as something distant and purely theoretical; they have no tangible impact on operations and do not mobilize the organization. Instead of such announcements and documents, we consider it essential to organize big events, including celebratory events, as well as meetings, work groups and project teams, and workshops for experimentation and implementation, and to focus on the handling of manager-employee relationships, the provision of new communication tools, and greater transparency regarding conduct and expected performance and the related bonuses and regular updates with regard to the process of change.

The Public Sector and the Private Sector Working Hand in Hand

A person's decision to work in the public sector may start out as a choice of a way of life, but it does not have to be a permanent choice.

Many people are more interested in dealing with the general interests of the community than with the problems associated with pursuing the specific objectives of a business, no matter how respectable these may be. In an ideal scenario, some of these people will find great personal gratification from their work in the public sector.

Other people are unable to overcome the basic anxiety that a choice is irreversible, and so they take a different path, not entering the public sector. Others approach the public sector driven by their ideals but soon become disappointed for various reasons and risk becoming "trapped" by them because they have no other prospects for work where there is a capacity to appreciate the public sector experience they have acquired.

This highlights a fundamental condition for improvements in the public sector: increasing its organizations and for-profit entities in the private sector. Several different types of obstacles must be overcome in order to achieve this. First, from a legal and formal point of view, the standardization of working relations must be strengthened by completing the privatization process of public sector employment.

This should be followed by attempts to standardize working conditions in the public and private sectors (working hours, rules, opportunities, risks, and so on), with similar pay conditions for comparable roles in comparable organizations and similar social security contributions.

It is also important to remove the cultural barriers between private companies and public agencies that usually emerge in situations marked by a potential conflict of interest or simply resulting from a lack of mutual knowledge and relationships. The idea of having public sector managers complete part of their professional training in private companies and vice versa would also be a positive development.

More Politics, Less Politicization

I close with an observation that might seem astonishing at first glance: there is a need for more politics in public agencies. From a technical and scientific point of view, the issue is the need to redesign corporate governance models, namely, the combination of organs, rules, and decisionmaking processes that ultimately define who in an organization is responsible for getting results.[14]

However, whereas the aim of corporate governance in a private company is to achieve shareholder satisfaction, corporate governance in the public sector aims to achieve something more valuable: the satisfaction of the entire community.

In private companies, the question is not easily resolved and lies in striking a balance between the role of the owners—the shareholders—and the role of management, the body designated to run the company. The creation of value and fulfilling shareholder expectations are essential parameters for any assessment of the quality of a company's conduct.

In recent decades, the growth of businesses and their transformation into public companies have typically done away with the direct control exercised by the owners in terms of the decisions taken, and more autonomy has been delegated to the management. As a result, the redesigning of corporate governance models has focused on removing the risks associated with too much managerial autonomy that could lead to the prevalence of objectives and behavior no longer in line with the interests of the owners, namely, the different and increasingly more complex shareholder categories (see chapter 13 of this volume).

The sensational scandals and bankruptcies that have recently involved leading companies and financial operators have shown how important it is to match the handing over of managerial autonomy with the correct and efficient implementation of the prerogatives for dictating strategies and exercising control by the owners.

What about public institutions? For a long time the role of the owners, which migrated to politicians through the mechanism of institutional representation, and the role of the management overlapped and were almost congruent, with politics exercising a direct influence on the actions and choices of the management and resulting in the granting of limited autonomy to the managers. It could be said that politics prevailed over management to a certain extent.

If this were the only question at stake, the issue of corporate governance in public agencies would not differ so much from governance in private companies, even though the starting points for their pursuit of the same ultimate goal of a new balance lie at opposite extremes. This can be summed up as more ownership in private companies and more management in public agencies to strike a balance in both cases.

However, this does not mean that public agencies should be independent from politics. On the contrary, managerial autonomy implies the active and qualified provision of policies via the definition of guidelines and strategic priorities to be followed by the management. In this sense, we can identify a virtuous and physiological relationship between politics and management that takes the specific aims of public administration into account, as well as the need to adjust economic targets to allow for the need to safeguard the interests of the public and a return in terms of social benefits.

However, all of this requires politics to resume its "higher" role, namely, the ability to express an innovative and long-term vision, conveying the emerging needs of the community and designing far-reaching strategies that lay down the direction to be followed by public agencies and monitor implementation, with the aim of driving ongoing improvements in the efficiency and quality of services delivered.

Conclusions

Comprehensive deployment of management concepts in the public sector implies a series of conditions that will only be ensured by reforms at the institutional level:

—Making improvements in the legal area by simplifying and coordinating current laws

—Clearly defining the tasks delegated to different levels of government and the degrees of freedom associated with them

—Redesigning the scheme of relationships within the public sector—whether financial or administrative—to ensure that individual institutions are more responsible for their own performance and to streamline complex decision-making processes involving several institutions

—Adapting the principles and systems associated with the delegation of responsibility to agencies or other bodies exercising temporary governance and management functions

—Outlining a competitive framework for the execution of public functions by defining the role to be played by the market and free competition as opposed to regulations specifying varying degrees of restrictions.

Beyond this, the quality and the efficacy of institutional reforms are strongly influenced by the contributions of the managerial approach and discipline in several other respects. First, it has played a prominent role in the identification of the basic principles and guidelines of reform processes and will continue to do so in the future. Established concepts such as efficacy, efficiency, and affordability have been incorporated in the reformers' agenda as a result of the influence of management. In a more advanced path of innovation in public intervention, the demand for decentralization typical of institutional reforms is confirmed and inspired by the principles of autonomy, cooperation, and integration that are typical of a managerial approach. In other words, in industrialized countries, management can simultaneously contribute to defining of the principles behind institutional reforms and make an active and constructive contribution to their actual implementation.

Furthermore, the governance of the implementation phase of reform is also a typical role of management, a traditional element of crisis in processes of change in complex systems, especially in the public sector. In this sense the ability to go beyond the project stage and formalize the scheme of the reform is crucial. Here, a managerial approach makes an essential contribution in the various linked phases of implementing the reform: defining the methods and timing of the implementation of the reforms; monitoring the actual level of implementation of the programs; analyzing and assessing the difficulties of implementation and the possible elimination of emerging obstacles; assessing the results obtained via the reform processes; and designing possible alterations to the reforms in light of results obtained after the various stages of implementation.

Finally, management guarantees the functioning and the efficacy of ongoing reforms, providing a decisive contribution to improvements in the methods used to run and develop individual public agencies. This is clearly an essential precondition for transforming institutional reforms and the general layout of the system into administrative processes and services that can generate end-value for the public.

These conclusions imply that trying to establish whether institutional reforms or managerial reforms come first, in terms of their contribution to improvements in the public sector, is a futile operation. The notion of autonomy for either of the two intervention plans is even less convincing. Nevertheless, one must not take too lightly the fact that the two approaches often seem to clash and express ideas, basic values, and approach problems in very different and sometimes conflicting manners.

Managerial and institutional reforms are, above all, increasingly faced with complex problems arising from the management of change. Although the processes to modernize the public sector may be innovative and rigorous as regards their basic setup and choices, they have clashed with well-established systems in ways that relate to power, functions, and responsibility.

The idea of central government control of the transformation of public administrations based on a general program of reform that agencies would be forced to adopt on pain of sanctions seems unrealistic and therefore ineffective. There are many examples of traditional bureaucracies that formally respect the policies for change defined at system level yet defend themselves against the changes needed to actually carry them out.

On the contrary, as we have shown, the comprehensive application of institutional reforms requires radical changes in the operational models and the management policies of the institutions targeted for transformation and is largely dependent on self-directed initiative, although this can be encouraged and guided by more general development projects at the system level.

This interpretation of management allows for an investigation of the value of the evolution or staticity of public administrations when faced with changes in their context and reform plans are being implemented.

Finally, the development of management within the public sector may contribute to the formation of new skills and expertise that are vital for negotiating the process of change. Entrepreneurship, risk propensity, the ability to manage uncertainty, leadership, the ability to promote involvement, propensity for innovation, a results-oriented approach, and managerial expertise are just some of the traits that are referred to most frequently in this regard.

Notes

1. Organization for Economic Cooperation and Development, "The Call for Innovative and Open Government," communiqué of the Ministerial Meeting of the OECD Governance Committee, Isola San Giorgio Maggiore, Venice, November, 15, 2010 (www.oecd.org/document/26/0,3746,en_21571361_45400858_46091546_1_1_1_1,00.html); (www.funzionepubblica.gov.it/media/601987/ocse_intervento_brunetta.pdf).

2. Gerald Caiden and Naomi Caiden, "Towards the Future of Comparative Public Administration," in *Public Administration in World Perspective*, edited by O. P. Dwivedi and Keith M. Henderson (Iowa State University Press, 1990).

3. Christopher Pollitt and Geert Bouckaert, *Continuity and Change in Public Policy and Management* (Cheltenham, UK, and Northampton, Mass.: Elgar, 2009).

4. Christopher Hood and David Heald, *Transparency: The Key to Better Governance?* (Oxford University Press, 2006); Vincente Pina, Lourdes Torres, and Sonia Royo, "E-Government Evolution in EU Local Governments: A Comparative Perspective," *Online Information Review* 33 (June 2009): 1137–68.

5. Gary M. Cunningham and Jean E. Harris, "Toward a Theory of Performance Reporting to Achieve Public Sector Accountability: A Field Study," *Public Budgeting & Finance* 25 (Summer 2005): 15–42.

6. Ibid.

7. Nils Brunsson, *Reform as Routine: Organizational Change and Stability in the Modern World* (Oxford University Press, 2009); Nils Brunsson and Johan P. Olsen, *The Reforming Organization* (Bergen, Norway: Fagbokforlaget, 1993); Christopher Hood, "A Public Management for All Seasons?" *Public Administration* 69 (Spring 1991): 3–19; Christopher Hood, "Contemporary Public Management: A New Global Paradigm?" *Public Policy and Administration* 10 (February 1995): 104–17; Edoardo Ongaro, *Public Management Reform and Modernization: Trajectories of Administrative Change in Italy,*

France, Greece, Portugal and Spain (Cheltenham, UK, and Northampton, Mass.: Elgar, 2009); Pollitt and Bouckaert, *Continuity and Change in Public Policy and Management.*

8. Donald F. Kettl, *The Global Public Management Revolution* (Brookings, 2000).

9. Ewan Ferlie, Jean Hartley, and Steve Martin, "Changing Public Service Organizations: Current Perspectives and Future Prospects," *British Journal of Management* 14, Supplement s1 (2003): S1–S14.

10. Hood, "Public Management for All Seasons?"; Kettl, *Global Public Management Revolution*; Donald F. Kettl, "The Global Revolution in Public Management: Driving Themes, Missing Links," *Journal of Policy Analysis and Development* 16, no. 3 (1991): 446–62.

11. J. Clifton and D. Díaz-Fuentes, "Evaluating EU Policies on Public Services: A Citizens' Perspective," *Annals of Public and Cooperative Economics* 81 (2010): 281–311.

12. J. Clifton, F. Comin, and D. Díaz Fuentes, "'Empowering Europe's Citizens'? Towards a Charter for Services of General Interest," *Public Management Review* 7, no. 3 (2005): 417–43.

13. Gary B. Brumback, "Getting the Right People Ethically," *Public Personnel Management* 25 (Fall 1996): 267–76; Brian K. Collins, "What's the Problem in Public Sector Workforce Recruitment? A Multi-Sector Comparative Analysis of Managerial Perceptions," *International Journal of Public Administration* 31, no. 4 (2008): 1592–608; Robert J. Lavigna and Steven W. Hays, "Recruitment and Selection of Public Workers: An International Compendium of Modern Trends and Practices," *Public Personnel Management* 33 (Fall 2004): 237–53; Jared J. Llorens, "Uncovering the Determinants of Competitive State Government Wages," *Review of Public Personnel Administration* 28 (December 2008): 308–26.

14. Oliver E. Williamson, *The Mechanisms of Governance* (Oxford University Press, 1999).

Contributors

Michael Barzelay
Professor of Public Management Department of Management, London School of Economics and Political Science

Nicola Bellé
Assistant Professor, Department of Institutional Analysis and Public Management, Bocconi University

Andrea Bonomi Savignon
Research Assistant, University of Rome "Tor Vergata"

Geert Bouckaert
Full Professor, Director, Instituut voor de Overheid, Public Management Institute, Katholieke Universiteit Leuven

Luca Brusati
Director, Laboratory for Research in Economics and Management (LAREM), Udine University

Paola Cantarelli
Research Assistant, SDA Bocconi School of Management

Denita Cepiku
Researcher and Assistant Professor in Strategic Management in the Public Sector, University of Rome "Tor Vergata"

Francesco Cerase

Luigi Corvo
Research Assistant, University of Rome "Tor Vergata"

Maria Cucciniello
Assistant Professor, SDA Bocconi School of Management

Isabell Egger-Peitler

Paolo Fedele
Lecturer, Udine University

Gerhard Hammerschmid

Mario Ianniello
Lecturer, Udine University

Elaine Ciulla Kamarck
Lecturer in Public Policy, Kennedy School of Government, Harvard University

Irvine Lapsley
Professor of Accounting and Director of the Institute of Public Sector Accounting Research (IPSAR), University of Edinburgh Business School

Peter Leisink

Mariannunziata Liguori
Lecturer, Belfast Queen's University

Renate Meyer

Greta Nasi
Associate Professor, Department of Institutional Analysis and Public Management, Bocconi University

James L. Perry
Distinguished Professor, Bloomington School of Public and Environmental Affairs, Indiana University

Christopher Pollitt
Research Professor in Public Management, Public Management Institute, Katholieke Universiteit Leuven

Adrian Ritz

Raffaella Saporito
Assistant Professor, SDA Bocconi School of Management

MariaFrancesca Sicilia
Assistant Professor, SDA Bocconi School of Management

Ileana Steccolini
Associate professor, Bocconi University, and Director of Public Management and Policy Department, SDA Bocconi School of Management

Bram Steijn

Giovanni Tria
President of SSPA—Italian National School of Public Administration

Giovanni Valotti
Dean, Bocconi Undergraduate School; Full Professor of Public Management, Bocconi University

Wouter Vandenabeele
Assistant Professor, Utrecht School of Governance, Utrecht University

Montgomery Van Wart
Full Professor, Interim Dean, College of Business and Public Administration, California State University–San Bernardino

Index